Published by

Richmond Law & Tax Ltd.
12-14 Hill Rise
Richmond TW10 6UA
United Kingdom
Tel. +44 (0) 20 8614 7652
Fax +44 (0) 20 8614 7651
info@richmondlawtax.com
www.richmondlawtax.com

Transnational Publishers, Inc.
410 Saw Mill River Road
Ardsley Park
United States
Tel. +1 (914) 693 5100
Fax +1 (914) 693 4430
info@transnationalpubs.com
www.transnationalpubs.com

Sold and Distributed in Europe and the Commonwealth (excluding Canada) by
Richmond Law & Tax Ltd.

Sold and Distributed in USA and Canada by
Transnational Publishers, Inc.

Library of Congress Cataloging-in-Publication Data

Moore, Jonathon R.
    International charitable foundations : an introduction by Jonathon R. Moore
        p. cm.
    ISBN 1-57105-281-X
    1. Charitable uses, trusts, and foundations.   2. Charity laws and
    legislation.   I. Title.

K658 .M66 2002
346. 73'064—dc21   2002028949

British Library CIP is available

ISBN 1-57105-281-X (Transnational Publishers, Inc.)
ISBN 1-904501-01-X (Richmond Law & Tax Ltd.)

Printed and bound in Great Britain and the United States.

"And above these things put on charity,
which is the bond of perfectness"

St. Paul, Epistle to the Colossians 3:14.

ABOUT THE AUTHOR

Jonathon R. Moore is a partner in the law firm of Moore & Bruce, LLP in Washington, D.C. His practice is comprised of planning and compliance matters for exempt organizations and for non-U.S. and U.S. corporate and individual clients interested in establishing chartitable organizations, estate planning for U.S. and multi-jurisdictional families, and international business transactions. He is a member of the District of Columbia and New York Bars, the Committee on Exempt Organizations of the American Bar Association's Section on Taxation, the Philanthropic Advisors Network of the Council on Foundations, and the District of Columbia Estate Planning Council.

He has contributed articles to numerous publications, including *The International Lawyer*, *Tax Management International Journal*, *The Journal Of Commerce*, *The International Tax Journal*, *International Law Enforcement Reporter* and *The Journal of International Law And Economics*. He is a graduate of the National Law Center of The George Washington University and Williams College.

Moore & Bruce, LLP is a law firm specializing in international taxation, private client work, trade and customs law, legislative and administrative representation, and "white-collar" defense litigation.

CONTENTS

INTRODUCTION—
WHO SHOULD READ THIS BOOK

You are successful. Perhaps you have become wealthy as an entrepreneur who has formed and grown a successful business. Perhaps you have achieved success as an investor by multiplying the capital you have accumulated from your family or the sale of a business. Now what?

Presumably the material wealth you have accumulated will be sufficient for maintaining the standard of living you have set for yourself and your family. Perhaps you no longer need to "make a living." So now is the time to ask yourself: what is your passion? For many, it will be golf, sailing or travel. But for many others such pursuits by themselves will not be fulfilling. For these persons, a wider cause—whether promoting education, alleviating poverty, promoting peace and understanding among nations, enhancing protection of the environment or advancing science— beckons. Having spent much of your adult life pursuing material well-being, success now accords the freedom to pursue goals that will benefit some segment of humankind. Just as your endeavors in business or investing have been notable, your philanthropic goals will likely target something significant.

This book is written for those families and individuals who are ready to pursue seriously such eleemosynary goals, as well as those who are already doing so. Its principles will also apply to businesses seeking to take some portion of their accumulated profits to devote to such pursuits and to existing U.S. foundations considering expansion of their scope.

The pages which follow will examine factors and decisions which are inherently *private*. As will be explained, U.S. tax disincentives drive numerous organizations to operate as public charities. Public charities, however, must direct a sizable portion of the gifts they receive each year to their charitable purposes, and then again each year raise additional resources to continue. If you contemplate funding an organization with a single or series of large gifts and wish to avoid raising new funding from outside sources on a continuing basis, you will not be interested in establishing a new public charity.

In evaluating whether to establish a private foundation, it is assumed that the purposes of the foundation will be innovative, uniquely responsive to a set of perceived problems—and perhaps controversial. Of course, if your philanthropic interests are being addressed entirely by an existing public charity, you may wish to devote your resources to furthering that entity's goals. In that case, join the organization and perhaps its

Board, and lend your financial support to its activities. If you can find such an organization, your charitable goals can be realized by "piggybacking" on an existing organizational and legal infrastructure created and maintained by a public charity, and you can stop reading now.

To the extent, however, that existing charities are not fulfilling your sense of what can or should be accomplished in any particular field of charitable endeavor—and in particular, what you want to accomplish personally—this book will provide guidance on alternatives to pursuing your vision. Your efforts have generated the resources; it is your prerogative to pursue and advance your values and philanthropic goals. The vehicle for doing so will allow you to instill in your children or other family members the values you are articulating and pursuing. Moreover, it will allow you to pass these values on to succeeding generations and serve as a uniting force for your family and/or close circle of friends.

So how do you set up a foundation? What type of legal structure do you use and where do you establish it? Most individuals in the United States, that is, U.S. citizens and residents for tax purposes (so called "green card" holders), pursuing philanthropic goals will either participate in existing entities or establish private foundations under the law of a particular state. Frequently, decisions on structure will be driven by tax considerations as to the deductibility from federal and state income taxes or estate taxes or exclusion from gift taxes. Indeed, most of the current structure of regulation of U.S. charitable organizations derives from the tax benefits granted to donors and the exemption from taxation to the organizations themselves.

This book will discuss the legal framework and mechanics of establishing a charitable entity which qualifies for tax benefits available under U.S. law. Those benefits, however, come with "strings attached" in the form of a complex regulatory regime, under which the charitable organization must initially qualify and then be maintained. Where some or all of the tax benefits available under U.S. law are not necessarily needed, foreign jurisdictions should be considered as the situs for the charity, as the foundation can then be operated flexibly—and privately—outside of the constraints of the U.S. regulatory regime. This book will describe the advantages and disadvantages of utilizing foreign structures for U.S. citizens and residents.

For some individuals, the U.S. tax advantages available are more than outweighed by the burdens and constraints of regulatory compliance. Such individuals may deliberately choose to forego short term tax benefits in favor of longer term freedom accorded from a foreign foundation structure.

This book is written for philanthropists—current and potential—and is not intended to present an exhaustive analysis of legal topics covered. The usual "law review" format and its emphasis on footnoted minuitiae are avoided. Although lawyers not expert in the area of exempt organizations may find the topics covered useful as a general overview, this book does not hold itself out as a legal treatise. It is written for lay persons making decisions to create charitable organizations and for their advisors. Nevertheless, primary authorities and references are cited.

FALSE CHARITY

Many of the ideas in this book are controversial. None of the suggestions offered, however, should be understood to offer a roadmap to those who would subvert charitable or philanthropic enterprises for illegitimate purposes. Much has been written recently about certain so-called Islamic charities, which although having names suggesting their purposes, for example, are to alleviate poverty and hunger among children, in fact have served as conduits for supporting terrorism. The subversion or perversion of charitable organizations for such purposes should not be permitted to constrain the vast array of legitimate philanthropic organizations which are working creatively to address numerous problems of the world, which are not or cannot be remedied by governments or private enterprise.

Nor is this a "how to" book on "gaming the system." There are certain foreign jurisdictions and service providers all too willing to establish charitable-sounding trusts or corporations, which would leave the door open for a future channeling of income or reversion of capital to private uses and purposes. This book seeks philanthropists with legitimate charitable intent. Its use does not invite subterfuge. Rather, its purpose is to offer insight on structuring charitable endeavors with far fewer governmental intrusions and constraints.

CHAPTER 1

CHARITABLE GIVING TODAY

Charitable organizations as a group are often referred to as the "third sector." Those unfamiliar with the scope of charitable endeavors may think this is a misnomer, as the size of the charitable sector is often perceived to be minuscule when compared with that of government or private enterprise. While the charitable sector is unquestionably the smallest of the three sectors, the number and diversity of charities is truly astounding.

SIZE

There are currently approximately 1.5 million organizations in the United States that are recognized as exempt from taxation by the Internal Revenue Service. Chart A, which is taken from the 1998 Data Book, Internal Revenue Service Publication 55B, lists various types of exempt organizations by statutory category. According to data compiled by the National Center for Charitable Statistics, a project of the Center on Nonprofits & Philanthropy at the Urban Institute, the total assets held by these entities is approaching $1.5 trillion.[1] A recent survey of the nonprofit sector published in *The Chronicle of Philanthropy* indicates that in 1999, this sector accounted for 8.5 percent of U.S. gross domestic product. Moreover, one of every twelve employees worked in the nonprofit sector.

According to published IRS figures, within this sector "domestic private foundations and charitable trusts provided $19.4 billion in contributions, gifts and grants" for 1998. The fair market value of total assets held was $397.1 billion.[2]

While already large, the sector is growing rapidly. In 1999, the last year for which figures are available, over 83,000 new charitable organizations sought recognition of tax-exempt status under Section 501(c)(3) from the Internal Revenue Service. These new institutions sought to join nearly 735,000 organizations already so recognized.

---

[1]   http://nccs.urban.org/factsht.htm.
[2]   Internal Revenue Service, 2001–2002 issue of Statistics of Income Bulletin, IR-2002-51 (22 April 2002), Doc 2002-9841, Tax Analysts Electronic Citation 2002-TNT-73-16.

Chart A: Number of Tax-Exempt Organizations Registered with the IRS, 1989–1998

IRS Section:	1992	1994	1995	1996	1997	1998
(1) Corporation organized under act of Congress	9	9	19	20	27	14
(2) Titleholding corps.	6,529	6,967	7,025	7,100	7,113	7,125
(3) Religious, charitable, etc. [1]	546,100	599,745	626,226	654,186	692,524	733,790
(4) Social welfare	142,673	140,143	139,451	139,512	141,776	139,533
(5) Labor, agriculture organizations	71,012	68,144	66,662	64,955	64,902	64,804
(6) Business leagues	70,871	74,273	75,695	77,274	78,406	79,864
(7) Social and recreation clubs	64,681	65,273	65,501	60,845	66,387	66,691
(8) Fraternal beneficiary societies	93,544	92,284	92,115	91,972	87,990	84,507
(9) Voluntary employees' beneficiary associations	14,986	14,835	14,681	14,486	14,464	14,240
(10) Domestic fraternal beneficiary societies	21,415	21,215	21,046	20,925	20,954	21,962
(11) Teachers' retirement funds	10	11	11	13	13	13
(12) Benevolent life insurance assns.	6,103	6,221	6,291	6,343	6,368	6,423
(13) Cemetery companies	9,025	9,294	9,433	9,562	9,646	9,792
(14) State chartered credit unions	5,559	5,391	5,225	5,157	4,959	4,378
(15) Mutual insurance companies	1,157	1,161	1,185	1,212	1,206	1,251
(16) Corps. to finance crop operations	23	23	23	253	25	25
(17) Supplemental unemployment benefit trusts	625	601	583	565	542	533
(18) Employee funded pension trusts	8	4	3	2	1	1
(19) War veterans' organizations	28,096	30,282	30,828	31,464	31,961	35,682
(20) Legal service organizations	217	181	141	131	92	56

Chart A: *(continued)*

(21) Black lung trusts	23	25	25	25	27	28
(22) Multiemployer pension plans	0	0	0	0	0	0
(23) Veterans associations founded prior to 1880	2	2	2	2	2	2
(24) Trusts described in section 4049 of ERISA	1	1	1	1	1	1
(25) Holding companies for pensions etc.	290	479	638	794	908	1,017
(26) State-sponsored high-risk health insurance organization [3]	N/A	N/A	N/A	N/A	N/A	7
(27) State-sponsored workers' compensation reinsurance organizations [4]	N/A	N/A	N/A	N/A	N/A	3
501(d) Religious and apostolic organizations	**92**	**99**	**107**	**113**	**115**	**118**
501(e) Cooperative hospital service organizations	**68**	**68**	**61**	**54**	**50**	**43**
501(f) Cooperative service organizations of operating educational organizations	**1**	**1**	**1**	**1**	**1**	**1**
521 Farmers' cooperatives	**2,086**	**1,866**	**1,810**	**1,773**	**1,754**	**1,442**
Sub-Total exempt organizations (EO)		1,138,598	1,164,789	1,188,510	1,232,214	1,273,346
Taxable farmers' cooperatives [5]		2,537	2,982	2,930	3,407	3,180
Nonexempt charitable trusts [5]		62,103	68,134	75,362	86,884	99,869
Total EOs and other entities		**1,203,238**	**1,235,905**	**1,266,802**	**1,322,505**	**1,376,395**

[1] All section 501(c) (3) organizations are not included because certain organizations, such as churches, integrated auxiliaries, subordinate units and conventions or associations of churches need not apply for recognition of exemption unless they desire a ruling.
[2] Granting of tax-exempt status under Internal Revenue Service Code section 501(c)(20) ceased, starting with tax years beginning after June 20, 1992. (These organizations continued to be included on the IRS Exempt Organizations Master File in years following expiration of their tax-exempt status.)
[3] Granting of Tax-exempt status under Internal revenue Code section 501(c)(26) was effective with tax years beginning after December 31, 1996.
[4] Granting of Tax-exempt status under Internal revenue Code section 501(c)(27) was effective with tax years beginning after August 21, 1996.
[5] These organizations are not exempt organizations, but are taxable entities for which the IRS tax-exempt organization function has program responsibility.
Source: Internal Revenue Service, 1998 Data Book, Publication 55B.

SCOPE

The focus of this book is on charitable organizations. In the broad classifications kept by the Internal Revenue Service, charities fall within Section 501(c)(3), which covers "religious, scientific, educational and charitable organizations." The term "charitable" in the statute is not defined, and the regulations, while listing numerous types of charitable endeavors, expressly decline to limit the type of activities which will be considered charitable under the law.[3]

A sense of the broad scope of charitable endeavors can be seen in Chart B, which was compiled by The Foundation Center.[4] Chart B gives an excellent overview of grant making by category of charitable use. Not only is the Chart useful in illustrating broad categories of charitable endeavors, *e.g.*, arts, culture, education, environment, human services, science, etc., but it breaks down these broad categories into typical activities.[5]

An independent analysis of charitable giving conducted by The Foundation Center indicates that over $15 billion in charitable grants were made in 2000 by various types of foundations [independent foundations, corporate foundations and community foundations], in addition to grants made by so-called public charities. These include, for example, nearly $525 million to museums, nearly $850 million for medical research and over $525 million for community improvement. Within each of these categories and subcategories numerous creative, innovative and visionary grants were made.

The foregoing statistics only include foundations and other tax-exempt organizations operating in the United States or reporting information to the Internal Revenue Service. Internationally, the levels of charitable activities without a doubt are certain to be several multiples of the foregoing, and therefore represent a significant contribution to the well-being of the world.

CAUSES

Manifestly, there is no shortage of problems in the world which are not being adequately addressed by governments or private enterprise. The breadth and imagination of charitable endeavors therefore should come as no surprise. For example,

---

3   Regulations Section 1.501(c)(3)-1(d)(2).

4   This data updated for 2001 appears at The Chronicle of Philanthropy (March 7, 2002) at 16.

5   An even more comprehensive list of the types of activities which are considered to be charitable has been developed by the National Center for Charitable Statistics. Its "National Taxonomy of Exempt Entities" breaks down the categories listed in Chart B into numerous additional subcategories. The system is accessible on the Internet at http://nccs.urban.org/ntee-cc/summary.htm.

Chart B Distribution of Foundation Grants by Subject Categories, circa 2000*

Subject	Dollar Value of Grants 2000 Amount	%	No. of Grants 2000 No.	%
Arts and Culture				
Policy, Management, and Information[1]	$14,191	0.1	200	0.2
Arts-Multipurpose	15B,490	1.1	2,032	1.7
Media and Communications	178,155	1.2	1,442	1.2
Visual Arts/Architecture	96,647	0.6	661	0.6
Museums	523,393	3.5	3,881	3.2
Performing Arts	579,144	3.9	7,256	6.1
Humanities	126,926	0.8	813	0.7
Historic Preservation	100,116	0.7	1,325	1.1
Other	21.553	0.1	225	0.2
Total Arts and Culture	**$1,798,615**	**12.0**	**17,835**	**14.9**
Education				
Policy, Management, and Information[1]	$22,127	0.1	275	0.2
Elementary and Secondary	1,206,912	8.0	8,423	7.0
Vocational and Technical	20,297	0.1	182	0.2
Higher Educabon	1,320,035	8.8	8,814	7.4
Graduate and Professional	643,172	4.3	2,537	2.1
Adult and Continuing	15,914	0.1	389	0.3
Library Science/Libraries	271,557	1.8	1,130	0.9
Student Services	94,198	0.6	678	0.6
Educational Services	184,797	1.2	2,187	1.8
Total Education	**$3.779,009**	**25.2**	**24,615**	**20.6**

Subject	Dollar Value of Grants 2000 Amount	%	No. of Grants 2000 No.	%
Human Services				
Crime, Justice, and Legal Services	$197,887	1.3	2,250	1.9
Employment	126,916	0.6	1,846	1.5
Food,Nutntion, and Agriculture	109,804	0.7	1,326	1.1
Housing and Shelter	199,979	1.3	2,670	2.2
Safety and Disaster Relief	25,004	0.2	400	0.3
Recreation and Sports	205,120	1.4	2,306	1.9
Youth Development	278,668	1.9	4,114	3.4
Human Services-Multipurpose	1,025,697	6.8	14,228	11.9
Total Human Services	**$2,169,075**	**14.4**	**29,140**	**24.3**
International Affairs, Development, Peace, and Human Rights	**$414,232**	**2.8**	**3,264**	**2.7**
Pubilc/Society Benefit				
Civil Rights and Social Action	$231,194	1.5	2,113	1.8
Community Improvement and	526,355	3.5	5,449	4.5
Philanthropy and Voluntarism	539,178	3.8	4,344	3.6
Public Affairs	395,019	2.6	2,953	2.5
Total Public/Society Benefit	**$1,691,746**	**11.3**	**14,859**	**12.4**

Chart B (continued)

Subject	Dollar Value of Grants 2000 Amount	%	No. of Grants 2000 No.	%
Environment and Animals				
Environment	$808,279	5.4	5,907	4.9
Animal and Wildlife	179,148	1.2	1,461	1.2
Total Environment and Animals	$987,425	6.6	7,368	6.2
Health				
General and Rehabilitative	$1,586,359	10.6	8,110	6.8
Policy, Management, and Information[1]	54,087	0.4	374	0.3
Hospitals and Medical Care	591,035	3.9	4,631	3.9
Reproductive Health Care	380,367	2.5	1,045	0.9
Public Health	412,006	2.7	1,121	0.9
Other	148,864	1.0	939	0.8
Specific Diseases	444,059	3.0	2,473	2.1
Medical Research	841,998	5.6	1,769	1.5
Mental Health	217,506	1.4	2,165	1.8
Total Health	$3,089,922	20.6	14,517	12.1

Subject	Dollar Value of Grants 2000 Amount	%	No. of Grants 2000 No.	%
Science and Technology				
Policy, Management, and Information[1]	$9,735	0.1	107	0.1
General Science	165,129	1.1	795	0.7
Physical Science	104,042	0.7	799	0.7
Technology	54,647	0.4	480	0.4
Life Science	80,473	0.5	217	0.2
Other	32	0.0	2	0.0
Total Science and Technology	$414,058	2.8	2,400	2.0
Social Science				
Social Science and Economics	$156,620	1.0	942	0.8
Interdisciplinary/Other	167,568	1.1	895	0.7
Total Social Science	$324,188	2.2	1,837	1.5
Religion	$329,937	2.2	3,819	3.2
Other	$17,260	0.1	124	0.1
Total Grants	$15,015,467	100.0	119,778	100.0

Source: Foundation Giving Trends (2002), The Foundation Center All dollar figures expressed in thousands; due to rounding, figures may not add up.

* Basedd on grants of $10,000 or more awarded bye national sample of 1,015 larger U.S. foundations (including 800 of the 1,000 largest ranked by total giving). For community foundations, only discretionary grants are included. Grants to individuals are not included in the file.

[1] Includes broad range of supporting activities or organizations identified by 12 "common codes."

- Jim Barksdale, founder of Netscape, has established the Barksdale Reading Institute in Oxford, Mississippi to address illiteracy in his home state.[6] Thus far, he has contributed $100 million in this project. Last year, the Institute delivered reading programs to 22,000 children from kindergarten to the third grade in Mississippi.
- Gordon Moore, founder of Intel, through a family foundation, has funded efforts to protect global biodiversity through Conservation International. Through a series of grants totaling $261 million over 10 years, his foundation has helped create an alliance of conservation partners which hopes to leverage $4.5 billion to acquire large parcels of land in 25 so-called biodiversity hot spots. Although these areas represent just 1.4 percent of the earth's land surface, they are said to claim more than 60 percent of all plant and animal species.[7]
- Richard C. Blum, a San Francisco investment banker, founded the American Himalayan Foundation following his visit to Nepal 23 years ago.[8] This foundation supports the construction of schools, retirement homes and health clinics and the restoration of cultural landmarks in rural areas of Nepal, Tibet, Bhutan and Pakistan. Its annual budget of approximately $2.5 million helps to support about 75 projects.[9]

As these individuals have demonstrated, meaningful progress on significant problems is achievable in each potential philanthropist's field of interest. The challenge is to identify a problem capable of ameliation/remediation, given the level of human and economic resources available. Virtually any cause that will benefit humankind generally can be pursued.

---

[6] *Barron's*, Investing in Philanthropy, December 17, 2001 at 30.

[7] Paul Rogers, Another Record Gift by Intel Co-Founder, *San Jose Mercury News*, December 9, 2001; Conservation International Press Release, December 9, 2001, www.conservation.org/xp/CIWEB/press_ releases/120901.xml.

[8] *The Chronicle of Philanthropy* (March 7, 2002) at 5.

[9] Additional examples of the imagination and vision of philanthropists may be found among the recipients of the President Bush's Daily Points of Light Award at http//pointsoflight.org.

CHAPTER 2

FUNDAMENTAL CONCEPTS RELATING TO
CHARITABLE ORGANIZATIONS

Before describing the legal framework regulating U.S. charitable organizations, it is appropriate to discuss some fundamental concepts. These concepts pervade both U.S. and foreign laws which recognize and enable the formation and functioning of charitable organizations.

PRIVATE INUREMENT

The key provision of the Internal Revenue Code granting tax exemption to U.S. charitable organizations includes the phrase: "no part of the net earnings [shall] inure . . . to the benefit of any private shareholder or individual. . .". As the reader considers whether to form a charitable organization, the basic concept of private inurement must be kept in mind.

The concept relates as much to the distinction between charitable endeavors and commerce as it does to the difference between for-profit entities and nonprofit entities. A for-profit entity, whether constituted as a corporation, partnership, limited liability company or sole proprietorship, has owners for whose benefit the enterprise is operated. As shareholders, partners or interest holders, these owners have a right to receive a share of profits or dividends and are entitled to receive any equity capital left in the business venture upon its dissolution or liquidation. Nonprofit entities, by contrast, are not operated for the benefit of any founder, contributor, executive or employee. Although under the laws of some states, nonprofit corporations, for example, might issue stock to the founders for control purposes, such stock ownership does not entitle the individual to share in the profits or in the value of the assets upon dissolution.

Of course, the difference between for-profit enterprises and nonprofit organizations relates fundamentally to purpose. Businesses are formed to make money; charities exist to provide some form of public benefit. It is important to note in this regard that the specific charitable purposes are expressly **not** for the benefit of any specific individuals. Accordingly, the founders, their families and associates may not receive economic benefit from the charity. The violation of this fundamental principle will contravene not only the tax laws granting benefits to the contributors and the charitable organizations, but may also risk intervention by applicable regulatory authorities, such as the Corporation Commissioner, the Secretary of State or the State's Attorney General. Although the level of supervision is frequently less strict in foreign jurisdictions, the same exposure for utilizing charitable contributions and assets for private inurement can arise. Nothing said in this book concerning the relative advantages or disadvantages of operating a charitable organization in a foreign jurisdiction should be construed to imply that any aspect of the charitable endeavors may inure to private individuals at any time.

Invariably, issues of private inurement involve "insiders" of the charity, whether Board members, Trustees, large donors or managers. Inherent in the analysis of whether an economic benefit has inured to an individual is the notion of control of the decision-making within the organization by the insider. Frequently the "insider" designation is also attributed to family members, including spouses and children, or to other entities, such as corporations, limited liability companies or partnerships, which are controlled by the insider.

Federal rules governing private foundations in United States have strict prohibitions against any dealings between designated insiders, called "disqualified persons," and the foundation (*see* Chapter 4). Prohibited transactions include sales or exchanges of property or services and borrowing or lending funds. Even if the proposed transaction is demonstrably fair and reasonable, it is "off-limits" under these rules.

PUBLIC BENEFIT VERSUS PRIVATE BENEFIT

A related concept is that of "private benefit." Charitable organizations must be dedicated to some form of public benefits, however broadly or narrowly defined. Use of the charity's assets for a **private** benefit, that is to say, to benefit an individual, therefore violates the fundamental charitable purpose. Unlike a private inurement, which benefits an insider of the charity, such as a significant contributor, an officer or a Board member, a private benefit occurs when the individual receiving benefits is not within the class of beneficiaries for which the charity is established.

This is not to say that *individuals* may not properly receive the benefits of charity; rather, for an individual properly to receive a charitable benefit, he or she must fall within the *charitable class* for which the charity is operated to benefit. Thus, if a charity is founded to alleviate hunger among indigent children, the charity might, for example, define the charitable class as including anyone whose family of four earns less than $20,000 per year.[10] Gifts to such individ-

---

[10] It was these distinctions which engendered controversy in the wake of the September 11 attacks. Both established charitable organizations and those created in response to the tragedies were confronted with difficult issues on defining the charitable class, e.g., where to "draw the line" in disbursing millions of dollars among the families of the victims.

uals would be constructed as rendering a private benefit.

As with the private inurement doctrine, the organization risks sanctions if it confers a private benefit. In essence, to do so violates its charitable purpose. Intervention by regulatory authorities, state and federal, can follow.

PUBLIC CHARITIES VERSUS PRIVATE FOUNDATIONS

Another fundamental distinction in the laws and regulations governing charitable organizations relates to public charities versus private foundations. Although the term "foundation" is sometimes used by entities which draw support from a wide cross-section of the public, for purposes of this book, the term will be used to refer to an independent entity funded by an individual, his or her family or a single corporation or business enterprise.

The major differences between the two categories of entities is that a public charity raises funds from a broad segment of the public on a continuous or repetitive basis, usually to meet its operating needs and charitable purposes, whereas a private foundation typically is funded by a small number of individuals, in a single or series of reasonably large gifts, which then form an endowment. Income from the endowment is then used to fund charitable activities, consistent with the private foundation's charitable purposes. Moreover, control of a private foundation usually remains with the donors, whereas a public charity is frequently governed by a more diverse Board of Directors or Trustees, some of which may be elected by members. Participation—as a member or otherwise—is usually open to anyone contributing financial or other support.

As discussed in Chapter 3, the characterization of an entity as a public charity gives rise to numerous tax benefits, both for the donors and the entity itself. On the other hand, characterization as a private foundation triggers multiple layers of regulation in the form of excise taxes and penalties, as described more fully in Chapter 4. It is necessary to discuss public charities, because in the typical "legal-speak" of the Internal Revenue Code, an entity is deemed to be a foundation only if it is **not** a public charity. As a matter of public policy in United States, public charities are the favored vehicle, and are viewed by the Congress as somewhat more capable of self governance. By contrast, based upon well-publicized abuses by a few wealthy families in the 1950s and '60s, the laws governing private foundations provide for closer scrutiny, enforced by escalating levels of penalties, both against the foundation and any individuals responsible for contravening the regulatory regime.[11]

---

[11] Certain aspects of the regulatory regime governing foundations have to a lesser extent over the years been extended to public charities as well.

The manner in which the Internal Revenue Code defines private foundations by means of various exceptions, which are generally referred to as "public charities," is illustrated in Chart C.[12] If the organization is described under one of the boxes numbered 1 through 4, it will be regarded as a public charity and not be subject to the complex regulatory regime applicable to private foundations described in Chapter 4.

> It will be assumed for purposes of this book that the reader is interested in establishing a private foundation, rather than a public charity. Accordingly, mention of public charities generally is limited to the extent needed to define private foundations for purposes of the U.S. legal regime.

NONPROFIT VERSUS TAX-EXEMPT VERSUS CHARITABLE

For the sake of clarity, brief mention is appropriate as to the distinction between these types of entities. Although all charitable institutions must be nonprofit, not all nonprofit entities are eligible to be tax-exempt. Section 501(c) of the Internal Revenue Code enumerates some 27 categories of organizations which can qualify for tax-exempt status. While broad, these categories are nevertheless specific and do not encompass the full range of nonprofit entities. Chart A, taken from the Internal Revenue Service Data Bank, and reprinted in Chapter 1, shows the range and usage of the various exempt categories from business leagues to pension funds to veterans associations.

The tax exemption process requires the nonprofit entity to apply to the Internal Revenue Service for recognition of exempt status, which will be granted upon showing that the organization is formed and operated for an exempt purpose. The process for charitable organizations is described in Chapter 3. Similar procedures apply to the other categories of exempt organizations.

As can be readily seen from the categories of exempt organizations shown in Chart C, not all are charitable in nature. Traditional charities include such organizations as schools, universities, community chests, and churches.[13]

The distinction between charitable, exempt and nonprofit can have enormous legal consequences, both under the laws of the United States and other jurisdictions. For example, tax-exempt status in United States

---

[12]   Chart C is based on a chart from J. Edie, First Steps In Starting a Foundation (4th Ed. 1997) Council on Foundations at 7.

[13]   Section 170(b)(i)(A).

is not available for political campaigns or funding for political advocacy. Nevertheless, organizations interested in various aspects of public policy, which may from time to time take positions on matters of public policy may, or may not, qualify as exempt, depending upon the type of activities in which the organizations may engage. If such organizations are primarily engaged in scholarly research, they may qualify as tax-exempt educational organizations. As the results of the research are used to shape public policy debate, at some point the line may be crossed to political activities, raising a "red flag" in terms of the entity obtaining or maintaining tax-exempt status.

As a matter of United States law, such issues can be extremely complex.[14] Under the laws of other jurisdictions, however, where an entity's purposes are described as public, as opposed to private or business, purposes, the entity may be specifically sanctioned by law.[15] Accordingly, the distinctions between nonprofit and tax-exempt and philanthropic or charitable may well have different implications under the laws of non-U.S. jurisdictions.

---

[14]   The intersection of regulation of political activities, particularly, lobbying and fundraising, with the First Amendment's guarantees of free speech and the right of assembly has always been controversial. When tax policy issues are overlaid, complexity is guaranteed.

[15]   *See* discussion of Bermuda Purpose Trusts in Chapter 8, *infra*.

Chart C Legal Definition of Private Foundations

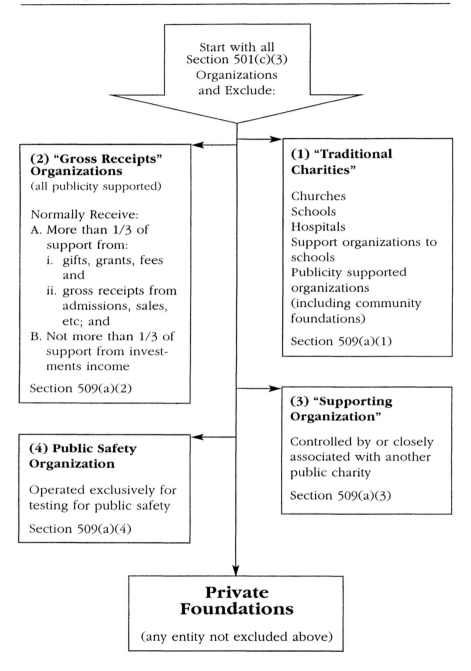

Start with all
Section 501(c)(3)
Organizations
and Exclude:

**(2) "Gross Receipts"
Organizations**
(all publicity supported)

Normally Receive:
A. More than 1/3 of
   support from:
   i. gifts, grants, fees
       and
   ii. gross receipts from
       admissions, sales,
       etc; and
B. Not more than 1/3 of
   support from invest-
   ments income

Section 509(a)(2)

**(1) "Traditional
Charities"**

Churches
Schools
Hospitals
Support organizations to
schools
Publicity supported
organizations
(including community
foundations)

Section 509(a)(1)

**(3) "Supporting
Organization"**

Controlled by or closely
associated with another
public charity

Section 509(a)(3)

**(4) Public Safety
Organization**

Operated exclusively for
testing for public safety

Section 509(a)(4)

**Private
Foundations**

(any entity not excluded above)

CHAPTER 3

U.S. LEGAL FRAMEWORK GOVERNING CHARITABLE ORGANIZATIONS

LEGAL STRUCTURES

In the United States, charitable organizations are usually organized as trusts or as nonprofit corporations. The laws governing trusts are typically common law in each state jurisdiction, and the laws governing nonprofit corporations are typically a subset of the state corporation laws. A charity may also take the form of an unincorporated association and, in some jurisdictions, a limited liability company ("LLC").

Nonprofit Corporations

Nonprofit corporations are by far the preferred vehicle for charitable organizations in the United States.[16] There are two principal reasons for this. First, a corporation is a limited liability entity, so that founders are insulated from any liabilities which may be incurred by the charity. Second, the corporate governance structure is familiar to most participants in charitable endeavors.

Since charities are not engaged in business as such, in theory isolating the founders against claims would not seem to be essential. Nevertheless, in the current litigious environment in the United States, a corporate structure is viewed by many potential donors as indispensable, as they do not want their charitable activities to give rise to personal legal exposure. Moreover, under the corporate laws of most states, a nonprofit corporation can provide for broad indemnity for its officers and directors. As a practical matter, unless the officers or directors are engaged in fraud or criminal activities, the indemnification provided by the charity should accord them sufficient protection.[17]

---

[16]   Most states have specific nonprofit or "not-for-profit" corporation statutes although there are many variations. Virginia, for example, has a Nonstock Corporation Act, § 13.1-801 *et seq.*, Virginia Code (2001), which although not limited to nonprofit entities, is generally utilized by them.

[17]   In addition, directors' and officers' liability insurance, so called "errors and omissions" policies, are generally available for nonprofit and charitable corporations.

Charitable entities organized as nonprofit corporations are usually governed by a Board of Directors. The Board appoints and supervises officers in charge of the charity's operations. The Board can be self-perpetuating, with the founders appointing the initial Board, and the Board itself filling any vacancies in directorships that may occur. Where charities have a large membership base, some portion of the Board can be selected by the membership at large, and different seats on the Board can be reserved for specific classes of members, for example, depending upon the size of donations.

Where a charity organized as a non-profit corporation operates in a state or in multiple jurisdictions other than the one where it is incorporated, it will be required to apply for a "certificate of authority" to conduct its operations in the "foreign" state. This allows charities to avail themselves of better corporate law in one state, even though they operate in another. For example, Delaware corporate law is universally recognized as preferable.[18] This is because it is complete, well thought-through and flexible. Of equal significance, the state bureaucracy which implements and interprets the law, the Office of the Delaware Secretary of State, has a well-deserved reputation for efficiency and responsiveness.[19] Accordingly, many charities are incorporated in Delaware as nonprofit corporations, and then qualify as foreign corporations in the state where they will actually be operating. The same mechanism could be used to qualify a truly foreign nonprofit entity, for example, one from the Channel Islands or Liechtenstein, in any state where it might be operating.

Trusts

Generally speaking, trusts are creatures of common law, and are recognized under state laws in the United States and in foreign jurisdictions which derive their law from the laws of England,[20] such as Bermuda, the

---

[18]   Delaware General Corporation Law, Title 8, Chapter 1, Delaware Code of 1953, as amended. Delaware is one of the few states that does not have a separate section of laws devoted exclusively to nonprofit corporations. Therefore, a charitable entity incorporating in Delaware would be a regular corporation, but might, for example, state in its charter that it does not issue stock.

[19]   Unlike the Secretary of State or Corporation Commission bureaucracies of many states, which pride themselves on strictly enforcing all requirements, down to the color of the ink used to sign documents filed, the Delaware Secretary of State has a number of "trouble shooters" readily available to work with nonprofit entities and their counsel to draft whatever filings are needed to carry out a specific transaction. Rather than having a filing rejected, counsel might receive a telephone call from the Delaware Secretary of State's office, and any difficulty or deficiency is quickly resolved or corrected. Corrected amendments can be filed via facsimile. This contrasts sharply with practices in other jurisdictions, which at times appear to be designed to demonstrate the power of low-level clerks to reject filings.

[20]   Trusts as a legal structure derive from the distinction in English common law between the *use* and *legal ownership* of property. The legal ownership and title to property in

Isle of Man, and the Cayman Islands.[21] In addition, a number of non-common law jurisdictions, such as Liechtenstein and the Netherlands Antilles, by statute permit trusts to be created. Unlike nonprofit corporations, charitable trusts usually do not need to qualify as a charity or otherwise obtain the official permission from a licensing authority to operate in any particular jurisdiction in United States. [If it is raising funds from the public, it may need to register with the applicable state authority which regulates such fund raising, but this would not typically be required by a private foundation.]

Normally grantors of charitable trusts should not be expected to be exposed to liability for claims against the trust, although trustees might be. Since trustees owe a fiduciary duty to the beneficiaries of the trust, for any claims against the trust or the trustee to be successful, in theory they would need to be based upon a breach of fiduciary duty. Professional fiduciaries, such as financial institutions, trust companies and lawyers, are well aware of this exposure and accept it as part of serving in a trustee capacity. Of course, most professional trustees maintain liability insurance and additionally require the trust to indemnify them against such claims. As is the case with indemnification of corporate officers and directors, standard indemnification clauses would not shield trustees in the event they were to engage in fraudulent or criminal activities.

Although most persons considering the establishment of charitable organizations in United States regard a corporate governance structure as being preferable to a trust structure, this most certainly is a misperception. It is possible to have multiple trustees or a Board of Trustees. As with a corporate Board of Directors, Co-Trustees or a Board of Trustees can appoint managers to run the charitable entity's operations. The grantor may expressly give power to remove trustee(s) to so-called trust "Protectors" or to a "Committee of Trust Advisors."[22] Moreover certain functions, such as advising on how the endowment fund is to be invested or how grants are to be made, can be delegated to individuals or committees other than the Trustee(s).

Generally speaking, trusts are viewed as a less flexible vehicle than corporations, which can amend their charters or by-laws, but again, this is a misperception. It all depends upon the Declaration of Trust or the Trust Agreement. Use of a discretionary trust, with power given to the Trustee to amend the trust document, perhaps subject to consent of the trust Protectors or a Committee of Trust Advisors, accords the trust the

---

trust is held by a trustee, whereas use, or beneficial ownership, runs to the beneficiaries of the trust. The origins date to feudal times when the King was the legal owner of all land, but granted the right to use the land to his lords.

[21]   Other common law jurisdictions include: the Bahamas, Barbados, Gibraltar and the Channel Islands.

[22]   See Chapter 7, *infra*.

ultimate flexibility in adapting to changing circumstances over time. Indeed, a trust can even migrate to a new jurisdiction, so that it can be governed by an entirely different set of laws.[23]

In comparing the relative advantages of operating a charity as a non-profit corporation or a trust, the charitable donor must first become comfortable with the concept of a trustee controlling the entity. To overcome this hurdle, there is no substitute for an in-depth interview of the persons or institutions under consideration for serving as trustees. Once a sufficient "comfort level" is attained, the potential grantor will realize that there can be far greater flexibility and control in utilizing a trust as the vehicle for the charity than he or she may have imagined.

Unincorporated Associations

A short word is also appropriate regarding unincorporated associations, which can also serve as a charitable vehicle. As with a corporate charter and by-laws, an unincorporated association will need a governing document, such as a "constitution." Of course, any governance structure imaginable can be created, including one where an authority over different aspects of the entity's work and administration can be delegated to various committees. These governance structures can be created at little or no cost, as lawyers would not necessarily be required to draft legal papers, and in many jurisdictions unincorporated associations are not required to register with any state or local regulatory body.[24]

The major downside of utilizing an unincorporated association is the potential for personal liability to the individuals involved in the work on behalf of the charity. For this reason alone, nonprofit corporations or trusts are usually preferred over unincorporated associations.

Limited Liability Companies

LLC's are a relatively new form of legal organization, which seeks to combine the limited liability benefits of operating as a corporation with the more flexible mechanisms for allocating profits, losses and capital

---

[23] By contrast, a corporation usually may not "migrate" to a new jurisdiction, because it is a creation of statutory law of a particular state. While a corporation can be "moved" to a new jurisdiction, the steps to do so are complex. Typically "re-incorporating" or "re-domiciling" a corporation requires liquidation of the old corporation and forming a new corporation in the new jurisdiction or forming a new corporation in a new jurisdiction and merging the old corporation into it, so that the new corporation is the surviving entity. As suggested by the foregoing description, such transactions are time consuming and expensive, both in terms of legal costs and filing fees. By contrast, migrating a trust is simple and fast.

[24] At least upon formation. Again, some form of registration may be required under state or local law if the charitable association will solicit donations from the public.

requirements among the principals, as can be done with partnerships.[25] Although the law of many states expressly limits the use of the LLC vehicle to for-profit enterprises,[26] Delaware permits LLC's to be used for non-profit purposes.[27]

Rather than using By-Laws to govern the structure of the organization, as would a corporation, LLC's utilize an Operating Agreement, under which the controlling parties typically delegate the authority to operate the organization to a Manager or group of managers. The Operating Agreement can also provide for the LLC to be managed by officers, like a corporation. The Operating Agreement is a flexible mechanism, and can provide for whatever form of administrative structure is required.

Because LLC's are not commonly used for charitable organizations, and the laws of relatively few states would appear to permit this, we will simply note that this vehicle continues to evolve and may become more common in the future.

U.S. TAXATION

Among the core issues which any potential philanthropist must address are the U.S. tax aspects of the gifts used to establish the charity and the tax status of the entity to be created. Depending upon the type of property being used to create a charitable entity, the timing of the gift and the charitable purposes of the proposed entity, different planning conclusions will follow an application of relevant tax rules. Accordingly, it is necessary to devote considerable detail to the U.S. tax regime governing charitable giving and charitable enterprises organized in United States and outside of it.

Unfortunately, this area is fraught with complexity. At the conclusion of perhaps the most comprehensive survey and evaluation written of the current U.S. tax laws on this subject, Professor Harvey Dale of New York University Law School and founder of the National Center on Philanthropy and the Law observed: "It is impossible to justify the incredible complexity, inconsistency, and impenetrability of the relevant statutory, regulatory, and other authorities bearing on foreign charities. There can be no reason—and there certainly is no rhyme—to the current pattern." 48 Tax Law Review 657 (1995). Nevertheless, an understanding of the basic structure governing U.S. taxation of charitable institutions is indispensable for proper planning.

---

[25]   Another variant of this theme is the Limited Liability Partnership.

[26]   For example, California, the District of Columbia, New York and Virginia.

[27]   Carolyn Klamp and David R. Heinen, State Law Survey, Delaware Law Concerning Exempt Organizations, Tax Analysts Electronic Citation: 2002 TNT 48-53 (1 November 2001).

U.S. Federal Charitable Income Tax Deduction

Any discussion of the tax deductibility of charitable donations should be prefaced by noting that there is nothing in the U.S. Constitution or in common law which inherently grants a tax benefit to charitable gifts or guarantees an exemption from taxes for charities. These features have been a part of the landscape for so long that it is easy to overlook the fact that Congress came close to not granting special tax benefits to charities when it adopted the income tax. Thus, it is important to remember that tax benefits accorded to various aspects of charitable endeavors are entirely a matter of statute, which can be amended at any time.[28]

1. *Individual Donors*

General Rules

Generally speaking, Section 170(a) of the Internal Revenue Code grants individuals a deduction for gifts to "charitable organizations." Different limitations on the extent of the deductibility apply depending upon whether the charitable organization is a public charity or a private foundation. Generally speaking, cash gifts to public charities are deductible up to 50% of adjusted gross income per year, whereas cash gifts to private foundations are limited to 30% of adjusted gross income. To the extent these limits are exceeded, a carry forward for up to five future tax years is permitted.

The deductibility of significant gifts is likely to be constrained by the Alternative Minimum Tax ("AMT"). Its impact will differ among taxpayers depending upon the level of "tax preference" items on the donor's individual return in the year in which a large charitable gift is made. Even though charitable deductions are not "tax preference" items for AMT purposes, the AMT frequently diminishes the post-tax value of deductions, and thus the tax benefit of the gift, because the AMT tax rate is typically lower than the donor's regular marginal rate.[29]

Different rules also apply to gifts of appreciated property, depending upon whether the donee organization is a public charity or a private foundation. The limitation on the deductibility of gifts of appreciated property to public charities is 30% of the taxpayer's adjusted gross income,

---

[28]   Indeed, proposals to modify the income tax deduction for charitable giving are perennially among the list of proposals before the U.S. Congress to amend the tax code.

[29]   Karen Hobe, "Silent Killer: the Alternative Minimum Tax is slaying taxpayers. Will you be next?" *Barron's* (February 11, 2002) at 23. Because the major rate reductions mandated by The Economic Growth and Tax Relief Reconciliation Act of 2001 did not modify the AMT, the number of taxpayers subject to the AMT is expected to increase dramatically in the coming years. For example, in 2000, 26% of taxpayers with incomes between $200,000 and $500,000 were subject to the AMT. By 2010 this is expected to increase to 98%.

as compared with 20% for gifts to private foundations. Additionally, gifts of such property to public charities is deductible to the extent of its fair market value, whereas the value of gifts of appreciated property private foundations is deductible only to the extent of the donor's adjusted basis (costs plus improvements) to the property.[30]

Non-deductibility of Gifts to Foreign Charities

Significantly, I.R.C. § 170(c) limits the deductibility of charitable contributions for U.S. federal income tax purposes to contributions to or for the use of ". . . a corporation, trust, community chest, fund or foundation" that is *"created or organized in the United States, or in any possession thereof, or under the law of the United States, any State*, the District of Columbia, or any possession of the United States." [Emphasis added.] I.R.C. § 170(c)(2). Moreoer, contributions to foreign charitable organizations or to U.S. organizations that merely act as conduits for foreign charitable organizations are **not** deductible for U.S. income tax purposes.[31]

The geographical limitation on the deductibility of charitable gifts has been part of the U.S. tax law since 1938, and was not an inadvertent decision on the part of the Congress. As explained in the legislative history: "the bill provides that the deduction . . . be also restricted to contributions made to domestic institutions. The exemption from taxation of money or property devoted to charitable and other purposes is based upon the theory that the Government is compensated for the loss of revenue by its relief from financial burden which would otherwise have to be made by appropriations from public funds, and by the benefits resulting from the promotion of the general welfare. The United States derives no such benefit from gifts to foreign institutions, and the proposed limitation is consistent with the above the theory. If the recipient, however, is a domestic organization, the fact that some portion of its funds is used in other countries for charitable and other purposes (such as missionary and educational purposes) will not affect the deductibility of the gift."[32] Nevertheless, charitable grants outside the United States by both public charities and private foundations are subject to considerable regulation by the Internal Revenue Service, as described in Chapter 4.

Even if the foregoing rationale were valid in 1938 [it has been extensively criticized in numerous law review articles], the policy behind the

---

[30]   Section 170(b).

[31]   *See generally*, Rev. Rul. 63-252, 1963-2 C.B. 101. Conduit status may be avoided if a U.S. charity is considered the actual recipient and does not act merely as a fund-raising mechanism for the foreign charity. The test is whether the U.S. charity has control over the donated funds and discretion as to their use so as to ensure that the funds will be used to carry out the U.S. charity's purposes. See also, Rev. Rul. 66-79, 1966-1 C.B. 48, and Rev. Rul. 76-1957, 1976-1 C.B. 61.

[32]   House Report No. 1860, 75th Congress, 3d Session 19–20 (1938).

non-deductibility of gifts to foreign charities is highly questionable as we enter the 21st century. This policy surely was borne of isolationism, the dominant post-World War I foreign policy theme. In today's world of multi-billion dollar foreign aid from the United States government, the legislative history's assertion that the United States derives no benefit from direct gifts to foreign institutions from its citizens is outdated. But more fundamentally, the world today is a much smaller place than it was in 1938. Protection of the environment outside of the United States benefits the United States as well. Alleviation of poverty and illiteracy outside the United States furthers over-all U.S. foreign policy, for example, by addressing the root causes of hopelessness that have led to the formation of terrorist organizations.

However anachronistic the prohibition on deductibility of gifts to foreign charities may be, there currently is no reasonable prospect that this aspect of U.S. tax law will be changed. Any enlargement of charitable gift deductibility should be expected to be opposed by those in Congress seeking to protect the tax revenues. Moreover, the lack of any domestic political constituency to advocate and support such a change would likely keep any initiative to permit the deductibility of gifts to foreign charities off of the legislative calendar.

Treaty Overrides

The general rule disallowing an income tax deduction for donations to foreign charitable organizations is overridden by bilateral income tax treaties between the U.S. and other countries, but in only three instances:

- *Mexico*. Under Article 22(2) of the U.S.-Mexico tax treaty, U.S. individuals are granted deductions for direct gifts to Mexican charities, as defined in Mexican law, provided the Mexican standards are "essentially equivalent" to U.S. law regulating charitable organizations.
- *Canada*. Under certain circumstances, U.S. individuals are eligible for tax deductions for direct gifts to Canadian charities under Article XXI (5). Significantly, U.S. standards for determining deductibility, rather than Canadian, apply.
- *Israel*. The most recent amendments to the U.S.-Israel tax treaty added a new Article 15A, which permits U.S. individuals to deduct direct contributions to charities organized in Israel. As with the Canadian treaty, U.S. standards apply.

In each instance, special rules may limit further the utility of these deductions in particular circumstances.[33]

---

[33] For example, under the Canadian Treaty, the applicable percentage limitations are further qualified by reference to Canadian source income. Thus, a U.S. citizen without Canadian source income is not eligible to deduct gifts to Canadian charities.

Practical Considerations

If the individual considering establishing a charitable entity requires the donation establishing the entity to be tax deductible, use of a charitable organization either formed in the United States or in a treaty exemption country is mandated.

There are many circumstances where a current charitable deduction from income tax may not be needed. For example, if an entrepreneur wishes to establish a charitable organization with 10% of the stock of a closely held corporation, for which there is no public market, an income tax deduction might have little value and therefore might not be required. Moreover, as discussed below, if the potential donor wishes only to establish the entity during his lifetime, and intends to defer funding of the charity until his death, there may be no current need for the deduction from federal income taxes.

2. *Corporate Donors*

As in the case of individual donors, the general rule of Section 170, which allows a deduction from gross income subject to the Federal corporate income tax also applies to gifts from corporations to charities. As with individuals, gifts to qualified charities are deductible from corporate taxable income if the charity is created or organized domestically. There is one additional qualifier, however: "a contribution or gift by a corporation to a *trust, chest, fund or foundation* shall be deductible by reason of this paragraph only if it is to be used within the United States. . . ." Section 170(c)(2). [Emphasis added.] This qualification does not apply to gifts to charitable organizations organized as corporations.

This additional condition appears to have been left over from legislation enacted in 1935, which was amended in 1938. Whether attributable to sloppy legislative drafting or to the nature of the legislative process, which charitably has been analogized to making sausage, the language remains. As a result, U.S. corporate donors have good reason to prefer charities which are in corporate form. Such entities may utilize gifts for charitable purposes outside of the United States without jeopardizing the tax deductibility of the contribution from the corporate donor.

As with charitable gifts from individuals, a cap is imposed on the amount of the deduction. For corporations, the limitation is 10% of its taxable income,[34] and any excess contributions may be carried forward for five years. As with individuals, the AMT can have an impact on tax benefit to be derived from corporate gifts to charity.

---

[34] Taxable income is computed without regard for the deduction for charitable contributions, the deductions for dividends received, and any net operating loss and capital loss carrybacks. I.R.C. § 170(b)(2); Treas. Reg. § 1.170-11(a).

3. Deduction for Trusts and Estates

Trusts and estates, of course, are subject to income tax. Therefore the question arises as to how they handle contributions to a charitable organization. In general, the rule that applies for a trust, applies for an estate. But as will be seen, not all trusts are treated alike.

Section 642(c) provides a special rule for amounts paid or permanently set aside for a charitable purpose. An estate or trust, but only a complex trust,[35] not a "simple" trust, is allowed a deduction against taxable income in lieu of the Section 170(c) deduction, for any amount paid for a charitable purpose (determined without regard to the provision described above which disallows the deduction to a foreign entity.)[36]

The legislative history makes it clear that this result was intended. These provisions date from 1919,[37] when there was no geographic restriction imposed on the charitable deduction for either individuals or trusts and estates. In 1938,[38] when the restriction sprang up for individuals and corporations, it was not—one can only assume deliberately—placed on trusts and estates. The Tax Court has confirmed the allowance of the charitable deduction for trusts and estates regardless of geography, and the Service has acquiesced.[39]

The outcome seems odd; two different results for two similarly situated taxpayers. But it has been argued that it makes sense. The thinking is that since a U.S. individual could make a gift (nondeductible) to a foreign charity, which invests the funds tax-free in the U.S., earning say, portfolio interest or capital gains, another individual should be able to make a gift to a U.S. trust (again, no deduction at this point), which invests the funds in the U.S. and which then makes gifts each year to a foreign charity, taking the deduction. In both cases the U.S. donor is not receiving a deduction, and in both the income is, when all is said and done, not taxed, either because it is earned by the non-U.S. charity or the donor-trust offsets income with the deduction. In a different light, the rule still

---

35   A complex trust, in brief, is a nongrantor trust, i.e., not subject to the special rules in Sections 671–679. Also, it is not a trust that by its terms is required to distribute all its income on a current basis and not to pay, set aside or use income for charitable purposes. Complex trusts and their beneficiaries are defined and taxed under Sections 661–663. Simple trusts—those that must distribute all their income on a current basis and not pay, set aside, etc. income for charitable purposes—are dealt with in Section 651.

36   "Thus, an amount paid to a corporation, trust, or community chest, fund, or foundation otherwise described in Section 170(c)(2) shall be considered paid for a purpose specified in Section 170(c) even though the corporation, trust, or community chest, fund, or foundation is not created or organized in the United States, any State, the District of Columbia, or any possession of the United States." Regulations § 1.642(c)-1(a)(2).

37   Revenue Act of 1918, Pub. L. No. 65-254, § 219(b), 40 Stat. 1057, 1071 (1919).

38   Revenue Act of 1938, Pub. L. No. 75-554 (1938).

39   *Est. of Tait v. Commissioner*, 11 T.C. 731, 736–37 (1948), acq. 1950-1 C.B. 5.

looks odd. How is it even-handed for an individual, who earns money however he or she earns money, to be denied a charitable deduction for a gift to a foreign charity and a trust, which earns money by investing in a portfolio, to be allowed the deduction? In any event, it should be noted that the allowance of the deduction to the trust is not a direct, simple-minded path to avoiding the geographic restriction.

U.S. Federal Estate & Gift Tax Deduction

1. *Federal Estate Tax Charitable Deduction*

Under existing U.S. tax law, an estate tax deduction is generally allowed for "all bequests, legacies, devises, or transfers," in unlimited amounts, to or for the use of certain qualified charities. Qualified charities are described broadly as any entity organized and operated exclusively for "religious, charitable, scientific, literary, or educational purposes . . . ," in the same manner as the entities eligible to receive gifts which are deductible for income tax purposes. Significantly, unlike the deductibility for income-tax purposes, the deduction for estate tax purposes is **not** premised upon the donee charitable organization being organized in the U.S. or the funds being utilized in the United States. I.R.C. § 2055(a)(2); Treas. Reg. § 20.2055-1(a).

There are numerous differences in the language describing gifts which are eligible for deductions from the income tax and the estate tax. These differences have been described by commentators as "inexplicable," "maddening" and "bizarre;" but there is no question that **the blanket prohibition on deductibility of gifts to non-U.S. charities that applies to income tax deductions, does not apply to estate tax deductions.** Nevertheless, other rules operate to limit the deductibility of testamentary gifts to foreign private foundations, unless such organizations receive more than 85% of their support from sources outside of the United States.[40] Therefore, as a practical matter, any U.S. individual desiring to fund a foreign private foundation in large or substantial measure by testamentary gift, must qualify the foreign foundation as tax-exempt. I.R.C. § 2055(e)(1) disallows estate tax deductions to foreign private foundations *unless* the foreign private foundation has qualified as tax-exempt under Section 501(c)(3).

The availability of an estate tax deduction for gifts to non-U.S. charities in unlimited amounts is among the most significant features of the applicable U.S. tax regime. While lifetime gifts to charities remain subject to both the percentage limitations [generally speaking, 50% of adjusted gross income for gifts to public charities and 30% for gifts to private foundations] *and* the Alternative Minimum Tax, testamentary gifts are not so

---

[40] I.R.C. § 4948(b).

limited. Accordingly, the establishment of private foundations, which will be funded in substantial or large measure upon the donor's death, are increasingly attractive.

2.   *Federal Gift Tax Charitable Deduction*

Rules that are similar to the U.S. federal estate tax deduction rules also allow a charitable contributions deduction for U.S. gift tax purposes. *Compare* the text of I.R.C. § 2522(a)(2) with §§ 170(c)(2) and 2055(a)(2). Again, there are inconsistencies in the applicable statutory language, but such inconsistencies do not qualify the conclusion that **gifts to non-U.S. charities generally qualify for exclusion from the gift tax.**

As with the estate tax, however, deductions from amounts subject to the gift tax are disallowed for gifts to foreign private foundations unless such entities receive more than 85% of their support from outside the United States,[41] or the foreign private foundation has been recognized by the IRS as tax-exempt under Section 501(c)(3). As a practical matter, therefore, philanthropists wishing to make substantial lifetime gifts to foreign charitable organizations will want to ensure that the donee is qualified as tax-exempt.

Exempt Status

Under applicable U.S. tax laws, a charitable corporation or trust which is qualified as exempt from taxation derives two primary benefits. First, all income earned on its investments and all donations received are exempt from income tax.[42] Second, fund-raising is facilitated, as it can inform potential donors that their contributions will be deductible, subject to the percentage limitations described above. Tax-exempt status, however, does not come automatically from establishing an organization whose purposes fit the statutory categories of being organized and operated exclusively for "religious, charitable, scientific, literary, or educational purposes. . . ." Rather, the organization must apply to the Internal Revenue Service to be recognized as tax-exempt, which status then is reviewed periodically for compliance with the applicable rules.[43]

---

[41]   The annual gift tax exclusion, currently $11,000 per donor per donee per year, plus the lifetime gift exclusion of $1 million for U.S. purposes, would have to be exceeded for the gift to be taxable.

[42]   Nevertheless, exempt organizations remain taxable on so-called "unrelated" business income. The rules for determining whether a particular activity is unrelated to the exempt organization's purposes are difficult and complex. Because private foundations are subject to excise taxes on so-called excess business holdings, as described in Chapter 4, private foundations usually are not subject to these taxes. Bruce Hopkins, Starting and Managing a Nonprofit Organization: A Legal Guide (3rd Ed. 2001) at 183.

[43]   Among the purposes behind the large quantity of information required by Form 990-PF, Appendix 2, is the monitoring of the organization's tax-exempt status.

For public charities and private foundations, the application for tax-exempt status is made on Form 1023, a copy of which, together with the instructions, is attached at Appendix 1.[44] Generally speaking, newly formed charitable organizations seek to obtain exempt status contemporaneously with being formed. Since qualification depends upon being both "organized" and "operated" for exempt purposes, and the organization will not have had much in the way of operating experience at the time it applies, the application places considerable emphasis on the organizational documents. Accordingly, particular care must be taken in drafting the corporate charter and by-laws, if applicable, or the Trust Agreement, to make clear the organization's charitable purposes.

The organizational documents should recite and restate the applicable provisions of law which form the basis for the tax exemption. An example of a form of organizational document which has been approved by the Internal Revenue Service is included as Appendix 7.

Under the law, the statement of purposes in the organizational documents can be quite broad, e.g., "educational," "charitable," etc. Nevertheless, the Internal Revenue Service requires a reasonable level of specificity in answering questions on Form 1023 regarding the organization's purposes. Where the organization will not qualify as a public charity, for example, because it will not rely upon broad public support, these organizational documents will also be required to spell out the entity's intended compliance with the various regulatory constraints governing private foundations. These are described in Chapter 4.

One conceptual difficulty invariably confronts the first time applicant for exempt status: until an entity has proven that it is a public charity, it is regarded as a private foundation, notwithstanding the fact that it has no operating history. Recognizing this "Catch 22," the Internal Revenue Service permits applicants to declare that they *intend* to be public charities, for purposes of immediately avoiding private foundation status and its attendant constraints. In these circumstances, the Internal Revenue Service will grant the organization provisional public charity status and then revisit this status following its initial five years of operations. In connection with seeking such an "advance ruling," the organization must agree to extend the statute of limitations for payment of any taxes which may become due as a result of failing to meet the tests of being a public charity.[45] In that case, the organization will be found to have been a

---

[44] Organizations qualifying for exempt status under § 501(c)(3) utilize Form 1023; organizations qualifying under the other provisions of § 501(c) (see Chart A, Chapter 1) generally utilize Form 1024. Form 1024 asks for similar information, but has specific sections tailored to the other bases for exempt status in Section 501(c), other than subsection (3).

[45] See Chapter 4.

private foundation, and potentially be subject to the various categories of excise taxes on a retroactive basis.[46]

In addition to providing organizational documents to the Internal Revenue Service, the Application for Recognition of Exemption must be supported by financial projections, which can be time-consuming and costly to prepare. Applicants must also obtain a taxpayer identification number and pay a user fee in connection with the application. Currently, for exempt organizations which have had or expect to have annual gross receipts of less than $10,000 annually for a four year period, the user fee is $150.00. Above this threshold, the user fee is $500.00.[47]

Termination of Exempt Status

Once a foundation has received a Determination Letter recognizing its status as an exempt organization, it must be operated in accordance with the charitable purposes set forth in its organizational documents, as represented to the Internal Revenue Service in obtaining exempt status. Failure to do so can trigger the imposition of penalties in the form of excise taxes, as summarized in Chapter 4. Repeated or flagrant disregard of applicable standards can result in the Internal Revenue Service revoking the organization's exempt status.

If the charitable organization decides to terminate its exempt status itself, it must formally notify the Internal Revenue Service.[48] The procedures to be followed in terminating exempt status are governed by a series of special rules, but usually this is accomplished by transferring all of the assets of the exempt entity to an existing public charity. The failure to do so triggers a penalty tax equal to the lesser amount of the aggregate tax benefits the organization has received as a result of its exempt status or the value of its net assets.[49]

---

[46] The various categories of excise taxes are described in Chapter 4.
[47] Applicants use Form 8718 to claim the lower user fee.
[48] Section 507(a)(1).
[49] Section 507(c).

CHAPTER 4

U.S. LEGAL CONSTRAINTS

PRIVATE FOUNDATION RULES

Background

Following public hearings which highlighted abuses by private foundations established by wealthy U.S. individuals, Congress enacted a comprehensive series of rules governing private foundations as part of the Tax Reform Act of 1969. As a result, any charitable organization which does not meet the legal definition of a public charity must be operated in compliance with a complex regulatory regime administered by the Internal Revenue Service if it is to maintain its tax-exempt status.

Prior to the enactment of these "reform" measures, the propriety of various transactions and practices was judged by an "arm's-length" standard—that is, whether the transaction or practice at issue was reasonable and fair when judged from the perspective of how unrelated parties might have acted. After focusing on several highly publicized cases involving wealthy families, Congress determined that objective tests should be substituted for the inherently subjective, "all facts and circumstances" evaluations of such practices, which had been the standard under existing law.

Congress criticized previous Internal Revenue Service enforcement efforts as ineffective. It found that the difficulty in proving a violation of law under the arm's-length standard tended to discourage the IRS from enforcing the law. Since the only sanction then available was to revoke the organization's tax-exempt status, which essentially put the charitable organization "out of business," both courts and prosecutors were reluctant to pursue less than egregious practices.

The congressional solution was to impose a series of penalties, in the form of excise taxes, which could be graduated and also targeted, not only against the exempt organization, but against responsible Directors or managers as well. These excise taxes are imposed in the context of a regulatory regime which substitutes "bright line" tests of behavior for the subjective, arm's-length standard under prior law.

Many of the standards imposed in 1969 represent reasonable, common sense practices, that might form the basis for a charitable organization's policy to ensure, for example, that benefits do not inure to any private individual. Taken as a whole, however, the regulatory regime is excessive and burdensome. Indeed, many professionals working in the charitable giving sector counsel against forming a private foundation, unless the donor is able to establish the foundation with a minimum of $500,000 to $1,000,000. Otherwise, the costs of regulatory compliance will likely outweigh the charitable benefits that the organization will be able to provide.

With the benefit of over 30 years of living under the private foundation excise tax rules, most observers would objectively say that Congress overreached and overreacted in response to a few highly publicized abuses.[50] Moreover, from the perspective of tax policy which has waxed and waned through multiple cycles of liberal and conservative political leadership since 1969, many of the "reforms" included in the Tax Reform Act package can be seen as modest revenue enhancing measures accomplished in the name of "regulating" wealthy donors. While the revenue consequences of these rules are modest, the regulatory burdens and constraints are not.[51]

The purpose of this book is to help potential donors considering formation of charitable organizations evaluate whether an entity should be formed in the United States or outside of it. An understanding of the existing regulatory framework applicable to charitable foundations organized under U.S. law is central to this evaluation, and therefore a summary of the principal features of the Internal Revenue Service's regulation of private foundations follows below.

---

[50] At the time these "reforms" were under consideration by Congress, few organizations or groups stepped forward to defend the existing practices or oppose the response which became enacted unto law. Without a constituency to defend the then current practices, Congressional advocates of a "clamp down" were largely unopposed.

[51] One of the by-products of the regulatory burdens on private foundations has been the growth of so-called Donor Advised Mutual Funds. The program established by the Vanguard Group, for example, requires donors to commit to making donations of a minimum of $25,000. These will allow the donor to "create a lasting philanthropic legacy without incurring the high costs and administrative requirements of a private foundation." http://www.vanguardcharitable.org/ProgramOverview. Such entities are in essence pass-though vehicles for donations to public charities, which accord donors considerable flexibility in timing their donations. Since the charitable gift (to the mutual fund) is irrevocable, the donor obtains the benefit of a tax deduction in the year the donation is made, even if the gifts to charities do not occur until subsequent years. In the interim, the mutual funds are pleased to invest the endowment fund for a management fee. Vanguard's Charitable Endowment Program raised approximately $165 million in its fiscal year ending June 30,

Excise Tax on Investment Income

The general rule is that the interest, dividends and net realized capital gains of private foundations are subject to a 2% excise tax. I.R.C. § 4940.[52] The primary justification given for this provision in the legislative history of the Tax Reform Act was that: "The Congress has concluded that private foundations should share some of the burden of paying the cost of government, especially for more extensive and vigorous enforcement of the tax laws relating to exempt organizations."[53]

Based on this rationale, this excise tax was initially set at 4%. After several years, the Council on Foundations petitioned Congress to revisit this tax, given that it was generating several multiples of revenue in excess of the annual budget of the Exempt Organizations Branch of the Internal Revenue Service. As a result, this tax was more recently re-characterized, at least by the Council, as a user fee. In addition, the law was amended so that in certain instances where a specific threshold of giving is exceeded, the excise tax called for by this section can be reduced to 1%. Even so, the complexity of establishing eligibility for the lower rate has resulted in relatively few private foundations claiming the lower rate.

Self-Dealing

Section 4941 imposes strict rules against self-dealing between private foundations and their insiders. To enforce the prohibitions against self-dealing, the law created a new category of "disqualified persons" which are defined to include trustees, directors, foundation managers, substantial contributors to the foundation, certain family members of the above, including spouses and children, and corporations, partnerships and other business entities related to or controlled by these individuals. A "substantial contributor" for these purposes is an individual, corporation or other entity that has contributed in the aggregate more than 2% of the total contributions to the foundation. Invariably, the founder of the foundation falls within this definition.

The following transactions between private foundations and any disqualified person are prohibited: (1) the sale, exchange or leasing of prop-

---

2001. See also http://www.charitablegift.org. Similar programs have been established by a member of major mutual fund families, including Fidelity, T. Rowe Price and the Calvert Group. The Calvert Group offers donors the opportunity to invest in its Social Investment Portfolio and its Community Investment Pool.

[52] For foreign private foundations, the tax is 4%, but only as to U.S. source interest and dividends. Section 4948(a).

[53] General Explanation of the Tax Reform Act of 1969, H.R. 13270, 91st Congress, Public Law 91-172 at 29 (1970) (the "General Explanation"). The original proposal as reported by the Committee on Ways and Means of the House of Representatives provided for a 7.5% excise tax on investment income of foundations. House Report No. 91-413 (Part 1), 91st Congress, 1st Session at 19 (1969).

erty; (2) the lending of money or other extension of credit; (3) the furnishing of goods, services or facilities; (4) the payment of compensation or expenses by the foundation to a disqualified person; and (5) the transfer to or use by or for the benefit of a disqualified person of the foundation's income or assets. Violations of the rules against self-dealing trigger a series of penalties, in the form of excise taxes, against both the foundation and the person responsible for the defined self-dealing.

For purposes of interpreting these rules, it does not matter that the transaction may be beneficial to the foundation. For example, the sale or leasing of real property to a foundation at below-market rates would fall within the purview of the prohibitions even if it were to save the foundation substantial resources from having to purchase or lease property on the open market. Nevertheless, it is clear that Congress perceived that nothing less than the integrity of private foundations itself was at stake when it substituted objective, "bright line" tests for existing arm's-length standards.[54]

Minimum Distributions

Among the evils Congress sought to remedy by the 1969 Act was the use of tax-exempt private foundations to accumulate and hold large amounts of capital resources. In its current form, Section 4942 requires foundations to pay out in "qualifying distributions" a minimum of 5% of the market value of their assets each year. Failure to do so triggers an initial penalty tax of 15% of the shortfall. If the foundation fails to make the necessary qualifying distributions by the end of the next tax year, an "additional tax" of 100% is imposed on any undistributed amounts below the 5% threshold. The foundation's choice therefore is a simple one: make the qualifying distributions to charitable purposes or have the amounts confiscated by the government.

Qualifying distributions include eligible grants to other charitable organizations, activities in furtherance of the foundation's exempt purposes, expenditures for assets acquired by the foundation for the conduct of its functions and reasonable and necessary administrative expenses. There are complex rules for the calculation and timing of the required minimum payouts.[55]

As a practical matter, unless the foundation's investments are yielding a minimum of 5% per year, which, at least in the current economic environment, has been challenging, the foundation in essence must move toward spending itself out of existence each year to comply with this rule.[56] As a result, private foundations which are begun with modest gifts

---

54 General Explanation at 30.
55 See the instructions to Form 990-PF, Appendix 2.
56 Declines in the value of the foundation's endowment do **not** constitute qualify-

may not let their endowment fund accumulate, so that more ambitious charitable goals might be accomplished in the future.[57] Moreover, the diminution of capital forced by this rule in the long run can impede the ability of the foundation to accomplish its charitable goals.

Excess Business Holdings

In the legislative history of the Tax Reform Act, Congress cited numerous instances where wealthy families utilized private foundations to acquire and aggregate large numbers of related (and sometimes unrelated) businesses. Even though all of the dividends and capital appreciation from such businesses were dedicated to charitable purposes (presumably regular corporate income taxes were paid on unrelated business activities), Congress denounced these activities as inappropriate and as inherently unfair competition to for-profit enterprises.[58] Like the rationale given by Congress for the adoption of the minimum distributions rules, Congress viewed the accumulation of capital within tax-exempt organizations suspiciously.

As a result, Section 4943 now requires that foundations and their "disqualified persons" together may not own more than 20 percent of the voting stock of business corporations or equivalent interests in business partnerships. This threshold is increased to 35% if effective control of a corporation's holdings in question are held by one or more persons who are not "disqualified persons," as would be the case with publicly held companies. If the foundation itself owns less than 2% of the corporate holdings under scrutiny, it does not matter what percentage is owned by disqualified persons.

The value of defined excess holdings is subject to an annual excise tax of 5%. In addition, divestiture of defined excess holdings must follow if the foundation is to avoid additional penalty taxes.

Jeopardy Investments

Notwithstanding fiduciary standards applicable to Trustees and Directors of foundations, Section 4944 imposes penalties for speculative investments by private foundations. The applicable standard is "ordinary business care and prudence" based on all relevant facts and circumstances prevailing at the time the investment is made and on the short-term and long-term financial needs of the foundation to carry out its exempt pur-

---

ing distributions. Therefore, in declining markets, the minimum distribution rules frequently exacerbate any decline in the foundation's net worth.

[57]   As noted above, one feature of Donor Advised Mutual Funds is to provide a vehicle for accumulating and growing a charitable endowment fund, which private foundations are hampered from doing by Section 4942.

[58]   General Explanation at 40.

poses.[59] No categories of investment are deemed *per se* violations, but the regulations indicate that margin trading, commodity futures trading, investments in oil and gas interests, puts, calls, straddles, warrants and selling short should all be viewed with a "red flag." When investments are found have jeopardized a foundation's purposes, penalty taxes, measured as a percentage of the amounts improperly invested, may be imposed on both the foundation and the managers responsible for the questionable investments.

Taxable Expenditures

The hearings leading to the 1969 legislation identified a number of abuses in grant making by private foundations. Congress addressed these in Section 4945. That provision imposes a penalty tax, initially 10% of the amount involved, against the foundation and 2.5% against the foundation's managers, on several areas of activities as follows:

- *Lobbying.* Expenditures to attempt to influence legislation are prohibited.
- *Electioneering and Voter Registration.* Expenditures to attempt to influence the outcome of any public election or to support voter registration drives are prohibited.
- *Grants to Individuals.* Travel, study and similar grants to individuals are prohibited.
- *Non-charities.* Qualified public charities alone are eligible to receive grants from private foundations, unless they are for charitable purposes and the foundation willing to exercise so-called "expenditure responsibility," as described in greater detail below.

The foregoing is a general summary of the prohibitions on disbursements in the above areas. In many cases, giving for related activities is possible, but subject to extensive and detailed qualifications.[60] As

---

[59]   Regulation 53.4944-1(a)(2)(i).

[60]   An excellent example of the type of difficulties charities encounter may be found the uproar which followed the revelation that the American Red Cross had distributed but a small portion of the hundreds of millions of dollars it collected on behalf of the victims of the terrorist incidents on September 11, 2001. In an Op Ed column by Daniel Henninger on November 16, 2001 in the *Wall Street Journal* entitled Charity Begins at Home, Ends Up Nowhere, it was stated: "there were something over 5000 victims of 9/11 . . . We know their names and where their families live. So what's the problem with letting Americans everywhere help them financially? The problem is that the U.S. tax code forbids it. . . . Seriously. Steven Miller of the Internal Revenue Service explained the relevant tax law to Congress last week: 'an affected individual generally is not entitled to charitable funds without a showing of need.' If a tax-exempt charity gives money to a person whose income is above a certain level, that charity could lose its tax-exempt status. Bureaucracy and formal procedures allow a complex society to function with a needed degree of predictability and,

a result, most private foundations make it a practice to "steer clear" of giving in these areas, if only to avoid complex and time-consuming compliance and oversight.

Reporting Requirements

The 1969 amendments also added extensive reporting requirements for private foundations.[61] These reports are filed on Form 990-PF, a copy of which is attached at Appendix 2. The information required is extensive, including gross income and expenses, balance sheet, grants for exempt purposes, total contributions and gifts, including the names and addresses of all "substantial contributors."[62] These returns are available for inspection and copying by the public, and must be made available for public inspection at the foundation's offices upon request. The various excise taxes under sections 4940 through 4945, described above, are imposed by the Schedules to Form 990-PF, some of which involve considerable complexity. Indeed, the reaction of most foundation founders upon seeing this form for the first time is to engage a professional accountant or lawyer.

Although entirely consistent with U.S. public policy requiring "full disclosure" in such areas, for example, as securities offerings and political campaign financing, many individuals regard charitable giving as a private matter. Anonymous gifts are hardly possible when a foundation's tax return is open for public inspection. This is particularly so where numerous self-appointed "watch dog" organizations are unconstrained in disseminating public information, widely and effortlessly, over the internet.[63] While "full disclosure" may be as American as apple pie, many donors are significantly constrained, if not offended, at having their eleemosynary objects subject to public scrutiny, and their IRS information returns readily disseminated to anyone typing in their organization's name on an internet search engine.

---

in theory, efficiency. . . . We've arrived at the point where our most important institutions must carry the cumulative burden of doing not only what they were created to do, but also making sure they never fail in any one decision to conform to our obsessions with fairness, inclusiveness and social rectitude. . . . It says something about the American people, all for the good, that when the call went out to help the September 11 families, they answered, thinking the monetary and moral transmission here should be as straightforward as anything ever gets. Well it's not. A simple act of charity has also become complicated."

[61] Section 6033.

[62] Defined as contributing more than 2% of the organization's funding.

[63] Guidestar, a service of Philanthropic Research, Inc., takes all raw data received by IRS on Forms 990 and 990-PF and posts the information on the internet. See, www.guidestar.org.

Conclusions

Any doubt as to the comprehensiveness of the regulatory environment governing private foundations in the U.S. is quickly dispelled by reviewing the information required of private foundations on Form 990-PF. If the 30 pages of instructions were not daunting enough, the disclosure as to the "estimated average time" to prepare the form, as required by the Paperwork Reduction Act,[64] is:

- Recordkeeping   140 hours, 37 minutes
- Learning about the law or the form   27 hours, 40 minutes
- Preparing the Form   32 hours, 7 minutes
- Copying and sending to the IRS   16 minutes.

This "information return" is used by the Internal Revenue Service to gather extensive information on all regulatory aspects of a foundation's activities, whether or not they involve payment of any excise taxes.

> Honest philanthropists have the right to ask whether the 30-year old U.S. regulatory scheme is appropriate—or, indeed, necessary. Many view the Internal Revenue Service's expansion into a number of the areas covered by the regulatory regime described above, whether under the aegis of imposing excise taxes or otherwise, as overreaching.[65] As with many areas of government regulation, once the Congress decides to intervene to remedy a perceived abuse, invariably the form of regulation goes farther than was required to remedy the problem. Nevertheless, potential philanthropists should not lose sight of the basic fact that acceptance of the regulatory regime is the price of income, estate and gift tax deductibility for gifts to private foundations. If this deductibility is not needed—or can be foregone—viable alternatives in the form of foreign foundations can be utilized to achieve the desired charitable purposes.

---

[64] Instructions to Form 999-PF at 28, Appendix 2.

[65] Part of the problem is that charitable organizations are creatures of state law and should be overseen and regulated by the states in which they are formed or incorporated. Few states, with the notable exceptions of New York and California, however, devote much in the way of enforcement resources to policing charitable organizations. Nevertheless, in being called upon to enforce the statutory scheme created by Congress in 1969, the Internal Revenue Service is required to work in areas far beyond its usual tax collection function.

CONSTRAINTS ON CROSS-BORDER GIVING

As noted in Chapter 3, the Internal Revenue Code draws numerous distinctions between charitable endeavors inside and outside of the United States. Sometimes the distinctions are "fine lines," and sometimes they are "bright lines." The distinctions frequently are arbitrary and for no apparent reason. As a matter of policy, there should be little difference between a charitable dollar spent to feed a hungry child in Alabama versus one spent to feed a hungry child in Azerbaijan. As a legal matter, however, there is.

At the time most of the provisions relating to the deductibility of charitable contributions from income, estate and gift taxes, and in particular, the imposition of the regulatory regime governing private foundations in 1969, were enacted into law, the world was a much larger place. Today, however, with fast, convenient and relatively inexpensive jet transportation available to any part of the world, together with the ability to communicate instantly with virtually every place in the world, whether by land line or wireless telephone, facsimile or the internet, the objects of philanthropy "know no boundaries." Nevertheless, U.S. law represents a significant constraint on borderless giving.

As mentioned above, unless a private foundation makes gifts to *public charities*, it runs the risk of incurring excise taxes for failing to meet its minimum distribution requirements under Section 4542. Moreover, if the gift is not a defined "qualifying distribution," it may also be deemed to be a taxable expenditure, which would potentially be subject to additional taxes. From a definitional standpoint, for a private foundation safely to make a gift to a public charity, that entity must be qualified as tax-exempt under Section 501(c)(3). While this is basic to U.S. public charities, many foreign charities will not have so qualified, and therefore gifts to such foreign charities do not automatically "pass muster" under the regulatory regime governing private foundations. For this reason, most U.S. private foundations make their gifts to U.S. public charities, following the "path of least resistance." If, however, a charitable donor's interests lie in areas which are partially or wholly outside the United States, an additional set of regulatory burdens must be faced.

Equivalency Determinations

Since payments from a U.S. private foundation to a U.S. public charity by definition are "qualifying distributions," the Internal Revenue Service has established a procedure whereby grantors can make a "reasonable judgment" and "good faith determination"[66] that the gift to the foreign

---

[66]   See Regulations 53.4945-6(c)(2)(ii), 53.4942(a)-3(a)(6) and 53.4945-5(a)(5).

entity has all of the indicia of a gift to a U.S. public charity, and therefore should be accorded the same legal status as a gift to a U.S. public charity. Revenue Procedure 92–94, a copy of which is attached at Appendix 3, in essence spells out "safe harbor" rules for having a grant to a foreign entity be deemed the legal equivalent of a grant to a U.S. public charity.

The "good faith determination" may be based on an affidavit of the grantee or an opinion of counsel of the grantor or the grantee. The form of the affidavit is set forth in Revenue Procedure 92–94, and its elements track essentially the same subjects as Form 1023, the Application for Recognition of Exempt Status under § 501(c)(3), Appendix 1. In summary, the affidavit must include:

- The purposes for which the grantee was organized;
- A description of the grantee's past, current and future activities and operations;
- A copy of the grantee's organizational and governing documents;
- A statement that none of the grantee's income and assets confer an improper private benefit;
- A statement that no person has a proprietary interest in the income or assets of the grantee;
- A copy of the relevant statutory law or prohibition in the grantee's governing instruments controlling the distribution of the grantee's assets upon dissolution;
- A statement that the grantee is not engaged, except to an insubstantial extent, in activities that further nonexempt purposes or influence legislation;
- A statement that the grantee does not engage in political or campaign activities on behalf of candidates for public office;
- A statement indicating whether the grantee is controlled by another organization, and, if so, what organization;
- A statement of what type of publicly supported charity the grantee is [*e.g.*, a school, hospital, church, etc.];
- If the grantee claims to be publicly supported, a Schedule of Financial Support for the four most recently completed taxable years.

If, instead of offering an affidavit, an opinion of counsel is to be substituted, counsel must have reviewed a sufficient number of facts concerning the grantee's operations and support to enable the Internal Revenue Service to reach a conclusion that the grantee would be characterized as a public charity under the Code. In other words, any counsel rendering an opinion based on anything less than a review of all the factors listed above would leave his client "on thin ice."

Notwithstanding laudable efforts on the part of the IRS to simplify and streamline the process of grant making to foreign charities, the equivalency determination process remains complex, time-consuming and costly.[67] Compliance frequently involves translating organizational documents and foreign laws into English, examining years of financial records, and attempting to reconcile differences between U.S. GAAP and foreign accounting methods. In addition, cultural differences can impede the ability of U.S. grantors to obtain all of the information necessary to make the equivalency determination.

In short, even though well articulated "safe harbors" are prescribed in Revenue Procedure 92–94 to allow grants to foreign charities, technical barriers to compliance significantly inhibit U.S. foundations from making foreign grants.

Expenditure Responsibility

Where an equivalency determination affidavit or opinion of counsel cannot be obtained, it is still possible for U.S. foundations to make a "qualifying distribution" grant to a foreign grantee. These are the same procedures that apply where grants are made to U.S.-based recipients which are not public charities. The so-called "expenditure responsibility" rules are designed to ensure that the grantee is utilizing the grant in the same manner and for analogous purposes as would a public charity.

The major elements of expenditure responsibility are summarized as follows:

Pre-grant inquiry. The private foundation must inquire of the potential grantee to be assured that the grant will be used for proper, charitable purposes. Typically the inquiry reviews past history and experience of the grantee and its practices.

Written agreement. Where the grantee is not a public charity, the terms of the grant must be memorialized in a written contract. The regulations are quite specific as to the elements which must be included in such agreements. In addition to basic identifying information, including the purposes of the grant, the grantee must make the following commitments in writing:

- To repay any portion of the grant that is not used for the stated purposes;

---

[67]   The experience of one private foundation is recited in a recent article: "When the Kunstadter Foundation made its first international grant of $2,500 to a project in China, . . . it sent the paperwork to its lawyer for review. A bill for $3,000 accompanied the lawyer's [equivalency determination] letter." Family Foundations Discuss How Small Grants Can Make a Difference, The Chronicle of Philanthropy (February 21, 2002) at 16.

- To submit thorough periodic or annual reports on the manner in which the funds were expended and the progress grantee has made towards achieving the purposes or goals set forth in the grant;
- To maintain receipts and records of all expenditures, which may be made available to the grantor at any time; and
- Not to use any of the grant for noncharitable, lobbying or campaign activities.[68]

Reports. The grantee must provide regular reports to the grantor on the progress and fulfillment of the grant.

Reports to the IRS. Form 990-PF requires that grantee add a schedule to its return on Form 990-PF providing a summary paragraph on each expenditure responsibility grant's status.

Financial Accounts. If the grantee is a private foundation itself, it must be able to prove that all of the grant funds have been expended and not retained as part of its endowment fund. These so-called "out of corpus" rules are administered in tandem with the minimum distribution rules described above, so that private foundations may not circumvent the minimum distribution rules by making grants to other private foundations, which themselves might hold the funds and not distribute them for charitable purposes. Any private foundation receiving a grant from another private foundation therefore must establish that these funds were expended on timely basis for the purposes of the grant. If the grantee is not a private foundation, the grantee must agree to segregate the grant in a separate bank account until all of the funds have been expended.

Until recently, the extent to which the equivalency determination and expenditure responsibility rules overlap or provided a hierarchy for foreign giving was not entirely clear. The Council on Foundations in 2001 secured an information letter from the IRS affirming that U.S. private foundations could invoke the expenditure responsibility rules for foreign grant making without first attempting to obtain an equivalency determination affidavit.[69] In other words, even though the grant was made to a foreign public charity, the U.S. foundation could dispense with the cumbersome equivalency determination rules, and instead be in compliance with the "qualifying distribution" rules by following the expenditure responsibility procedures.

Conclusions

Although the equivalency determination and expenditure responsibility rules can be seen to represent good administrative practices for any

---

[68]   *See* the discussion of taxable expenditures under Section 4945, *supra*.

[69]   The April 18, 2001 letter from the Internal Revenue Service to John A. Edie, Esq. Senior Vice President and General Counsel, Council on Foundations, can be downloaded from the Council's website at http://WWW.cof.org/government/index .htm.

charitable organization in safeguarding the integrity of its grant making process, unquestionably these rules represent a significant constraint on international grant making by U.S. foundations. Accordingly, if the primary focus of a charitable organization is to be grant making outside the United States, strong consideration should be given to forming the foundation under the laws of another jurisdiction.

CHAPTER 5

WHY CREATE A FOREIGN CHARITY?

THE BIAS IN U.S. LAW AGAINST PRIVATE FOUNDATIONS

As suggested in the previous chapter, once a potential philanthropist sets out to establish a charitable organization, it is quickly learned that it will be far easier to create a public charity, rather than face the regulatory burdens and constraints of creating and maintaining a private foundation. Fundamentally, the entire private foundation regulatory regime can be avoided by broadening support of the organization so that at least 35% of the funds each year come from the general public. Moreover, founders frequently quickly come to the conclusion that the compliance efforts that are entailed in equivalency determinations and expenditure responsibility on grants to non-public charities can be avoided by limiting grants to entities which are already qualified as public charities.

The burdens and complexities of the U.S. regulatory regime governing private foundations has had the predictable effect of discouraging philanthropists from establishing private foundations. Among the more visible manifestations of this effect are the rise of donor advised mutual funds. According to a recent issue of *Philanthropy News Digest*, for the eighth year in a row, the Fidelity Investments Charitable Giving Fund ranked fifth on *The Chronicle of Philanthropy's* annual ranking of the top fund-raising charities. This was behind such well-known public charities as the Salvation Army, the YMCA, the American Red Cross and the American Cancer Society.[70]

Donor advised mutual funds are now generating over a billion dollars per year for charity.[71] All of the gifts transferred to such funds sooner or later will flow to public charities. Therefore, it is the public charities, and not organizations directly overseen by the donors themselves, which will utilize the charitable resources. From a public policy standpoint, it is appropriate to ask how much of the creative spirit of charitable giving is lost by channeling these funds to existing public charities. Stated dif-

---

[70]   *Philanthropy News Digest*. Volume 7, Issue 4 (January 23, 2001).

[71]   The May 20, 2002 issue of The Chronicle of Philanthropy at pages 7–9 published figures for 2001 for donor advised funds, showing total assets, distributions and number of participants.

ferently, had these donors, many of whom are giving substantial amounts, not been encumbered by regulatory burdens—whether actual or perceived—might not new and innovative solutions for the various problems facing our society have been funded?[72]

It is impossible to measure the extent to which the regulatory burdens imposed by the Internal Revenue Code on private foundations have discouraged the establishment of charitable endeavors. Many potential philanthropists, who have accumulated sufficient wealth to consider endowing a charitable fund, have mastered the hyper-technical legal and accounting expertise necessary to succeed in the current business regulatory environment. For those who have achieved fluency in complex legal or accounting matters, compliance with the regulatory regime governing private foundations may not be viewed as being particularly burdensome. For others, however, perhaps more skeptical of intrusive government, the regulatory landscape will first invoke fear, then avoidance.

ADVANTAGES OF A FOREIGN CHARITABLE ORGANIZATION

Fortunately, a potential philanthropist need not choose either burdensome regulation or a pass-through vehicle, such as a donor advised mutual fund. Instead, a charitable organization can be established in a foreign jurisdiction, outside of the constraints applicable to private foundations organized in United States.

Perhaps the perspective brought to philanthropy through use of a foreign entity may be best understood by an example. Charles F. Feeney was a successful businessman who developed a chain of duty-free shops at international airports around the world. As his business grew, he decided to devote an increasing share of the profits to philanthropy. He established the Atlantic Foundation and the Atlantic Trust under Bermuda law and contributed a substantial portion of his stockholdings in his businesses to these charitable entities.

Mr. Feeney was particularly interested in providing increased educational opportunities in poor communities in United States and Ireland. Mr. Feeney, however, believed that his charitable interests were best

---

[72] One by-product of the legal and regulatory landscape favoring public charities, has been the significant expansion of large public charities. This expansion has been accomplished by an ever growing charitable infra-structure, which some observers have characterized as the bureaucratization of American philanthropy. The recent criticism of the American Red Cross began when it was revealed that the Red Cross planned to hold back an astronomical sum from the funds raised in the name of helping the victims of the September 11, 2001 terrorist attacks to fund administrative expenses. After its Chairman resigned and the organization came under a barrage of criticism, it announced that every dollar collected in the name of addressing the 9/11 attacks would be disbursed to the victims.

served by anonymity. Accordingly, among the conditions attached to the grants which his foundations made were that the source of the funds would remain anonymous.

The foundations continued their generous support of education in this manner for over a decade, extending grants in excess of $600 million. The source of these gifts came to light when Mr. Feeney's business agreed to be acquired by a publicly traded corporation, and applicable securities laws required disclosure of the ownership of its shares. It was then revealed that the subject shares were owned by Bermuda charitable trusts. Shortly thereafter, Mr. Feeney agreed to be interviewed by the *New York Times*, and the full scope of his charitable work came to light.[73] Today, the Bermuda charitable trusts established by Mr. Feeney are estimated to have between $4 billion to $10 billion in assets.

Mr. Feeney's charitable objectives could never have been achieved if his foundations had been organized under U.S. law. As discussed in Chapter 4, Section 4943 would have prohibited the foundations from owning more than 20 percent of the stock of Mr. Feeney's enterprises. Had they done so, the value of the holdings would have been subject to excise taxes, and the foundations would have been required to divest a sufficient number of shares to be in compliance. Of equal significance from Mr. Feeney's perspective, the gifts made could not have been on an anonymous basis. The "information returns" required by the Internal Revenue Service, *see* Appendix 2, would have resulted in public disclosure of certain of the gifts, and probably most of the ones to foreign donees. Although he might have requested the donees to show the gifts as "anonymous," surely the magnitude of the gifts would have caught the attention of persons reviewing the public records and would have resulted in publication of their sources.

Of course, establishing a private foundation in a foreign jurisdiction is not appropriate in all circumstances. If a deduction from federal income tax is a fundamental consideration for establishing the foundation, there is little choice but to establish it in United States and abide by the private foundation rules. Nevertheless, there are a number of situations where this may not be the case:

- Where a foundation can be established by early contribution of "founders shares" in a start-up company, which shares have little or no value, little or no tax benefit will be derived from the contribution.

---

[73] J. Miller and D.C. Johnston, "He Gave Away $600 Million, and No One Knew." *New York Times* (January 23, 1997) at 1. Now that the silence has been broken, his charities have become more visible and are seeking to broaden their grant making activities. To this end, charities have established a website, www.atlanticphilanthropies.org.

- Where the foundation will be funded principally from testamentary gifts, potential donors will also not be motivated by incentives accorded by income tax deductibility.
- If the donor has significant assets, but these generate little or no income, the ceiling on deductibility may render any deduction from income taxes relatively insignificant.

Different aspects of the U.S. regulatory regime governing private foundations will have different levels of significance for different donors. For Mr. Feeney, the excess holdings and disclosure requirements of U.S. law were apparently undesirable. For others, the mandatory annual minimum distributions might be a significant impediment. For others, the strict rules against dealings between the foundation and disqualified persons might be offensive. [Presumably, the propriety or legality of such dealings under the laws of foreign jurisdictions might more typically be governed by the type of arm's-length standards which were applied in United States prior to the adoption of the private foundation excise tax rules in 1969.]

> In conclusion, the formation of a charitable organization under the laws of foreign jurisdiction can accord potential philanthropists the opportunity to conduct their charitable activities outside of the constraints of the regulatory framework applicable to U.S. foundations.

CHAPTER 6

PICKING A JURISDICTION

From the perspective of advising U.S. persons on the formation of charitable organizations, the fundamental distinction is between the laws of United States and the laws of other, *non-U.S.*, jurisdictions. Of course, United States represents but one of several dozen "good" jurisdictions where a philanthropist might confidently form a charitable organization. Unless the potential founder of a charitable organization is familiar with a specific foreign jurisdiction, the notion of entrusting a substantial endowment to unfamiliar persons or institutions in an unfamiliar setting can be daunting. This chapter will analyze the factors to be taken into consideration in choosing a foreign jurisdiction in which to locate a charitable organization.

The search for an appropriate jurisdiction should be undertaken without haste and with the objective of finding a comfort level in dealing with individuals and organizations in the foreign jurisdiction, which is in every respect equivalent to the level of trust and comfort the founder currently has with his own professional advisers in his home jurisdiction. **If that comfort level is not reached, the search should be abandoned and more familiar alternatives—direct gifts to U.S. public charities, establishing a U.S. private foundation or donating to a donor advised mutual fund—should be pursued.**

Over years of experience in working with individuals, families and companies, we have often been surprised at the speed at which persons evaluating foreign jurisdictions have become comfortable, even where the exercise initially may have begun with skepticism. The sophistication and experience of many foreign professionals sometimes comes as a surprise to U.S. persons. This experience is not universal, however. Unless and until an appropriate comfort level is reached with the jurisdiction being evaluated, our recommendation is to defer making a final decision, and consider evaluating additional jurisdictions.

This chapter will discuss, in no particular order or level of significance, the primary considerations in selecting a foreign jurisdiction in which to establish a charitable organization.

LAW

Sometimes U.S. persons are not fully aware of the extent to which they desire and rely upon a fully developed legal system until they encounter one which is not. While culturally one of the distinguishing factors of contemporary life in the United States is the over-emphasis on law and legal process (and therefore, collaterally, lawyers), a careful review of the foreign law and legal system which will become the basis for the formation and operation of a foreign charity is critical. The primary areas for evaluation are corporate or trust law, the regulations and institutions governing charitable organizations and the procedures governing access to the courts. The evaluation may also want to consider the legal oversight mechanisms and the enforcement policy of the government agency or bureau charged with regulating charities.

Not surprisingly, there is frequently an enormous variation in the comprehensiveness of governing statutes and the quality of decisional law among jurisdictions. Jurisdictions such as Bermuda, which have relied heavily on "offshore" corporate insurance and trust businesses, have well-developed laws and legal infrastructure. The sheer volume of transactions in such jurisdictions makes it far more likely that any particular problem that might arise will be governed by a specific statute or will have decisional law that provides the necessary guidance.[74]

Fundamentally, the type of structure envisioned by the charitable donor—a corporation or a trust—will come into play. If the donor is looking to establish a trust, he or she will want a common law jurisdiction, such as England, Bermuda, Cayman Islands, Bahamas, Isle of Man, etc., and not a jurisdiction having a civil code.[75] If a corporate entity will be utilized, the evaluation may well find that the corporate law of particular jurisdictions under review is significantly more developed. Our recommendation is to stay away from jurisdictions which are actively promoting new financial products or services based upon recently enacted laws.[76]

FINANCIAL SERVICES INFRASTRUCTURE

The foreign charity will require banking services. If organized as a trust, it may also choose to utilize the trust services of a financial insti-

---

[74]   By analogy, New York or Delaware corporate law is far more developed (and, therefore, usually "better") than the corporate law, for example, of Vermont or the District of Columbia.

[75]   Switzerland has enacted trust statutes, even though it is a code jurisdiction. Nevertheless, charitable donors considering utilizing trust structures should look to the various jurisdictions whose laws are derived from laws of England.

[76]   For example, particular advisors might urge donors to form a charitable organization as a trust having "asset protection" features. A number of jurisdictions have actively promoted newly enacted "asset protection" laws, sometimes drafted by American lawyers. The Cook Islands is one of the more notorious jurisdictions for this and should be avoided.

tution. If organized as a corporation, requirements of local law may mandate local officers or directors. Nominee officers, directors or stockholders might be customary when utilizing a corporate form for the charitable organization. For all these reasons, the financial strength and professional reputations of financial services firms should form an important part of evaluating a foreign jurisdiction.

In most jurisdictions it is possible to engage a "brand-name" bank or trust company, as many worldwide financial services institutions headquartered, for example, in New York, London or Geneva often have branch offices in such jurisdictions as Bermuda. This is not to suggest that a local bank or trust company might not provide better services. Indeed, some of the preeminent private banks and trust companies in the world operate in only a single or a few jurisdictions.

The selection process will be no different than the process utilized to select banking relationships in the United States. Not only will financial stability be essential, but reputation and service are important factors to be considered. The potential philanthropist's existing banking relationships or professional advisors may be used to gain introductions to appropriate candidates. "Due diligence" will likely also require a personal visit by the potential charitable donor to the offices where the services will be provided.

PROFESSIONAL INFRASTRUCTURE

Ultimately, the security and soundness of a particular jurisdiction will depend upon the quality of the legal and accounting professionals that are available. Few jurisdictions have the scale and the scope of legal and accounting firms that are common United States. Many of the so-called "final four" accounting firms will have branches or affiliated offices in many of the jurisdictions that would typically be considered. It is less common for large United States law firms to have branch offices in these jurisdictions.

Foreign law firms should be evaluated much in the same way as U.S. law firms. The Martindale Hubbell law directory lists law firms in virtually all jurisdictions. The same format is followed for law firms in Barbados as in the United States, listing bar admissions, educational background and professional memberships. A review of the Martindale Hubbell listings can identify those law firms having attorneys, solicitors or barristers who have been trained in the United States or abroad or have been affiliated with law firms in larger jurisdictions.[77] More importantly, potential donors should utilize their own professional advisers to "network" to locate appropriate candidates for assistance.[78] In many foreign jurisdic-

---

[77]   Martindale Hubbell, however, does not rate foreign law firms and lawyers as it does in the United States.

[78]   Increasingly, U.S. law firms participate in international affiliations of law firms in multiple jurisdictions, such as Lex Mundi.

tions, law firms or departments within law firms specialize in so-called private client practice, which usually encompasses the types of services needed by potential donors and philanthropic enterprises.[79] The strength and depth of a particular law firm's private client practice department is probably as important a consideration as would be the overall reputation of that firm.

While prospective new counsel or accountants can be interviewed by telephone, there is no substitute for a personal interview. Again, unless the professional under consideration inspires confidence, the potential philanthropist should keep looking. Such interviews are best conducted at the home offices of the firms which will be providing the services. Accordingly, even if the professional adviser under consideration is planning a trip to the United States on other business or will be visiting the United States on a promotional trip, the prospective charitable donor will gain a more accurate view of the professional by interviewing him on his "home turf."

PROXIMITY/ACCESS TO THE UNITED STATES

Although the world is a much smaller place than it was a decade or two ago, certain jurisdictions are far more convenient to deal with and travel to than others. The popularity and extensive use of Bermuda and the Bahamas derives in large measure from their proximity to the United States. There are daily flights to Bermuda from New York, Philadelphia, Washington, D.C., Baltimore and Charlotte, North Carolina. Each day there are multiple flights to the Bahamas from New York, Miami and Atlanta. This is in stark contrast to jurisdictions like the Isle of Man or the Channel Islands, where a transatlantic flight must be followed by poor connections on small aircraft.

In this day and age, most of the jurisdictions under consideration will have "state of the art" telecommunications services for both voice and data. This is not always the case, however. If a jurisdiction such as Barbados, for example, is under consideration, additional investigation should be made into telecommunications capabilities to ensure that proper communications can be maintained with local professionals and service providers.

REPUTATION

Unfortunately, lax law enforcement and laissez-faire bank regulators in a number of jurisdictions opened the way for money laundering by

---

[79]   These firms often have "captive" trust companies which are available to serve a fiduciary role in the charitable entity to be established. For example, the law firm of Conyers, Dill & Pearman, based in Bermuda, has established an affiliated Trust company, Codan Trust Company Limited, which has branches in a number of jurisdictions.

drug traffickers, terrorists and other international criminals. The clamp down which followed revelations of certain of these practices in some jurisdictions did not come soon enough to salvage the jurisdiction's reputation. Once lost, reputations are difficult to regain. Thus, potential philanthropists seeking to evaluate foreign jurisdictions should play close attention to the general reputation of the jurisdiction.

Even jurisdictions which have worked very hard to regulate banking activities and corporate formations closely have from time to time been tarred by scandal. For example, in Jersey several highly publicized incidents demonstrated that the highest level of scrutiny is required to protect the reputation of the jurisdiction.

Operating in a jurisdiction which maintains stricter controls, however, often results in higher costs, both in setting up the entity and in maintaining it. One way these jurisdictions screen out undesirable business and ensure that such business will seek to go elsewhere is to require relatively high filing fees and annual maintenance/franchise tax assessments. For example, the high filing fees applicable to forming corporations in Bermuda[80] and Jersey often result in the corporations being formed in lower cost jurisdictions such as the British Virgin Islands.

Increasingly, another mechanism certain jurisdictions utilize to scrutinize new entities seeking to operate within their borders is to require a review by a government agency of the principals seeking to establish a new entity there. These would be in addition to the almost universal "know your customer" requirements being implemented by most financial services institutions.[81] For example, the Bermuda Monetary Authority requires persons forming a new corporation in Bermuda to answer a lengthy questionnaire and submit extensive supporting documentation. This review is well-known to be far more than a "rubber stamp," and not infrequently results in denying the applicant the authorization to form a new corporation in Bermuda.

LANGUAGE

The ability to conduct business in a particular jurisdiction in English can be important to potential philanthropists. Although English has become the universal business language, not all jurisdictions have uniformly high-

---

[80] Higher costs in Bermuda relate directly to the requirement of the Bermuda Monetary Authority which strictly scrutinizes applications for new corporations, and often requires financial intermediaries to conduct additional due diligence of new clients.

[81] Typically, the "know your customer" requirements of most financial institutions in non-U.S. jurisdictions [and increasingly so in U.S. jurisdictions as well, at least as to non-U.S. persons] include a review of passports, proof of residency, such as requiring copies of utility bills, and reference letters from another financial institution with which the customer has maintained relationship for least five years, and from professionals, such as a law or accounting firm.

quality English-speaking professionals. The good news is that many of the more favored foreign jurisdictions in which to locate a private foundation are former British colonies or remain so-called crown dependencies, and therefore English remains the dominant language, if not the official one.

COSTS

Most, but not all, of the above factors will have an impact on the total costs of establishing a charitable entity in a foreign jurisdiction. As with any "benefit/cost analysis," intangibles will often come into play, and may in fact be the determining factor. Nevertheless, all the relative costs of these different components will need to be balanced in reaching a final decision on an appropriate jurisdiction.

CHAPTER 7

ESTABLISHING A FOREIGN CHARITABLE FOUNDATION

You have made the major decisions. After lengthy discussions with your advisors and due diligence visits to various fiduciaries and professionals, you have chosen a foreign jurisdiction. You have also decided to form a trust or a new corporation. You have selected a trustee or a registered agent and perhaps nominee officers or directors. Now what?

U.S. TAX CONSIDERATIONS

As stated above, since your organization will be formed in a foreign jurisdiction, any donations used to establish it will not be deductible for federal income tax purposes.[82] Nevertheless, any future gifts or testamentary bequests can be fully deductible, without limitation, from both U.S. estate[83] and gift[84] taxes.

If a corporate vehicle is utilized, the transfer of funds or property to form the entity will not be taxable to either the donor or the corporation. Nor will the transfer cause any gain to be recognized in the case of the transfer of appreciated property.[85] Assuming that the laws of the foreign jurisdiction make clear that a charitable organization has no shareholders as such, the entity, though labeled a corporation, should not rule afoul of the U.S. Subpart F rules applicable to controlled foreign corporations.[86]

If a trust is utilized, presumably it will be an irrevocable trust, and the trust agreement or declaration of trust will provide the trustee with

---

[82]   Section 170(c)(2). See also Chapter 3, *supra*.

[83]   Section 2055 (a).

[84]   Section 2522 (a)(2).

[85]   Section 351.

[86]   The U.S. shareholders of a controlled foreign corporation ("CFC") are taxed, generally speaking, on all the income of the CFC except active business income. (Note that active business income is just the type of income that a charity should not be earning.) "Controlled foreign corporation" means, again abbreviating, any foreign corporation of which more than 50% of either (1) the total combined voting power of all classes of stock of the corporation entitled to vote; or (2) the total value of the stock of the corporation, is owned, directly or indirectly by United States shareholders. U.S. shareholder is any person owning 10% or more of the total combined voting power of all classes of stock of the corporation. Sections 957 and 951(b).

specific guidance as to the types and purposes of charitable endeavors the entity will pursue. The trust should be a "non-grantor" trust, so that income earned by the trust is not taxable to the U.S. settlor.[87] It should be noted that there are a number of special rules in the Internal Revenue Code governing transfers to foreign trusts, which, on their face, appear to complicate the establishment of a foreign charitable trust.[88] Fortunately, the Internal Revenue Service by rulemaking has clarified that these constraints do not apply to foreign trusts which are established for charitable purposes as described in Section 501(c)(3).[89] Significantly, the foreign trust need not obtain a Determination Letter from the IRS recognizing its tax-exempt status to qualify for exclusion from these rules.

Distributions to U.S. grantees from the foreign charitable organization may be taxable to the U.S. grantees. Of course, if the grantee is tax-exempt under Section 501(c)(3), it will not be taxed on the distribution. If, however, the grantee is an individual, he or she may be taxed depending upon the use to which the grantee will put the funds received. Grants to foreign entities or persons generally should not be taxed by the United States.

SHOULD THE FOREIGN ENTITY APPLY FOR EXEMPT STATUS IN THE UNITED STATES?

Foreign charitable organizations often apply for and obtain exempt status. Eligibility for tax-exempt status under Section 501(c)(3) is based on charitable purposes and not limited geographically to entities formed in the United States.[90] The Service's policy on qualifying foreign charities under Section 501(c)(3) is clear: "The fact that an organization has been formed under foreign law will not preclude its qualification under Section

---

[87] Under the rules governing grantor trusts, Section 671 *et seq.*, if the settlor, for example, retains the right to amend the trust, change the beneficiaries or revoke the trust, the trust assets are deemed to have remained the taxpayer's property for tax purposes notwithstanding the transfer of legal title to the trustee, and the taxpayer remains taxable on any income or capital gains earned by the trust. See generally, C. M. Bruce, *U.S. Taxation of Foreign Trusts* (Kluwer, 2000) at 106–115.

[88] Section 684 triggers the recognition of gain on transfers of appreciated property to foreign trusts. Section 679 deems any foreign trust having U.S. beneficiaries to be a grantor trust, so that income of the foreign trust is treated as income to the U.S. grantor.

[89] The exception to the tax imposed by Section 684 is set forth in Section 1.684-3(b) of the Regulations. The exception to treatment as a grantor trust under Section 679 is set forth at Section 1.679-4(a)(3). When both of these regulations were proposed, no exemption for foreign charitable trusts was included. The explanation for the change given by the Internal Revenue Service is set forth at T.D. 8956 (July 20, 2001) and T.D. 8955 (July 20, 2001).

[90] By contrast, Sections 501(c)(1), (19), (21) and (22) do contain geographic limitations. Under Section 509(a), all private foundations, both domestic and foreign, are described by Section 501(c)(3).

501(c) . . . if it meets the test of exemption. . . ."[91]

The Internal Revenue Service generally applies the same standards to foreign charities as it would to U.S. entities seeking exempt status.[92] Thus, to qualify, the foreign charitable organization must be both organized and operated for charitable purposes, must not be operated for private benefit or inurement and may not engage in lobbying or political activities. Whether the foreign charity should seek exempt status under U.S. tax rules, however, involves evaluating a number of factors, pro and con.

Notice Requirements

All newly formed Section 501(c)(3) domestic organizations are required to notify the Service that they are applying for tax-exempt status. The normal rule is that this must be done within fifteen months of formation, although a twelve month "grace period" automatically permits the application to be made within 27 months of formation. As described in Chapter 3, Form 1023, Appendix 1, is used to give the requisite statutory notice and apply for exempt status. Domestic charitable organizations failing to apply or which have their applications rejected will be taxable as regular corporations or trusts.

Certain foreign charities are exempted by statute from the notice and filing requirements applicable to domestic private foundations. Section 4948(b) and the regulations issued thereunder state that these requirements do not apply to foreign charities which receive at least 85% of their support from non-U.S. sources.[93] Thus, if more than 15% of the support for a foreign charity will come from U.S. sources, the entity by law is required to apply for exempt status. Failure to do so will result in characterization of the foreign charity as a foreign corporation or a foreign trust for U.S. tax purposes.

Tax Implications of Exempt Status for Foreign Private Foundations

There are four primary aspects of U.S. law which should be evaluated before determining whether or not a foreign foundation established by a U.S. person should seek exempt status under U.S. law.

---

[91]   Revenue Ruling 66-177, 1966-1 C.B. 13.

[92]   Professor Dale discusses the problem foreign entities typically have in meeting IRS standards at 48 Tax Law 657. This can be particularly problematic for foreign educational institutions with respect to meeting standards of non-discrimination for private universities and schools in the wake of *Bob Jones University v. U.S.*, 461 U.S. 574 (1983).

[93]   Such entities are deemed to be tax-exempt for U.S. tax purposes without so qualifying. They are expressly exempted from the excise tax regulatory regime in Chapter 42 applicable to private foundations. Nevertheless, Section 4648(c) further provides that any such organization which engages in any acts or practices which would result in the imposition of excise taxes under the private foundation rules applicable to U.S. private foundations shall not be accorded exempt status, and, where it has been notified by the Internal Revenue Service of such disqualification, deductions for any donations to it are disallowed.

1. Deductibility of Lifetime Gifts and Testamentary Bequests of U.S. Donors

The non-deductibility of gifts to foreign charities for U.S. federal *income* tax purposes is a fundamental part of the legal landscape.[94] The ban on deductibility applies to both foreign public charities and foreign private foundations. As discussed above, this statutory restriction dates from isolationist sentiments in Congress in the 1930s and has never been repealed. Although this restriction does not on its face apply in the context of estate and gift taxes, the private foundation notice requirements operate to bar estate and gift tax deductions for lifetime gifts and testamentary bequests to foreign private foundations, where the foreign private foundation has not qualified for tax-exempt status under Section 501(c)(3).[95] Accordingly, this rule is among the most central considerations in determining whether to seek exempt status in United States for foreign private foundations.

As discussed above, mandatory notice provisions applicable to private foundations apply to both foreign and domestic private foundations. Section 508(a) states that unless a private foundation has given notice to the Service and has been recognized as exempt, it "shall not be treated as a organization described in section 501(c)(3)." The effect of this provision is to render the entity taxable for U.S. purposes. Section 508(d)(2)(B) disallows the deductibility of gifts to "taxable private foundations" under both the estate tax and the gift tax provisions. **Accordingly, if the donor is establishing a foreign private foundation with a relatively small initial gift, with the expectation that the foundation will be largely funded upon his or her demise, the foreign private foundation should be qualified as tax-exempt.**

The need to qualify a foreign private foundation as tax-exempt for the purpose of claiming an estate tax deduction may become less important in the upcoming years, with the escalation of amounts exempt from the U.S. estate tax. The chart on page 57 summarizes the scheduled reductions of estate taxes called for by the Economic Growth and Tax Relief Reconciliation Act of 2001.

As can be seen from this chart, in the years 2006 through 2010, deductibility of testamentary gifts to foreign private foundations will become relatively less important. Whether it is irrelevant in any particular situation will depend upon, among other things, the size of the testamentary gift, the testator's dispositive plan and the extent to which other

---

[94] See chapter 3, *supra*.

[95] I.R.C. §§ 2055(e)(1) and 508(d)(2)(B). If a foreign private foundation does not obtain exempt status pursuant to the notice requirements of § 508(a), it is regarded as a taxable private foundation. Nevertheless, donations to foreign *public charities* are fully deductible for estate and gift tax purposes. See, e.g., PLR 9853037.

Calendar year	Estate and GST tax deathtime transfer exemption	Highest estate and gift tax rates
2002	$1 million	50%
2003	$1 million	49%
2004	$1.5 million	48%
2005	$1.5 million	47%
2006	$2 million	46%
2007	$2 million	45%
2008	$2 million	45%
2009	$3.5 million	45%
2010	N/A (taxes repealed)	top individual rate under the bill (gift tax only)
2011	Current tax regime reinstated.	

gifts to family members may be taxable. Under current law, the existing estate tax rates will be reinstated[96] unless Congress acts to extend the outright repeal scheduled for 2010, or reimposes estate taxes to some extent. The uncertainty presented by the 2001 Act makes it difficult for estate planners to take actions based upon current law, and therefore the best advice that can be given at this juncture is to continue watching the legislative calendar, as Congress will likely revisit these issues before the end of this decade.[97]

2. Excise/Income Taxes

If the foreign private foundation is regarded as a foreign corporation or a foreign trust,[98] only its U.S. source dividends, interest, and similar passive income generally will be subject to U.S. taxation. Generally speaking, this will subject the foreign entity to the statutory withholding rate of 30% for U.S. source interest, dividends, rent, salaries, wages, annuities, compensations, remunerations, emoluments, or other fixed or determinable annual or periodical gains, profits, and similar income, unless a

---

[96] In 2011, the time of reinstatement, the maximum exempt amount will revert to $1,000,000.

[97] Congressional efforts to make the repeal of estate taxes permanent failed by a narrow margin in the Spring of 2002.

[98] that is, it is **not** as tax-exempt for U.S. purposes

lower tax treaty rate applies.[99] This type of income is from U.S. sources if it is paid by domestic U.S. corporations, U.S. citizens or resident aliens, or entities formed under the laws of the U.S. or a state. Income is also from U.S. sources if the property that produces the income is located in the U.S. or services for which the income is paid were performed in the U.S. By structuring investments to be in securities and property outside of the U.S., the foreign entity may avoid U.S. taxation altogether.

For a foreign private foundation which has qualified as tax-exempt under Section 501(c)(3), its U.S. source interest and dividends would also be taxable, but under a special rule in Section 4948(a), which substitutes a 4% excise tax on such income for the 2% excise tax on defined net investment income, which is applicable to domestic private foundations under Section 4940. The difference in the tax base applicable to foreign versus domestic private foundations is that net capital gains are taxed to domestic entities, but are not taxed to foreign entities. This mirrors the tax rules applicable to non-tax-exempt persons and entities. Treaty rules may also apply to reduce the usual rate of withholding on U.S. source dividends and interest earned by foreign private foundations.[100] Of course, as with non-tax-exempt foreign private foundations, the 4% Section 4648(a) excise tax can be avoided entirely by investing the foreign private foundation's endowment in non-U.S. securities.

Withholding at the lower rate is claimed by filing Form W-8EXP. If the foreign foundation has not received a Determination Letter from the IRS, it may claim the lower rate by supporting the Form W-8EXP by an opinion of counsel that the foundation is described in Section 501(c). A copy of Form W-8EXP, together with instructions, is attached as Appendix 4.

3. Private Foundation Regulatory Regime

The most significant difference between qualifying a foreign private foundation as tax-exempt under Section 501(c)(3) and not doing so is that entities so qualified are brought within the excise tax regulatory regime of Chapter 42 described above.[101] Thus, for example, the foreign private foundation would be subject to the minimum distribution requirements of Section 4942, the penalties applicable to excess business holdings under Section 4943 and the prohibitions on self-dealing in Section 4941. This curious extraterritorial reach of the private foundation regula-

---

[99] Sections 1441 & 1442. There are currently 64 bilateral income tax treaties in effect. The treaty between the U.S. and Switzerland, for example, provides for withholding at the rate of zero on interest and as low as 5% on dividends.

[100] For example, the treaty rate with Barbados applicable to interest payments is 5%. Protocol Amending The Convention Between The U.S. And Barbados For The Avoidance Of Double Taxation And The Prevention Of Fiscal Evasion With Respect To Taxes On Income (signed Dec. 18, 1991).

[101] Sections 4940 *et seq.*, described in Chapter 4.

tory provisions derives from the definition of *private foundation* to include "a domestic or foreign organization" in Section 509(a). But before the foreign private foundation ever files its first Form 990-PF, the Service extends the regulatory regime to foreign private foundations by requiring the organizational documents[102] of the entity applying for exempt status to include provisions which require compliance with the regulatory regime as a precondition to approval of exempt status.[103]

In addition to bringing the foreign foundation within the Chapter 42 regime, once the foundation receives a Determination Letter, it must comply with all rules and pay all required excise taxes and penalties. Failure to do so or taking action to withdraw from exempt status will trigger special rules governing termination of exempt status.[104] In summary, any foundation withdrawing from exempt status must transfer all of its assets to public charities or pay a tax equal to the lesser of the net assets of the foundation or the aggregate tax benefits the organization has received from its inception as a result of its exemption from tax.

4. Grant Making Activities

Where the foreign charitable organization intends to engage in collaborative efforts with U.S. private foundations or public charities, or will itself from time to time be seeking grants from U.S. charitable entities, it may want to qualify as exempt under U.S. law, so as to minimize the compliance actions required by the U.S. grant-making entities. As discussed in Chapter 4, if a foreign charitable entity is qualified as tax-exempt under U.S. law, no equivalency determination would need to be to be undertaken by the U.S. donor. Moreover, expenditure responsibility becomes somewhat less burdensome for the U.S. grant-making entity where the grantee has qualified as tax-exempt under Section 501(c)(3).[105]

GOVERNANCE ISSUES

The overwhelming majority of the legal documents used to create a trust or corporation will be legal "boilerplate" and will take relatively little time to draft when compared to the efforts that potential philanthropists would typically go through to determine what kind structure they will utilize and what jurisdiction they will choose. Invariably, however, a significant amount of customization will be required to establish the mechanism for managing and overseeing the organization and providing

---

[102]   E.g., Memorandum and Articles of Association, By-Laws or Trust Agreement.

[103]   Section 508(e). An example of documentation required is attached as Appendix 6, discussed in Chapter 8, *infra*.

[104]   These are set forth in I.R.C. § 507 and are summarized in Chapter 3.

[105]   For example, the grantee would not be required to maintain a separate bank account for the grant. Rather, the "out of corpus" rules would apply. See Chapter 4, *supra*.

for an orderly succession of powers following the demise of the founder.

Often families seeking to establish an independent private foundation are doing so to provide a structure for implementing the family's charitable values. Indeed, founders frequently are looking to involve family members in the grant making process. Part of this involvement will be a form of "training" younger generation(s) to carry on the charitable work and values of the family after the demise of the founding members. Succession issues therefore are central to the family's efforts to establish —and perpetuate—its charitable vision.

Fundamentally, governance issues must address the basic need of the enterprise for guidance, both in investment decisions and grant making. The mechanisms decided upon must also ensure the safety and security of the endowment, considerations having added significance when dealing with trustees or corporate board members and officers in foreign jurisdictions.

Board of Directors/Trustees

The basic repository of management power of the entity will be the Board of Directors, if the entity is organized as a corporation, or the Trustee(s), if organized as a Trust. Applicable foreign law may require at least one member of the Board or one Trustee, and perhaps a majority, to be a citizen of the country where the entity is organized. If a corporation, the founding family invariably will want to have one or more of its members on the Board. If a Trust, the family may want a member to serve as co-Trustee with a local bank, trust company or attorney. Alternatively, the perception of "distance" and independence for the Trustee or co-Trustees can be achieved by use of a Trust Protector or a Committee of Trustee Advisors, described below.

Compensation of professional fiduciaries is typically established by standard, published fee schedules if a bank or trust company is selected to serve. There is usually room for negotiating such fee schedules, at least in the short term. Negotiating fees with potential fiduciaries is always a worthwhile exercise. Even if it does not yield a reduction in administrative costs, negotiations frequently reveal institutional biases. For example, it is better to know up front if the institution you are engaging fundamentally is not interested in your business, whether because of the size of the initial gift[106] or because of differences in "style" or culture. After all, costs will be lower in the long term, and service will be better, if the initial relationship can be maintained over the years.

---

[106] In recent years a number of "brand name" fiduciaries have sought to pare down client lists to those having relatively significant endowments. This is frequently accomplished by manifestly non-competitive fee schedules, designed to drive lower net worth individuals and families elsewhere. It seems that "80/20" or "90/10" management theories

Family members serving on Boards or as Trustees can be compensated as well, notwithstanding the self-dealing prohibitions applicable to defined "disqualified persons" under Section 4942. Likewise, expenses for attending Board or Trustee meetings can be reimbursed. Care should be taken to follow established guidelines of reasonableness, so that neither the compensation nor the expenses are deemed to be excessive, thereby trigging penalties.

The Council on Foundations publishes an annual survey on standards and practices for such compensation.[107] Fundamentally, whether compensation is "reasonable" or "excessive" will be based on all relevant factors, which will include a review of the scope of the duties being performed, the size of the foundation, and the experience and professional qualifications of the person being compensated.

At the end of the day, common sense should prevail.[108] It will always be inappropriate to place the founder's 23 year old son on the Board and pay him a $200,000 per year salary where the foundation makes only minimal grants annually to public charities. Likewise, it will be hard to justify reimbursement of expenses for annual Board meetings in the South of France in August, with a suite at the Grand Hotel de Cap, where the foundation is formed in Bermuda and all of its grant-making activities and all of its members are in the Western Hemisphere.

Compensation issues are usually less problematic for foundations established by corporations. It is usually possible to staff the foundation, including the Board, officers and key committees, with employees of the donor corporation. Frequently, such employees will work part time for the foundation and part time for the corporate donor, and their remuneration from the foundation may reflect the relative portion of time devoted to foundation matters.

Committees

Depending on the basic management structure, use of committees can be a convenient way to segregate or delegate discrete functions to those family members or trusted colleagues having expertise in a particular area. If the entity is organized as a corporation, this might typically be done as a committee of the Board. Alternatively, the committee members might have consulting agreements with the foundation. If organized as a Trust, the committee might be one or more of the Trustees, or might be entirely made up of non-trustees who have been engaged in con-

---

are now even being extended to private banking. ["80% of revenues derive from 20% of the business," or its corollary, "80% of the headaches are caused by 20% of the clients."]

[107] www.cof.org. On the Council's home page, scroll down on "topics of interest" to the current year's Salary and Benefits Report Summary.

[108] Or its alternative, the "smell test"

sulting capacities. Thus, use of committees might permit the family to engage a member in grant making decisions, without involving him or her in the charity's other management decisions.

The two most common areas for utilizing committees are to oversee or manage investment of the endowment fund and to recommend grant making. Depending on the size and scope of the endowment fund or the grant making activities, this mechanism can be a convenient and flexible one for involving family members, utilizing their particular skills and experience, and for formalizing communications regarding the desires and goals of the founding family to the Trustees or the Board.

A structure involving Committees also works well with corporate foundations. The donor corporation can provide highly qualified members to particular committees based on the employee's expertise or professional training.

Control

Unlike an ordinary business corporation set up to earn a profit, a foundation organized as a corporation would not usually have voting stock. Accordingly, the usual control by stockholders over the Board (and thus, indirectly, over the officers and employees) is not typically present. Control over the Board, therefore, which includes power to hire and fire "outside" directors, must be maintained in the family by means of the initial structure. The By-laws or Memorandum of Association must be drafted to provide a mechanism for succession that will ensure that future generations of the family will control the charity.

Such mechanisms are invariably customized and drafted to accommodate family idiosyncrasies. It would be inappropriate to describe a "typical" arrangement, because so many different approaches are used. Suffice it to say that the arrangement must be specific, yet flexible. Like a good estate plan, it must contemplate different orders for the deaths of principal family members, as well as potential disabilities and the possibility that "the plane might go down" on the way to the family reunion, creating multiple vacancies on the governing body.

With trusts, a "Committee of Trust Advisors" can be used. If the trust is to be characterized for U.S. tax purposes as a foreign non-grantor trust, so that the gift establishing the charity is complete *and* the charitable endowment no longer is deemed to be part of the Settlor's property for U.S. income and estate tax purposes, the Settlor must have parted with most, if not all, incidents of control over the Trust, such as the ability to revoke or amend the Trust Agreement.

If a Trust document granting broad discretionary powers to the Trustees is to be used, a Committee of Trust Advisors might be given the responsibility to advise, but not direct, the Trustees on appropriate invest-

ment of the funds. The Trustees, in keeping with their fiduciary responsibilities, will receive the advice of the Committee, but will retain the discretion as to whether to follow it. Nevertheless, the Committee will also
be granted the power to terminate any Trustee, in accordance with ascer-
tainable standards,[109] or otherwise. A typical mechanism utilizing a
Committee of Trust Advisors may be found in Appendix 5, which is a
Bermuda charitable trust.[110]

---

[109] e.g., conflicts of interest, breach of fiduciary responsibility.

[110] The power to "hire and fire" Trustees may also be exercised by a so-called "Trust
Protector." As with a Committee of Trust Advisors, the Protector's powers, responsibilities
and activities may be broad or narrow, depending upon the perceived need for controls
over the Trustees, but great care should be exercised not, in effect, to negate the creation
of the trust by not "letting go" of the property being transferred, or not really putting the
trustee in actual possession of the property, behaving as if the trust did not exist, or behaving as though the Committee or the Protector were in fact a co-trustee with all the fiduciary duties that befall a trustee. *See* C. M. Bruce, *United States Taxation of Foreign Trusts*
(Kluwer, 2000), Chapter 3 (Definitions of Trust and Foreign Trust) and discussion of incomplete transfers and "sham" trusts, therein. The use of a "Protector" should be avoided, as
this formulation has a history of abuse, which can be seen in a host of cases involving abu-
sive trusts.

CHAPTER 8

REPRESENTATIVE STRUCTURES

This chapter will describe a few typical organizational structures for establishing a charitable organization in a foreign jurisdiction. Forms for each of the representative vehicles are included as Appendices, and the text below will describe a number of the salient features of each template.

BERMUDA CHARITABLE TRUSTS

As a common law jurisdiction, Bermuda has well-established laws regarding trusts. Where the common law has needed improvement to facilitate new types of family and business transactions, the Bermuda Legislature has passed a series of statutes, which have permitted Bermuda to stay at the forefront of preferred "offshore" jurisdictions. Trusts are a common vehicle for achieving charitable purposes in Bermuda, and if the new charity will not solicit charitable contributions in Bermuda, no registration of the charity is required. Likewise, unlike the United States, the charity need not apply to the tax authorities for recognition of exempt status, as no income taxes or taxes on earnings or capital gains are levied by the Bermuda government.

A representative Bermuda charitable trust template is attached as Appendix 5.[111] It is a fairly straightforward Declaration of Trust taking the form of a discretionary trust, the major portions of which are standard "boilerplate" administrative provisions. The identity of the grantor does not appear in the document, since the Trust is established by the Trustee's declaration, rather than in the form of an agreement between the grantor and the Trustee. Except for several references to Bermuda law, and specifically, the Charities Act 1978, the trust instrument could serve as a Declaration of Trust in a number of common law jurisdictions.

Among the significant provisions of the template in Appendix 5 are the recitals of the objects of charitable purposes in Article 3. The template presented makes none of the recitals required of organizational documents for entities which will be qualified in the United States as tax-exempt under Section 501(c)(3), as it is intended that this charity

---

[111] The template attached as Appendix 5 is based upon a template provided by Michael J. Mello QC, JP, of Mello Jones & Martin, Reid House, 31 Church Street, Hamilton, Bermuda.

would not apply to the Internal Revenue Service for exempt status.

The governance procedures vest control in a Committee of Trust Advisors in Article 26. The Committee is given the power to appoint or replace the Trustee in Article 7. Although it is a committee, Article 26.4 empowers the first Chairman, in essence, to act for the Committee. The initial Chairman is appointed by the Trustee by separate Deed appended to the Declaration of Trust.

BARBADOS CHARITABLE TRUSTS

Barbados, like Bermuda, is a common law jurisdiction. The trust template attached as Appendix 6 differs in approach from the template under Bermuda law previously discussed. In terms of form, this document is a Trust Agreement, to which the Settlor is a party, rather than a Declaration of Trust, executed only by the Trustee. More significantly, this template includes all of the necessary recitals which the Internal Revenue Service requires in organizational documents of charitable organizations seeking tax-exempt status.[112] These recitals are woven throughout the document, but in particular, Article VI, tracks the regulatory regime governing private foundations operating as Section 501(c)(3) entities.

It should be noted that specific charitable purposes are not enumerated; rather, the Trustees are given the discretion to distribute income and principal of the trust fund for general charitable purposes. As indicated in Chapter 3, the Internal Revenue Service requires more specificity before a Determination Letter can be issued. Descriptions of specific projects and purposes should therefore be set forth in responses to Form 1023. See Appendix 1, Part II, question 1. The Internal Revenue Service has issued a Determination Letter to a charitable entity which utilized a Trust Agreement based on this template.

A few other points are relevant to philanthropists considering Barbados as a situs for a charitable trust. Because none of the contributions to this trust came from within Barbados and no charitable solicitation will be done in Barbados, the trust is not required to register with the government under the Barbados Charities Act. Moreover, the charitable purpose of the trust automatically exempts it from taxation in Barbados.

BERMUDA PURPOSE TRUSTS

Bermuda, as well as a number of other jurisdictions, has enacted legislation permitting the creation of so-called purpose trusts. In Bermuda the concept was developed because charitable trusts under Bermuda law

---

[112] Section 508(e).

had been construed restrictively to require a public purpose, so that a number of philanthropic trusts failed to meet the required test and became void. Under the new statutory authorization of the Trusts (Special Provisions) Act 1989, purpose trusts need not benefit a specified class of beneficiaries, but rather can be devoted to a general public purpose.

Purpose trusts can be a useful vehicle for accomplishing broad, public interest or policy purposes, which, because of the proscriptions in U.S. law against lobbying and political activities, may not qualify for tax-exempt status under U.S. law. For example, if a philanthropist wished to promote controversial ideas regarding limiting or ameliorating air pollution, with the intention that his ideas might be implemented into law, a purpose trust might be considered.

The template included as Appendix 7 was drafted to create a vehicle authorized by the Trusts (Special Provisions) Act 1989.[113] The purposes, which need not necessarily fit the definition of "charitable" for purposes of U.S. law, are to be enumerated in Paragraph 4. Unlike some charitable trust declaration or agreements, which merely grant discretion to the Trustee to distribute funds for charitable purposes, specific purposes should be included. [Under Bermuda law, the use of purpose trusts is not confined to quasi-charitable or philanthropic endeavors, but may be used for specific business transactions, such as holding shares of a company pending fulfillment of particular conditions, much like an escrow or custodial arrangement under U.S. law.]

Bermuda law requires the inclusion of a number of specific provisions. For example, an "Enforcer" must be named in the trust deed, which should provide for the appointment of a successor. By law, the Trustee is required to advise the Attorney General of Bermuda in the event that the Enforcer is unable to act, after which the Attorney General may apply to the courts for the appointment of a successor. The template cross references the duties of the Enforcer to the statute in Paragraph 14.

The template utilizes a "Trust Protector" mechanism to maintain control over the structure. As with the Committee of Trust Advisors in the other templates discussed above, the Protector has the power to appoint new or additional Trustees and to remove Trustees. Paragraph 12. The attached form also includes typical protective features, whereby the trust will automatically migrate to another jurisdiction and the Trustee be replaced by an "Emergency Trustee" upon the occurrence of specified "emergency events," such as war, civil insurrection or governmental intervention in the affairs of the Trust or the Trustee.

---

[113] This template was provided by Grosvenor Trust Company, 33 Church Street, Hamilton, Bermuda.

One other difference under Bermuda law between a charitable trust and a purpose trust is that the purpose trust is subject to the rule against perpetuities, which by statute, permits purpose trusts to remain in existence for up to 100 years. Compliance with the Perpetuities and Accumulations Act 1989 of Bermuda is covered in the definitional provisions of the template.

CHAPTER 9

FURTHER RESOURCES

Additional resources and guidance on the subjects discussed in this book are readily available on the Internet. The best sources of information on establishing and maintaining private foundations are the following:

- Council on Foundations, 1828 L Street, NW, #300, Washington, D.C. 20036-5168; Web address: www.cof.org. Although this is a member organization, the Council's website is an extraordinary resource for anyone working with private foundations. Most of the publications from previous issues of the Council's periodicals can be readily downloaded, and helpful leads to additional resources are easily accessible.
- The Foundation Center, 1627 K. Street, NW, Washington, D.C. 20036 and 79 Fifth Avenue, New York, NY 10003; Web address: http://www.foundationcenter.org.
- National Center for Charitable Statistics, a project of the Center on Nonprofits & Philanthropy at the Urban Institute, 2100 M. Street, NW, Washington, D.C. 20037; Web address: www.urban.org/centers/cnp.html. The Center takes raw data from the information returns filed by public charities and foundations with the Internal Revenue Service and generates a broad range of statistics, which show the extent and scope of charitable and nonprofit endeavors in the United States.
- GuideStar, c/o Philanthropic Research, Inc., 427 Scotland Street, Williamsburg, VA 23185; Web address: http://www.guidestar.org. This organization has created a database using all of the information provided by the Internal Revenue Service on Forms 990, 990-PF and 990 EZ. Any member of the public can access data on any tax-exempt organization from this website. Subscribers can create customized reports on specific exempt sectors.
- National Center on Philanthropy and the Law, New York University Law School, 110 West 3rd Street, 2nd Floor, New York, NY 10012-1074; Web site address: www.law.nyu.edu/ncpl/. This organization

is preparing a comprehensive bibliography of all English language resources pertaining to the law of nonprofit organizations.

All of the above Web sites contain numerous links to other organizations offering additional resources on charitable activities on the Web.

GLOSSARY OF TERMS

Additional Tax—Under the regulatory regime applicable to private foundations, excise taxes are initially assessed on the foundation and its managers. If the infraction which gave rise to the initial penalty is not corrected, additional excise taxes, sometimes called "second-tier taxes," are imposed.

AMT—Alternative Minimum Tax. A stand-alone, separate income tax computation applicable to both individuals and corporations, which can have the effect of diminishing the tax-saving value of all deductions, including charitable donations.

Annual Information Return—Required of all tax-exempt entities. Form 990 is required for public charities and Form 990-PF for foundations.

Articles of Organization—The documents used to create a foundation; Articles of Incorporation for a domestic corporation; Memorandum and Articles of Association for a foreign corporation; a Trust Agreement or Declaration of Trust for a trust.

Board of Directors—The governing body of a corporation.

Declaration of Trust—A form of trust established by the Trustee only. It may be contrasted with a settlement or Trust Agreement where both Settlor and Trustee execute the trust instrument.

Determination Letter—Evidence issued by the Internal Revenue Service that the charitable organization is recognized as tax-exempt.

Disqualified Person—A person who is a Trustee, Director or officer of or a substantial contributor to a private foundation.

Electioneering—Participating in a campaign for the election of a candidate for public office.

GAAP—Generally Accepted Accounting Principles. The standards applied by licensed CPA's in the United States, and licensed or chartered accountants in other jurisdictions.

Grantor—A person establishing a Trust by a gift of property. Sometimes also called a Settlor.

Grantor Trust—Under U.S. tax laws, characterization of assets and income of a Trust as remaining with the grantor for tax purpose only.

GST Tax—Generation Skipping Transfer Tax. Part of the U.S. Federal estate tax regime, which imposes an additional tax on bequests which skip a generation, for example, testamentary gifts from a grandparent to grandchildren when their parents are surviving.

IRC—Internal Revenue Code. Federal tax law in the United States, formally referred to as the Internal Revenue Code (IRC) of 1986, as amended.

IRS—Internal Revenue Service. The agency of the United States federal government charged with tax collection and enforcement, including regulation of tax-exempt organizations. The IRS is a branch of the Department of the Treasury.

Lobbying—Political activities for the purpose of influencing the legislative process or executive branch decision making.

Protector—A person (other than a Trustee) whose consent is required to the exercise of powers conferred upon the Trustees, or who may have power to appoint or remove Trustees.

Settlement—A document which creates a trust in circumstances where a person, known as a Settlor, transfers his property to a trustee to be held in trust in accordance with the arrangements set out in the settlement. Also called a Trust Agreement.

Settlor—A person establishing a Trust by a gift of property. Sometimes also referred to as a Grantor.

Trust—A legal relationship where a person (known as the Trustee) holds the legal title to property (of which he is not the owner in his own right) for the benefit of any person (known as a beneficiary) or purpose which is not solely for the benefit of the Trustee.

Trustee—A person who holds trust property for beneficiaries of a Trust.

APPENDICES

 Department of the Treasury
Internal Revenue Service

Application for Recognition of Exemption

Under Section 501(c)(3) of the Internal Revenue Code

Contents:
Form 1023 and
  Instructions
Form 872-C

Note: *For the addresses for filing* **Form 1023,** *see* **Form 8718,** *User Fee for Exempt Organization Determination Letter Request.*

For obtaining an employer identification number (EIN), see **Form SS-4,** *Application for Employer Identification Number.*

Package 1023
(Rev. September 1998)

Cat. No. 47194L

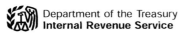

Department of the Treasury
Internal Revenue Service

Instructions for Form 1023

(Revised September 1998)

Application for Recognition of Exemption Under Section 501(c)(3) of the Internal Revenue Code

Note: *Retain a copy of the completed Form 1023 in the organization's permanent records. See **Public Inspection of Form 1023** regarding public inspection of approved applications.*

General Instructions

Section references are to the Internal Revenue Code unless otherwise noted.

User Fee.—Submit with the Form 1023 application for a determination letter, a **Form 8718,** User Fee for Exempt Organization Determination Letter Request, and the user fee called for in the Form 8718. You may obtain Form 8718, and additional forms and publications, through your local IRS office or by calling 1-800-829-3676 (1-800-TAX-FORM). User fees are subject to change on an annual basis. Therefore, be sure that you use the most current Form 8718.

Helpful information.—For additional information, see:

● **Pub. 557,** Tax-Exempt Status for Your Organization

● **Pub. 598,** Tax on Unrelated Business Income of Exempt Organizations

● **Pub. 578,** Tax Information for Private Foundations and Foundation Managers

● **Internet site,** www.irs.ustreas.gov/bus_info/eo/

Purpose of Form

1. Completed Form 1023 required for section 501(c)(3) exemption.—Unless it meets one of the exceptions in **2** below, any organization formed after October 9, 1969, must file a Form 1023 to qualify as a section 501(c)(3) organization.

The IRS determines if an organization is a private foundation from the information entered on a Form 1023.

2. Organizations not required to file Form 1023.—The following types of organizations may be considered tax-exempt under section 501(c)(3) even if they do not file Form 1023:

1. Churches,

2. Integrated auxiliaries of churches, and conventions or associations of churches, or

3. Any organization that:

(a) Is not a private foundation (as defined in section 509(a)), and

(b) Has gross receipts in each taxable year of normally not more than $5,000.

Even if the above organizations are not required to file Form 1023 to be tax-exempt, these organizations may choose to file Form 1023 in order to receive a determination letter that recognizes their section 501(c)(3) status.

Section 501(c)(3) status provides certain incidental benefits such as:

● Public recognition of tax-exempt status.

● Advance assurance to donors of deductibility of contributions.

● Exemption from certain state taxes.

● Exemption from certain Federal excise taxes.

● Nonprofit mailing privileges, etc.

3. Other organizations.—Section 501(e) and (f) cooperative service organizations, section 501(k) child care organizations, and section

501(n) charitable risk pools use Form 1023 to apply for a determination letter under section 501(c)(3).

4. Group exemption letter.—Generally, Form 1023 is not used to apply for a group exemption letter. See Pub. 557 for information on how to apply for a group exemption letter.

What To File

All applicants must complete pages 1 through 9 of Form 1023. These organizations must also complete the schedules or form indicated:

1. Churches	. . . .	Schedule A
2. Schools	. . . .	Schedule B
3. Hospitals and Medical Research	. . . . . .	Schedule C
4. Supporting Organizations (509(a)(3))	. . . . .	Schedule D
5. Private Operating Foundations	. . . . .	Schedule E
6. Homes for the Aged or Handicapped	. . . .	Schedule F
7. Child Care	. . . .	Schedule G
8. Scholarship Benefits or Student Aid	. . . .	Schedule H
9. Organizations that have taken over or will take over a "for profit" institution	. . . .	Schedule I
10. Organizations requesting an advance ruling in Part III, Line 10	. . . .	Form 872-C

Attachments.—For any attachments submitted with Form 1023.—

● Show the organization's name, address, and employer identification number (EIN).

● Identify the Part and line item number to which the attachment relates.

● Use 8½ x 11 inch paper for any attachments.

● Include any court decisions, rulings, opinions, etc., that will expedite processing of the application. Generally, attachments in the form of tape recordings are not acceptable unless accompanied by a transcript.

When To File

An organization formed after October 9, 1969, must file Form 1023 to be recognized as an organization described in section 501(c)(3). Generally, if an organization files its application within 15 months after the end of the month in which it was formed, and if the IRS approves the application, the effective date of the organization's section 501(c)(3) status will be the date it was organized.

Generally, if an organization does not file its application (Form 1023) within 15 months after the end of the month in which it was formed, it will not qualify for exempt status during the period before the date of its application. For exceptions and special rules, including automatic extensions in some cases, see Part III of Form 1023.

The date of receipt of the Form 1023 is the date of the U.S. postmark on the cover in which an exemption application is mailed or, if no postmark appears on the cover, the date the application is stamped as received by the IRS.

Private delivery services.—See the instructions for your income tax return for information on certain private delivery services designated by the IRS to meet the "timely mailing as timely filing/paying rule." The private delivery service can tell you how to get written proof of the mailing date.

Caution: *Private delivery services cannot deliver items to P.O. boxes. You must use the U. S. Postal Service to mail any item to an IRS P.O. box address. See the Form 8718 for the P.O. box address as well as the express mail or a delivery service address.*

Where To File

File the completed Form 1023 application, and all required information, with the IRS at the address shown in Form 8718.

The IRS will determine the organization's tax-exempt status and whether any annual returns must be filed.

Signature Requirements

An officer, a trustee who is authorized to sign, or another person authorized by a power of attorney, must sign the Form 1023 application. Attach a power of attorney to the application. You may use **Form 2848,** Power of Attorney and Declaration of Representative, for this purpose.

Deductibility of Contributions

Donors can take a charitable contribution deduction if their gift or bequest is made to a section 501(c)(3) organization.

The effective date of an organization's section 501(c)(3) status determines the date that contributions to it are deductible by donors. (See **When To File** on page 1.)

Contributions by U.S. residents to foreign organizations generally are not deductible. Tax treaties between the U.S. and certain foreign countries provide limited exceptions. Foreign organizations (other than those in Canada or Mexico) that claim eligibility to receive contributions deductible by U.S. residents must attach an English copy of the U.S. tax treaty that provides for such deductibility.

Appeal Procedures

The organization's application will be considered by the IRS which will either:

1. Issue a favorable determination letter;

2. Issue a proposed adverse determination letter denying the exempt status requested; or

3. Refer the case to the National Office.

If the IRS sends you a proposed adverse determination, it will advise you of your appeal rights at that time.

Language and Currency Requirements

Language requirements.—Prepare the Form 1023 and attachments in English. Provide an English translation if the organizational document or bylaws are in any other language.

You may be asked to provide English translations of foreign language publications that the organization produces or distributes and that are submitted with the application.

Financial requirements.—Report all financial information in U.S. dollars (specify the conversion rate used). Combine amounts from within and outside the United States and report the total for each item on the financial statements.

For example:

Gross Investment Income	
From U.S. sources	$4,000
From non-U.S. sources	1,000
Amount to report on income statement	$5,000

Annual Information Return

If an annual information return is due while the organization's application for recognition of exempt status is pending with the IRS (including any appeal of a proposed adverse determination), the organization should file at the following address:

Internal Revenue Service
Ogden Service Center
Ogden, Utah 84201-0027

● **Form 990,** Return of Organization Exempt From Income Tax, **or**

● **Form 990-EZ,** Short Form Return of Organization Exempt From Income Tax, **and,**

● **Schedule A (Form 990),** Organization Exempt Under Section 501(c)(3), **or**

● **Form 990-PF,** Return of Private Foundation, if the organization acknowledges it is a private foundation, **and**

Indicate that an application is pending.

If an organization has unrelated business income of more than $1,000, file **Form 990-T,** Exempt Organization Business Income Tax Return.

Public Inspection of Form 1023

Caution: *Note the discussion below for the potential effect of the Taxpayer Bill of Rights 2 (TBOR2) on these instructions.*

IRS responsibilities for public inspection.—If the organization's application for section 501(c)(3) status is approved, the following items will be open to public inspection in any District office and at the National Office of the IRS (section 6104):

1. The organization's application and any supporting documents.

2. Any letter or other document issued by the IRS with regard to the application.

Note that the following items are not available for public inspection:

1. Any information relating to a trade secret, patent, style of work, or apparatus that, if released, would adversely affect the organization, or

2. Any other information that would adversely affect the national defense.

IMPORTANT: Applicants must identify this information by clearly marking it, "NOT SUBJECT TO PUBLIC INSPECTION," and must attach a statement to explain why the organization asks that the information be withheld. If the IRS agrees, the information will be withheld.

Organization's responsibilities for public inspection.—The organization must make available a copy of its approved application and supporting documents, along with any document or letter issued by the IRS for public inspection.

These documents must be available during regular business hours at the organization's principal office and at each of its regional or district offices having at least three paid employees. See Notice 88-120,1988-2 C.B. 454.

A penalty of $20 a day will be imposed on any person under a duty to comply with the public inspection requirements for each day a failure to comply continues.

Furnishing copies of documents under TBOR2.—The Taxpayer Bill of Rights 2 (TBOR2), enacted July 30, 1996, modified prospectively the section 6685 penalty and the rules for the public inspection of returns and exemption applications. An organization must furnish a copy of its Form 990, Form 990-EZ, or exemption application, and certain related documents, if a request is made in writing or in person.

For a request made in person, the organization must make an immediate response.

For a response to a written request, the organization must provide the requested copies within 30 days.

The organization must furnish copies of its Forms 990, or Forms 990-EZ, for any of its 3 most recent taxable years. No charge is to be made other than charging a reasonable fee for reproduction and actual postage costs.

An organization need not provide copies if:

1. The organization has made the requested documents widely available in a manner provided in Treasury regulations, or

2. The Secretary of the Treasury determined, upon application by the organization, that the organization was subject to a harassment campaign such that a waiver of the obligation to provide copies would be in the public interest.

Penalty for failure to allow public inspection or provide copies.—The section 6685 penalty for willful failure to allow public inspections or provide copies is increased from the present-law level of $1,000 to $5,000 by TBOR2.

Effective date of TBOR2.—These public inspection provisions governing tax-exempt organizations under TBOR2 generally apply to requests made no earlier than 60 days after the date on which the Treasury Department publishes the regulations required under the provisions. However, Congress, in the legislative history of TBOR2, indicated that organizations would comply voluntarily with the public inspection provisions prior to the issuance of such regulations.

Special Rule for Canadian Colleges and Universities

A Canadian college or university that received **Form T2051,** Notification of Registration, from Revenue Canada (Department of National Revenue, Taxation) and whose registration has not been revoked, does not need to complete all parts of Form 1023.

Such an organization must complete only Part I of Form 1023 and Schedule B (Schools, Colleges, and Universities). It must attach a copy of its **Form T2050,** Application for Registration, together with all the required attachments submitted to Revenue Canada. It must furnish an English translation if any attachments were prepared in French.

Other Canadian organizations.—Other Canadian organizations that seek a determination of section 501(c)(3) status must complete Form 1023 in the same manner as U.S. organizations.

Specific Instructions

The following instructions are keyed to the line items on the application form:

Part I. Identification of Applicant

Line 1. Full name and address of organization.—Enter the organization's name exactly as it appears in its creating document including amendments. Show the other name in parentheses, if the organization will be operating under another name.

For a foreign address, enter the information in the following order: city, province or state, and country. Follow the country's practice in placing the postal code in the address. **Do not** abbreviate the country name.

Line 2. Employer identification number (EIN).—All organizations must have an EIN. Enter the nine-digit EIN the IRS assigned to the organization. See **Form SS-4,** Application for Employer Identification Number, for information on how to obtain an EIN immediately by telephone, if the organization does not have an EIN. Enter, "applied for," if the organization has applied for an EIN number previously. Attach a statement giving the date of the application and the office where it was filed. **Do not** apply for an EIN more than once.

Line 3. Person to contact.—Enter the name and telephone number of the person to contact during business hours if more information is needed. The contact person should be an officer, director, or a person with power of attorney who is familiar with the organization's activities and is authorized to act on its behalf. Attach Form 2848 or other power of attorney.

Line 4. Month the annual accounting period ends.—Enter the month the organization's annual accounting period ends. The accounting period is usually the 12-month period that is the organization's tax year. The organization's first tax year depends on the accounting period chosen. The first tax year could be less than 12 months.

Line 5. Date formed.—Enter the date the organization became a legal entity. For a corporation, this is the date that the articles of incorporation were approved by the appropriate state official. For an unincorporated organization, it is the date its constitution or articles of association were adopted.

Line 6.—Indicate if the organization is one of the following:

- 501(e)   Cooperative hospital service organization
- 501(f)   Cooperative service organization of operating educational organization
- 501(k)   Organization providing child care
- 501(n)   Charitable risk pool

If none of the above applies, make no entry on line 6.

Line 7.—Indicate if the organization has ever filed a Form 1023 or **Form 1024,** Application for Recognition of Exemption Under Section 501(a), with the IRS.

Line 8.—If the organization for which this application is being filed is a private foundation, answer "N/A." If the organization is not required to file Form 990 (or Form 990-EZ) and is not a private foundation, answer "No" and attach an explanation. See the Instructions for Form 990 and Form 990-EZ for a discussion of organizations not required to file Form 990 (or Form 990-EZ). Otherwise, answer "Yes."

Line 9.—Indicate if the organization has ever filed Federal income tax returns as a taxable organization or filed returns as an exempt organization (e.g., Form 990, 990-EZ, 990-PF, or 990-T).

Line 10. Type of organization and organizational documents.—**Organizing instrument.**—Submit a conformed copy of the organizing instrument. If the organization does not have an organizing instrument, it will not qualify for exempt status.

A conformed copy is one that agrees with the original and all amendments to it. The conformed copy may be:

- A photocopy of the original signed and dated organizing document, OR

- A copy of the organizing document that is unsigned but is sent with a written declaration, signed by an authorized individual, that states that the copy is a complete and accurate copy of the original signed and dated document.

Corporation.—In the case of a corporation, a copy of the articles of incorporation, approved and dated by an appropriate state official, is sufficient by itself.

If an unsigned copy of the articles of incorporation is submitted, it must be accompanied by the written declaration discussed above.

Signed, or unsigned, copies of the articles of incorporation must be accompanied by a declaration stating that the original copy of the articles was filed with, and approved by, the state. The date filed must be specified.

Unincorporated association.—In the case of an unincorporated association, the conformed copy of the constitution, articles of association, or other organizing document must indicate, in the document itself, or in a written declaration, that the organization was formed by the adoption of the document by two or more persons.

Bylaws.—If the organization has adopted bylaws, include a current copy. The bylaws do not need to be signed if they are submitted as an attachment to the Form 1023 application. The bylaws of an organization alone are not an organizing instrument. They are merely the internal rules and regulations of the organization.

Trust.—In the case of a trust, a copy of the signed and dated trust instrument must be furnished.

Dissolution clause.—For an organization to qualify for exempt status, its organizing instrument must contain a proper dissolution clause, or state law must provide for distribution of assets for one or more section 501(c)(3) purposes upon dissolution. If the organization is relying on state law, provide the citation for the law and briefly state the law's provisions in an attachment. Foreign organizations must provide the citation for the foreign statute and attach a copy of the statute along with an English language translation.

See Pub. 557 for a discussion of dissolution clauses under the heading, **Articles of Organization, Dedication and Distribution of Assets.** Examples of dissolution clauses are shown in the sample organizing instruments given in that publication.

Organizational purposes.—The organizing instrument must specify the organizational purposes of the organization. The purposes specified must be limited to one or more of those given in section 501(c)(3). See Pub. 557 for detailed instructions and for sample organizing instruments that satisfy the requirements of section 501(c)(3) and the related regulations.

Part II. Activities and Operational Information

Line 1.—It is important that you report all activities carried on by the organization to enable the IRS to make a proper determination of the organization's exempt status.

Line 2.—If it is anticipated that the organization's principal sources of support will increase or decrease substantially in relation to the organization's total support, attach a statement describing anticipated changes and explaining the basis for the expectation.

Line 3.—For purposes of providing the information requested on line 3, "fundraising activity" includes the solicitation of contributions and both functionally related activities and unrelated business activities. Include a description of the nature and magnitude of the activities.

Line 4a.—Furnish the mailing addresses of the organization's principal officers, directors, or trustees. Do not give the address of the organization.

Line 4b.—The annual compensation includes salary, bonus, and any other form of payment to the individual for services while employed by the organization.

Line 4c.—Public officials include anyone holding an elected position or anyone appointed to a position by an elected official.

Line 4d.—For purposes of this application, a "disqualified person" is any person who, if the applicant were a private foundation, is:

1. A "substantial contributor" to the foundation (defined below);

2. A foundation manager;

3. An owner of more than 20% of the total combined voting power of a corporation that is a substantial contributor to the foundation;

4. A "member of the family" of any person described in 1, 2, or 3 above;

5. A corporation, partnership, or trust in which persons described in 1, 2, 3, or 4 above, hold more than 35% of the combined voting power, the profits interest, or the beneficial interests; and

6. Any other private foundation that is effectively controlled by the same persons who control the first-mentioned private foundation or any other private foundation substantially all of whose contributions were made by the same contributors.

A substantial contributor is any person who gave a total of more than $5,000 to the organization, and those contributions are more than 2% of all the contributions received by the organization from the date it was created up to the end of the year the contributions by the substantial contributor were received. A creator of a trust is treated as a substantial contributor regardless of the amount contributed by that person or others.

See Pub. 578 for more information on "disqualified persons."

Line 5.—If your organization controls or is controlled by another exempt organization or a taxable organization, answer "Yes." "Control" means that:

1. Fifty percent (50%) or more of the filing organization's officers, directors, trustees, or key employees are also officers, directors, trustees, or key employees of the second organization being tested for control;

2. The filing organization appoints 50% or more of the officers, directors, trustees, or key employees of the second organization; or

3. Fifty percent (50%) or more of the filing organization's officers, directors, trustees, or key employees are appointed by the second organization.

Control exists if the 50% test is met by any one group of persons even if collectively the 50% test is not met. Examples of special relationships are common officers and the sharing of office space or employees.

Line 6.—If the organization conducts any financial transactions (either receiving or distributing cash or other assets), or nonfinancial activities with an exempt organization (other than a 501(c)(3) organization), or with a political organization, answer "Yes," and explain.

Line 7.—If the organization must report its income and expense activity to any other organization (tax-exempt or taxable entity), answer "Yes."

Line 8.—Examples of assets used to perform an exempt function are: land, building, equipment, and publications. Do not include cash or property producing investment income. If you have no assets used in performing the organization's exempt function, answer "N/A."

Line 10a.—If the organization is managed by another exempt organization, a taxable organization, or an individual, answer "Yes."

Line 10b.—If the organization leases property from anyone or leases any of its property to anyone, answer "Yes."

Line 11.—A membership organization for purposes of this question is an organization that is composed of individuals or organizations who:

1. Share in the common goal for which the organization was created;

2. Actively participate in achieving the organization's purposes; and

3. Pay dues.

Line 12.—Examples of benefits, services, and products are: meals to homeless people, home for the aged, a museum open to the public, and a symphony orchestra giving public performances.

Note: *Organizations that provide low-income housing should see Rev. Proc. 96-32, 1996-1 C.B. 717, for a "safe harbor" and an alternative facts and circumstances test to be used in completing line 12.*

Line 13.—An organization is attempting to influence legislation if it contacts or urges the public to contact members of a legislative body, for the purpose of proposing, supporting, or opposing legislation, or if it advocates the adoption or rejection of legislation.

If you answer "Yes," you may want to file **Form 5768,** Election/Revocation of Election by an Eligible Section 501(c)(3) Organization To Make Expenditures To Influence Legislation.

Line 14.—An organization is intervening in a political campaign if it promotes or opposes the candidacy or prospective candidacy of an individual for public office.

Part III. Technical Requirements

Line 1.—If you check "Yes," proceed to line 7. If you check "No," proceed to line 2.

Line 2a.—To qualify as an integrated auxiliary, an organization must not be a private foundation and must satisfy the affiliation and support tests of Regulations section 1.6033-2(h).

Line 3.—Relief from the 15-month filing requirement is granted automatically if the organization submits a completed Form 1023 within 12 months from the end of the 15-month period.

To get this extension, an organization must add the following statement at the top of its application: "Filed Pursuant to Section 301.9100-2." No request for a letter ruling is required to obtain an automatic extension.

Line 4.—See Regulation sections 301.9100-1 and 301.9100-3 for information about a discretionary extension beyond the 27-month period. Under these regulations, the IRS will allow an organization a reasonable extension of time to file a Form 1023 if it submits evidence to establish that:

(a) It acted reasonably and in good faith, and

(b) Granting relief will not prejudice the interests of the government.

Showing reasonable action and good faith.—An organization acted reasonably and showed good faith if at least one of the following is true.

1. The organization filed its application before the IRS discovered its failure to file.

2. The organization failed to file because of intervening events beyond its control.

3. The organization exercised reasonable diligence but was not aware of the filing requirement.

To determine whether the organization exercised reasonable diligence, it is necessary to take into account the complexity of filing and the organization's experience in these matters.

4. The organization reasonably relied upon the written advice of the IRS.

5. The organization reasonably relied upon the advice of a qualified tax professional who failed to file or advise the organization to file Form 1023. An organization cannot rely on the advice of a qualified tax professional if it knows or should know that he or she is not competent to render advice on filing exemption applications or is not aware of all the relevant facts.

Not acting reasonably and in good faith.—An organization has not acted reasonably and in good faith if it chose not to file after being informed of the requirement to file and the consequences of failure to do so. Furthermore, an organization has not acted reasonably and in good faith if it used hindsight to request an extension of time to file. That is, if after the original deadline to file passes, specific facts have changed so that filing an application becomes advantageous to an organization, the IRS will not ordinarily grant an extension. To qualify for an extension in this situation, the organization must prove that its decision to file did not involve hindsight.

No prejudice to the interest of the government.—Prejudice to the interest of the government results if granting an extension of time to file to an organization results in a lower total tax liability for the years to which the filing applies than would have been the case if the organization had applied on time. Before granting an extension, the IRS may require the organization requesting it to submit a statement from an independent auditor certifying that no prejudice will result if the extension is granted.

Procedure for requesting extension.—To request a discretionary extension, an organization must submit the following with its Form 1023:

● A statement showing the date Form 1023 should have been filed and the date it was actually filed.

● An affidavit describing in detail the events that led to the failure to apply and to the discovery of that failure. If the organization relied on a qualified tax professional's advice, the affidavit must describe the engagement and responsibilities of the professional and the extent to which the organization relied on him or her.

● All documents relevant to the election application.

● A dated declaration, signed by an individual authorized to act for the organization, that includes the following statement: "Under penalties of perjury, I declare that I have examined this request, including accompanying documents, and, to the best of my knowledge and belief, the request contains all the relevant facts relating to the request, and such facts are true, correct, and complete."

● A detailed affidavit from individuals having knowledge or information about the events that led to the failure to make the application and to the discovery of that failure. These individuals include accountants or attorneys knowledgeable in tax matters who advised the organization concerning the application. Any affidavit from a tax professional must describe the engagement and responsibilities of the professional as well as the advice that the professional provided to the organization. The affidavit must also include the name, current address, and taxpayer identification number of the individual making the affidavit (the affiant). The affiant must also forward with the affidavit a dated and signed declaration that states: "Under penalties of perjury, I declare that I have examined this request, including accompanying documents, and, to the best of my knowledge and belief, the request contains all the relevant facts relating to the request, and such facts are true, correct, and complete."

The reasons for late filing should be specific to your particular organization and situation. Regulation section 301.9100-3 (see above) lists the factors the IRS will consider in determining if good cause exists for granting a discretionary extension of time to file the application. To address these factors, your response for line 4 should provide the following information:

1. Whether the organization consulted an attorney or accountant knowledgeable in tax matters or communicated with a responsible IRS employee (before or after the organization was created) to ascertain the organization's Federal filing requirements and, if so, the names and occupations or titles of the persons contacted, the approximate dates, and the substance of the information obtained;

2. How and when the organization learned about the 15-month deadline for filing Form 1023;

3. Whether any significant intervening circumstances beyond the organization's control prevented it from submitting the application timely or within a reasonable period of time after it learned of the requirement to file the application within the 15-month period; and

4. Any other information that you believe may establish reasonable action and good faith and no prejudice to the interest of the government for not filing timely or otherwise justify granting the relief sought.

A request for relief under this section is treated as part of the request for the exemption determination letter and is covered by the user fee submitted with Form 8718.

Line 5.—If you answer "No," the organization may receive an adverse letter limiting the effective date of its exempt status to the date its application was received.

Line 6.—The organization may still be able to qualify for exemption under section 501(c)(4) for the period preceding the effective date of its exemption as a section 501(c)(3) organization. If the organization is qualified under section 501(c)(4) and page 1 of Form 1024 is filed as directed, the organization will not be liable for income tax returns as a taxable entity. Contributions to section 501(c)(4) organizations are generally not deductible by donors as charitable contributions.

Line 7.—Private foundations are subject to various requirements, restrictions, and excise taxes under Chapter 42 of the Code that do not apply to public charities. Also, contributions to private foundations may receive less favorable treatment than contributions to public charities. See Pub. 578. Therefore, it is usually to an organization's advantage to show that it qualifies as a public charity rather than as a private foundation if its activities or sources of support permit it to do so. Unless an organization meets one of the exceptions below, it is a private foundation. In general, an organization is **not** a private foundation if it is:

1. A church, school, hospital, or governmental unit;

2. A medical research organization operated in conjunction with a hospital;

3. An organization operated for the benefit of a college or university that is owned or operated by a governmental unit;

4. An organization that normally receives a substantial part of its support in the form of contributions from a governmental unit or from the general public as provided in section 170(b)(1)(A)(vi);

5. An organization that normally receives not more than one-third of its support from gross investment income and more than one-third of its support from contributions, membership fees, and gross receipts related to its exempt functions (subject to certain exceptions) as provided in section 509(a)(2);

6. An organization operated solely for the benefit of, and in connection with, one or more organizations described above (or for the benefit of one or more of the organizations described in section 501(c)(4), (5), or (6) of the Code and also described in **5** above), but not controlled by disqualified persons other than foundation managers, as provided in section 509(a)(3); or

7. An organization organized and operated to test for public safety as provided in section 509(a)(4).

Line 8.—Basis for private operating foundation status: (Complete this line **only** if you answered "Yes" to the question on line 7.)

A "private operating foundation" is a private foundation that spends substantially all of its adjusted net income or its minimum investment return, whichever is less, directly for the active conduct of the activities constituting the purpose or function for which it is organized and operated.

The foundation must satisfy the income test and one of the three supplemental tests: **(1)** the assets test; **(2)** the endowment test; or **(3)** the support test. For additional information, see Pub. 578.

Line 9.—Basis for nonprivate foundation status: Check the box that shows why your organization is not a private foundation.

Box (a). A church or convention or association of churches.

Box (b). A school.—See the definition in the instructions for Schedule B.

Box (c). A hospital or medical research organization.—See the instructions for Schedule C.

Box (d). A governmental unit.—This category includes a state, a possession of the United States, or a political subdivision of any of the foregoing, or the United States, or the District of Columbia.

Box (e). Organizations operated in connection with or solely for organizations described in (a) through (d) or (g), (h), and (i).—The organization must be organized and operated for the benefit of, to perform the functions of, or to carry out the purposes of one or more specified organizations described in section 509(a)(1) or (2). It must be operated, supervised, or controlled by or in connection with one or more of the organizations described in the instructions for boxes **(a)** through **(d)** or **(g)**, **(h)**, and **(i)**. It must not be controlled directly or indirectly by disqualified persons (other than foundation managers or organizations described in section 509(a)(1) or (2)). To show whether the organization satisfies these tests, complete Schedule D.

Box (f). An organization testing for public safety.—An organization in this category is one that tests products to determine their acceptability for use by the general public. It does not include any organization testing for the benefit of a manufacturer as an operation or control in the manufacture of its product.

Box (g). Organization for the benefit of a college or university owned or operated by a governmental unit.—The organization must be organized and operated exclusively for the benefit of a college or university that:

- Is an educational organization within the meaning of section 170(b)(1)(A)(ii) and is an agency or instrumentality of a state or political subdivision of a state;

- Is owned or operated by a state or political subdivision of a state; OR

- Is owned or operated by an agency or instrumentality of one or more states or political subdivisions.

The organization must also normally receive a substantial part of its support from the United States or any state or political subdivision of a state, or from direct or indirect contributions from the general public or from a combination of these sources.

An organizaton described in section 170(b)(1)(A)(iv) will be subject to the same publicly supported rules that are applicable to 170(b)(1)(A)(vi) organizations described in box (h) below.

Box (h). Organization receiving support from a governmental unit or from the general public.—The organization must receive a substantial part of its support from the United States or any state or political subdivision, or from direct or indirect contributions from the general public, or from a combination of these sources.

The organization may satisfy the support requirement in either of two ways.

(1) It will be treated as publicly supported if the support it normally receives from the above-described governmental units and the general public equals at least one-third of its total support.

(2) It will also be treated as publicly supported if the support it normally receives from governmental or public sources equals at least 10% of total support and the organization is set up to attract new and additional public or governmental support on a continuous basis.

If the organization's governmental and public support is at least 10%, but not over one-third of its total support, the questions on lines 1 through 14 of Part II will apply to determine both the organization's claim of exemption and whether it is publicly supported. Preparers should exercise care to assure that those questions are answered in detail.

Box (i). Organization described in section 509(a)(2).—The organization must satisfy the support test under section 509(a)(2)(A) and the gross investment income test under section 509(a)(2)(B).

To satisfy the support test, the organization must normally receive more than one-third of its support from: **(a)** gifts, grants, contributions, or membership fees; and **(b)** gross receipts from admissions, sales of merchandise, performance of services, or furnishing of facilities, in an activity that is not an unrelated trade or business (subject to certain limitations discussed below).

This one-third of support must be from organizations described in section 509(a)(1), governmental sources, or persons other than disqualified persons.

In computing gross receipts from admissions, sales of merchandise, performance of services, or furnishing of facilities in an activity that is not an unrelated trade or business, the gross receipts from any one person or from any bureau or similar agency of a governmental unit are includible only to the extent they do not exceed the greater of $5,000 or 1% of the organization's total support.

To satisfy the gross investment income test, the organization must not receive more than one-third of its support from gross investment income.

Box (j).—If you believe the organization meets the public support test of section 170(b)(1)(A)(vi) or 509(a)(2) but are uncertain as to which public support test it satisfies, check box **(j)**. By checking this box, you are claiming that the organization is not a private foundation and are agreeing to let the IRS compute the public support of your organization and determine the correct foundation status.

Line 10.—An organization must complete a tax year consisting of at least 8 months to receive a definitive (final) ruling under sections 170(b)(1)(A)(vi) and 509(a)(1), or under section 509(a)(2).

However, organizations that checked box **(h)**, **(i)**, or **(j)** on line 9 that do not meet the 8-month requirement must request an advance ruling that covers their first 5 tax years instead of requesting a definitive ruling.

An organization that meets the 8-month requirement has two options:

1. It may request a definitive ruling. The organization's public support computation will be based on the support the organization has received to date; or

2. It may request an advance ruling. The organization's public support computation will be based on the support it receives during its first 5 tax years.

An organization should consider the advance ruling option if it has not received significant public support during its first tax year or during its first and second tax years, but it reasonably expects to receive such support by the end of its fifth tax year.

An organization that receives an advance ruling is treated, during the 5-year advance ruling period, as a public charity (rather than a private foundation) for certain purposes, including those relating to the deductibility of contributions by the general public.

Line 11.—For definition of an unusual grant, see instructions for Part IV-A, line 12.

Line 12.—Answer this question only if you checked box **(g)**, **(h)**, or **(j)** on line 9.

Line 13.—Answer the question on this line only if you checked box **(i)** or **(j)** on line 9 and are requesting a definitive ruling on line 10.

Line 14.—Answer "Yes" or "No" on each line. If "Yes," you must complete the appropriate schedule. Each schedule is included in this application package with accompanying instructions. For a brief definition of each type of organization, see the appropriate schedule.

Part IV. Financial Data

Complete the Statement of Revenue and Expenses for the current year and each of the 3 years immediately before it (or the years the organization has existed, if less than 4).

Any applicant that has existed for less than 1 year must give financial data for the current year and proposed budgets for the following 2 years.

The IRS may request financial data for more than 4 years if necessary.

All financial information for the current year must cover the period beginning on the first day of the organization's established annual accounting period and ending on any day that is within 60 days of the date of this application.

If the date of this application is less than 60 days after the first day of the current accounting period, no financial information is required for the current year.

Financial information is required for the 3 preceding years regardless of the current year requirements. Please note that if no financial information is required for the current year, the preceding year's financial information can end on any day that is within 60 days of the date of this application.

Prepare the statements using the method of accounting and the accounting period (entered on line 4 of Part I) the organization uses in keeping its books and records. If the organization uses a method other than the cash receipts and disbursements method, attach a statement explaining the method used.

A. Statement of Revenue and Expenses

Line 1.—Do not include amounts received from the general public or a governmental unit for the exercise or performance of the organization's exempt function. However, include payments made by a governmental unit to enable the organization to provide a service to the general public.

Do not include unusual grants. See the explanation for unusual grants in Line 12 of this section.

Line 2.—Include amounts received from members for the purpose of providing support to the organization. These are considered as contributions. Do not include payments to purchase admissions, merchandise, services, or use of facilities.

Line 3.—Include on this line the income received from dividends, interest, and payments received on securities loans, rents, and royalties.

Line 4.—Enter the organization's net income from any activities that are regularly carried on and are not related to the organization's exempt purposes.

Examples of such income include fees from the commercial testing of products; income from renting office equipment or other personal property; and income from the sale of advertising in an exempt organization's periodical. See Pub. 598 for information about unrelated business income and activities.

Line 5.—Enter the amount collected by the local tax authority from the general public that has been allocated for your organization.

Line 6.—To report the value of services and/or facilities furnished by a governmental unit, use the fair market value at the time the service/facility was furnished to your organization. Do not include any other donated services or facilities in Part IV.

Line 7.—Enter the total income from all sources that is not reported on lines 1 through 6, or lines 9, 11, and 12. Attach a schedule that lists each type of revenue source and the amount derived from each.

Line 9.—Include income generated by the organization's exempt function activities (charitable, educational, etc.) and its nontaxable fundraising events (excluding any contributions received).

Examples of such income include the income derived by a symphony orchestra from the sale of tickets to its performances; and raffles, bingo, or other fundraising-event income that is not taxable as unrelated business income because the income-producing activities are not regularly carried on or because they are conducted with substantially all (at least 85%) volunteer labor. Record related cost of sales on line 22, Other.

Line 11.—Attach a schedule that shows a description of each asset, the name of the person to whom sold, and the amount received. In the case of publicly traded securities sold through a broker, the name of the purchaser is not required.

Line 12.—Unusual grants generally consist of substantial contributions and bequests from disinterested persons that:

1. Are attracted by reason of the publicly supported nature of the organization;

2. Are unusual and unexpected as to the amount; and

3. Would, by reason of their size, adversely affect the status of the organization as normally meeting the support test of section 170(b)(1)(A)(vi) or section 509(a)(2), as the case may be.

If the organization is awarded an unusual grant and the terms of the granting instrument provide that the organization will receive the funds over a period of years, the amount received by the organization each year under the grant may be excluded. See the regulations under sections 170 and 509.

Line 14.—Fundraising expenses represent the total expenses incurred in soliciting contributions, gifts, grants, etc.

Line 15.—Attach a schedule showing the name of the recipient, a brief description of the purposes or conditions of payment, and the amount paid. The following example shows the format and amount of detail required for this schedule:

Recipient	Purpose	Amount
Museum of Natural History	General operating budget	$29,000
State University	Books for needy students	14,500
Richard Roe	Educational scholarship	12,200

Colleges, universities, and other educational institutions and agencies subject to the Family Educational Rights and Privacy Act (20 U.S.C. 1232g) are not required to list the names of individuals who were provided scholarships or other financial assistance where such disclosure would violate the privacy provisions of the law. Instead, such organizations should group each type of financial aid provided, indicate the number of individuals who received the aid, and specify the aggregate dollar amount.

Line 16.—Attach a schedule showing the name of each recipient, a brief description of the purposes or condition of payment, and amount paid. Do not include any amounts that are on line 15. The schedule should be similar to the schedule shown in the line 15 instructions above.

Line 17.—Attach a schedule that shows the name of the person compensated; the office or position; the average amount of time devoted to the organization's affairs per week, month, etc.; and the amount of annual compensation. The following example shows the format and amount of detail required:

Name	Position	Time devoted	Annual salary
Philip Poe	President and general manager	16 hrs. per wk.	$27,500

Line 18.—Enter the total of employees' salaries not reported on line 17.

Line 19.—Enter the total interest expense for the year, excluding mortgage interest treated as if an occupancy expense on line 20.

Line 20.—Enter the amount paid for the use of office space or other facilities, heat, light, power, and other utilities, outside janitorial services, mortgage interest, real estate taxes, and similar expenses.

Line 21.—If your organization records depreciation, depletion, and similar expenses, enter the total.

Line 22.—Attach a schedule listing the type and amount of each **significant** expense for which a separate line is not provided. Report other miscellaneous expenses as a single total if not substantial in amount.

B. Balance Sheet

Line 1.—Enter the total cash in checking and savings accounts, temporary cash investments (money market funds, CDs, treasury bills, or other obligations that mature in less than 1 year), change funds, and petty cash funds.

Line 2.—Enter the total accounts receivable that arose from the sale of goods and/or performance of services, less any reserve for bad debt.

Line 3.—Enter the amount of materials, goods, and supplies purchased or manufactured by the organization and held to be sold or used in some future period.

Line 4.—Attach a schedule that shows the name of the borrower, a brief description of the obligation, the rate of return on the principal indebtedness, the due date, and the amount due. The following example shows the format and amount of detail required:

Name of borrower	Description of obligation	Rate of return	Due date	Amount
Hope Soap Corporation	Debenture bond (no senior issue outstanding)	8%	Jan. 2004	$37,500
Big Soap Company	Collateral note secured by company's fleet of 20 delivery trucks	10%	Jan. 2003	262,000

Line 5.—Attach a schedule listing the organization's corporate stock holdings.

For stock of closely held corporations, the statement should show the name of the corporation, a brief summary of the corporation's capital structure, and the number of shares held and their value as carried on the organization's books. If such valuation does not reflect current fair market value, also include fair market value.

For stock traded on an organized exchange or in substantial quantities over the counter, the statement should show the name of the corporation, a description of the stock and the principal exchange on which it is traded, the number of shares held, and their value as carried on the organization's books.

The following example shows the format and the amount of detail required:

Name of corporation	Capital structure (or exchange on which traded)	Shares	Book amount	Fair market value
Little Spool Corporation	100 shares nonvoting preferred issued and outstanding, no par value; 50 shares common issued and outstanding, no par value.			
	Preferred shares:	50	$20,000	$24,000
	Common shares:	10	25,000	30,000
Flintlock Corporation	Class A common N.Y.S.E.	80	6,000	6,500

Line 6.—Report each loan separately, even if more than one loan was made to the same person. Attach a schedule that shows the borrower's name, purpose of loan, repayment terms, interest rate, and original amount of loan.

Line 7.—Enter the book value of government securities held (U.S., state, or municipal). Also enter the book value of buildings and equipment held for investment purposes. Attach a schedule identifying and reporting the book value of each.

Line 8.—Enter the book value of buildings and equipment **not** held for investment. This includes plant and equipment used by the organization in conducting its exempt activities. Attach a schedule listing these assets held at the end of the current tax year/period and the cost or other basis.

Line 9.—Enter the book value of land **not** held for investment.

Line 10.—Enter the book value of each category of assets not reported on lines 1 through 9. Attach a schedule listing each.

Line 12.—Enter the total of accounts payable to suppliers and others, such as salaries payable, accrued payroll taxes, and interest payable.

Line 13.—Enter the unpaid portion of grants and contributions that the organization has made a commitment to pay to other organizations or individuals.

Line 14.—Enter the total of mortgages and other notes payable outstanding at the end of the current tax year/period. Attach a schedule that shows each item separately and the lender's name, purpose of loan, repayment terms, interest rate, and original amount.

Line 15.—Enter the amount of each liability not reported on lines 12 through 14. Attach a separate schedule.

Line 17.—Under fund accounting, an organization segregates its assets, liabilities, and net assets into separate funds according to restrictions on the use of certain assets. Each fund is like a separate entity in that it has a self-balancing set of accounts showing assets, liabilities, equity (fund balance), income, and expenses. If the organization does not use fund accounting, report only the "net assets" account balances, such as: capital stock, paid-in capital, and retained earnings or accumulated income.

Paperwork Reduction Act Notice.—We ask for the information on this form to carry out the Internal Revenue laws of the United States. If you want your organization to be recognized as tax-exempt by the IRS, you are required to give us this information. We need it to determine whether the organization meets the legal requirements for tax-exempt status.

The organization is not required to provide the information requested on a form that is subject to the Paperwork Reduction Act unless the form displays a valid OMB control number. Books or records relating to a form or its instructions must be retained as long as their contents may become material in the administration of any Internal Revenue law. The rules governing the confidentiality of the Form 1023 application are covered in Code section 6104.

The time needed to complete and file these forms will vary depending on individual circumstances. The estimated average times are:

Form	Recordkeeping	Learning about the law or the form	Preparing, and sending the form to IRS
1023 Parts I to IV	55 hr., 58 min.	5 hr., 1 min.	8 hr., 33 min.
1023 Sch. A	7 hr., 10 min.	-0- min.	7 min.
1023 Sch. B	4 hr., 47 min.	30 min.	36 min.
1023 Sch. C	5 hr., 1 min.	35 min.	43 min.
1023 Sch. D	4 hr., 4 min.	42 min.	47 min.
1023 Sch. E	9 hr., 20 min.	1 hr., 5 min.	1 hr., 17 min.
1023 Sch. F	2 hr., 39 min.	2 hr., 53 min.	3 hr., 3 min.
1023 Sch. G	2 hr., 38 min.	-0- min.	2 min.
1023 Sch. H	1 hr., 55 min.	42 min.	46 min.
1023 Sch. I	3 hr., 35 min.	-0- min.	4 min.
872-C	1 hr., 26 min.	24 min.	26 min.

If you have comments concerning the accuracy of these time estimates or suggestions for making these forms simpler, we would be happy to hear from you. You can write to the Tax Forms Committee, Western Area Distribution Center, Rancho Cordova, CA 95743-0001. **DO NOT** send the application to this address. Instead, see **Where To File** on page 1.

Procedural Checklist

Make sure the application is complete.

If you do not complete all applicable parts or do not provide all required attachments, we may return the incomplete application to your organization for resubmission with the missing information or attachments. This will delay the processing of the application and may delay the effective date of your organization's exempt status. The organization may also incur additional user fees.

Have you . . .

_____ Attached **Form 8718** (User Fee for Exempt Organization Determination Letter Request) and the appropriate fee?

_____ Prepared the application for mailing? (See **Where To File** addresses on Form 8718.) Do **not** file the application with your local Internal Revenue Service Center.

_____ Completed Parts I through IV and any other schedules that apply to the organization?

_____ Shown the organization's **Employer Identification Number (EIN)**?
   a. If your organization has an EIN, write it in the space provided.
   b. If this is a newly formed organization and does not have an Employer Identification Number, obtain an EIN by telephone. (See Specific Instructions, Part I, Line 2, on page 3.)

_____ Described your organization's **specific activities** as directed in Part II, line 1, of the application?

_____ Included a **conformed copy** of the complete organizing instrument? (See Specific Instructions, Part I, Line 10, on page 3.)

_____ Had the application signed by one of the following?
   a. An officer or trustee who is authorized to sign (e.g., president, treasurer); **or**
   b. A person authorized by a power of attorney (Submit Form 2848, or other power of attorney.)

_____ Enclosed **financial statements** (Part IV)?
   a. Current year (must include period up to within 60 days of the date the application is filed) and 3 preceding years.
   b. Detailed breakdown of revenue and expenses (no lump sums).
   c. If the organization has been in existence less than 1 year, you must also submit proposed budgets for 2 years showing the amounts and types of receipts and expenditures anticipated.

Note: _During the technical review of a completed application, it may be necessary to contact the organization for more specific or additional information._

Do not send this checklist with the application.

Form **1023**
(Rev. September 1998)
Department of the Treasury
Internal Revenue Service

Application for Recognition of Exemption
Under Section 501(c)(3) of the Internal Revenue Code

OMB No. 1545-0056

Note: *If exempt status is approved, this application will be open for public inspection.*

Read the instructions for each Part carefully.
A User Fee must be attached to this application.
If the required information and appropriate documents are not submitted along with Form 8718 (with payment of the appropriate user fee), the application may be returned to you.
Complete the Procedural Checklist on page 8 of the instructions.

Part I Identification of Applicant

1a Full name of organization (as shown in organizing document)		**2** Employer identification number (EIN) (If none, see page 3 of the **Specific Instructions**.)
1b c/o Name (if applicable)		**3** Name and telephone number of person to be contacted if additional information is needed
1c Address (number and street)	Room/Suite	
		( )
1d City, town, or post office, state, and ZIP + 4. If you have a foreign address, see **Specific Instructions** for Part I, page 3.		**4** Month the annual accounting period ends
		5 Date incorporated or formed
1e Web site address		**6** Check here if applying under section: **a** ☐ 501(e) **b** ☐ 501(f) **c** ☐ 501(k) **d** ☐ 501(n)

7 Did the organization previously apply for recognition of exemption under this Code section or under any other section of the Code? . . . . ☐ **Yes** ☐ **No**
If "Yes," attach an explanation.

8 Is the organization required to file Form 990 (or Form 990-EZ)? . . . . ☐ **N/A** ☐ **Yes** ☐ **No**
If "No," attach an explanation (see page 3 of the **Specific Instructions**).

9 Has the organization filed Federal income tax returns or exempt organization information returns? . . ☐ **Yes** ☐ **No**
If "Yes," state the form numbers, years filed, and Internal Revenue office where filed.

10 Check the box for the type of organization. ATTACH A CONFORMED COPY OF THE CORRESPONDING ORGANIZING DOCUMENTS TO THE APPLICATION BEFORE MAILING. (See **Specific Instructions** for Part I, Line 10, on page 3.) See also Pub. 557 for examples of organizational documents.)

a ☐ Corporation—Attach a copy of the Articles of Incorporation (including amendments and restatements) showing approval by the appropriate state official; also include a copy of the bylaws.

b ☐ Trust— Attach a copy of the Trust Indenture or Agreement, including all appropriate signatures and dates.

c ☐ Association— Attach a copy of the Articles of Association, Constitution, or other creating document, with a declaration (see instructions) or other evidence the organization was formed by adoption of the document by more than one person; also include a copy of the bylaws.

If the organization is a corporation or an unincorporated association that has not yet adopted bylaws, check here ▶ ☐

I declare under the penalties of perjury that I am authorized to sign this application on behalf of the above organization and that I have examined this application, including the accompanying schedules and attachments, and to the best of my knowledge it is true, correct, and complete.

Please Sign Here ▶

_____ (Signature) _____ (Type or print name and title or authority of signer) _____ (Date)

For Paperwork Reduction Act Notice, see page 7 of the instructions.   Cat. No. 17133K

Part II   Activities and Operational Information

1   Provide a detailed narrative description of all the activities of the organization—past, present, and planned. **Do not merely refer to or repeat the language in the organizational document.** List each activity separately in the order of importance based on the relative time and other resources devoted to the activity. Indicate the percentage of time for each activity. Each description should include, as a minimum, the following: **(a)** a detailed description of the activity including its purpose and how each acitivity furthers your exempt purpose; **(b)** when the activity was or will be initiated; and **(c)** where and by whom the activity will be conducted.

2   What are or will be the organization's sources of financial support? List in order of size.

3   Describe the organization's fundraising program, both actual and planned, and explain to what extent it has been put into effect. Include details of fundraising activities such as selective mailings, formation of fundraising committees, use of volunteers or professional fundraisers, etc. Attach representative copies of solicitations for financial support.

Part II   **Activities and Operational Information** *(Continued)*

4   Give the following information about the organization's governing body:

a Names, addresses, and titles of officers, directors, trustees, etc.	**b** Annual compensation

c Do any of the above persons serve as members of the governing body by reason of being public officials or being appointed by public officials? . . . . □ **Yes** □ **No**
If "Yes," name those persons and explain the basis of their selection or appointment.

d Are any members of the organization's governing body "disqualified persons" with respect to the organization (other than by reason of being a member of the governing body) or do any of the members have either a business or family relationship with "disqualified persons"? (See **Specific Instructions** for Part II, Line 4d, on page 3.) . . . . □ **Yes** □ **No**
If "Yes," explain.

5 Does the organization control or is it controlled by any other organization? . . . . □ **Yes** □ **No**
Is the organization the outgrowth of (or successor to) another organization, or does it have a special relationship with another organization by reason of interlocking directorates or other factors? . . . . □ **Yes** □ **No**
If either of these questions is answered "Yes," explain.

6 Does or will the organization directly or indirectly engage in any of the following transactions with any political organization or other exempt organization (other than a 501(c)(3) organization): **(a)** grants; **(b)** purchases or sales of assets; **(c)** rental of facilities or equipment; **(d)** loans or loan guarantees; **(e)** reimbursement arrangements; **(f)** performance of services, membership, or fundraising solicitations; or **(g)** sharing of facilities, equipment, mailing lists or other assets, or paid employees? . . . . . . □ **Yes** □ **No**
If "Yes," explain fully and identify the other organizations involved.

7 Is the organization financially accountable to any other organization? . . . . □ **Yes** □ **No**
If "Yes," explain and identify the other organization. Include details concerning accountability or attach copies of reports if any have been submitted.

Part II   Activities and Operational Information *(Continued)*

8   What assets does the organization have that are used in the performance of its exempt function? (Do not include property producing investment income.) If any assets are not fully operational, explain their status, what additional steps remain to be completed, and when such final steps will be taken. If none, indicate "N/A."

9   Will the organization be the beneficiary of tax-exempt bond financing within the next 2 years? . . . . ☐ **Yes** ☐ **No**

10a   Will any of the organization's facilities or operations be managed by another organization or individual under a contractual agreement?. . . . . ☐ **Yes** ☐ **No**
b   Is the organization a party to any leases? . . . . ☐ **Yes** ☐ **No**
If either of these questions is answered "Yes," attach a copy of the contracts and explain the relationship between the applicant and the other parties.

11   Is the organization a membership organization? . . . . ☐ **Yes** ☐ **No**
If "Yes," complete the following:
a   Describe the organization's membership requirements and attach a schedule of membership fees and dues.

b   Describe the organization's present and proposed efforts to attract members and attach a copy of any descriptive literature or promotional material used for this purpose.

c   What benefits do (or will) the members receive in exchange for their payment of dues?

12a   If the organization provides benefits, services, or products, are the recipients required, or will they be required, to pay for them? . . . . ☐ **N/A** ☐ **Yes** ☐ **No**
If "Yes," explain how the charges are determined and attach a copy of the current fee schedule.

b   Does or will the organization limit its benefits, services, or products to specific individuals or classes of individuals? . . . . ☐ **N/A** ☐ **Yes** ☐ **No**
If "Yes," explain how the recipients or beneficiaries are or will be selected.

13   Does or will the organization attempt to influence legislation? . . . . ☐ **Yes** ☐ **No**
If "Yes," explain. Also, give an estimate of the percentage of the organization's time and funds that it devotes or plans to devote to this activity.

14   Does or will the organization intervene in any way in political campaigns, including the publication or distribution of statements? . . . . ☐ **Yes** ☐ **No**
If "Yes," explain fully.

Part III   **Technical Requirements**

1 Are you filing Form 1023 within 15 months from the end of the month in which your organization was
created or formed? . . . . ☐ **Yes** ☐ **No**
If you answer "Yes," do not answer questions on lines 2 through 6 below.

2 If one of the exceptions to the 15-month filing requirement shown below applies, check the appropriate box and proceed
to question 7.
Exceptions—You are not required to file an exemption application within 15 months if the organization:

☐ **a** Is a church, interchurch organization of local units of a church, a convention or association of churches, or an
integrated auxiliary of a church. See **Specific Instructions,** Line 2a, on page 4;

☐ **b** Is not a private foundation and normally has gross receipts of not more than $5,000 in each tax year; or

☐ **c** Is a subordinate organization covered by a group exemption letter, but only if the parent or supervisory organization
timely submitted a notice covering the subordinate.

3. If the organization does not meet any of the exceptions on line 2 above, are you filing Form 1023 within
27 months from the end of the month in which the organization was created or formed?. . . . . . ☐ **Yes** ☐ **No**

If "Yes," your organization qualifies under Regulation section 301.9100-2, for an automatic 12-month
extension of the 15-month filing requirement. Do not answer questions 4 through 6.

If "No," answer question 4.

4 If you answer "No" to question 3, does the organization wish to request an extension of time to apply
under the "reasonable action and good faith" and the "no prejudice to the interest of the government"
requirements of Regulations section 301.9100-3? . . . . ☐ **Yes** ☐ **No**

If "Yes," give the reasons for not filing this application within the 27-month period described in question 3.
See **Specific Instructions,** Part III, Line 4, before completing this item. Do not answer questions 5 and 6.

If "No," answer questions 5 and 6.

5 If you answer "No" to question 4, your organization's qualification as a section 501(c)(3) organization can
be recognized only from the date this application is filed. Therefore, do you want us to consider the
application as a request for recognition of exemption as a section 501(c)(3) organization from the date
the application is received and not retroactively to the date the organization was created or formed?   ☐ **Yes** ☐ **No**

6 If you answer "Yes" to question 5 above and wish to request recognition of section 501(c)(4) status for the period beginning
with the date the organization was formed and ending with the date the Form 1023 application was received (the effective
date of the organization's section 501(c)(3) status), check here ▶ ☐ and attach a completed page 1 of Form 1024 to this
application.

Part III   **Technical Requirements** *(Continued)*

7   Is the organization a private foundation?
☐ **Yes**   (Answer question 8.)
☐ **No**   (Answer question 9 and proceed as instructed.)

8   If you answer "Yes" to question 7, does the organization claim to be a private operating foundation?
☐ **Yes**   (Complete Schedule E.)
☐ **No**

After answering question 8 on this line, go to line 14 on page 7.

9   If you answer "No" to question 7, indicate the public charity classification the organization is requesting by checking the box below that most appropriately applies:

THE ORGANIZATION IS NOT A PRIVATE FOUNDATION BECAUSE IT QUALIFIES:

a	☐	As a church or a convention or association of churches (CHURCHES MUST COMPLETE SCHEDULE A.)	Sections 509(a)(1) and 170(b)(1)(A)(i)
b	☐	As a school (MUST COMPLETE SCHEDULE B.)	Sections 509(a)(1) and 170(b)(1)(A)(ii)
c	☐	As a hospital or a cooperative hospital service organization, or a medical research organization operated in conjunction with a hospital (These organizations, except for hospital service organizations, MUST COMPLETE SCHEDULE C.)	Sections 509(a)(1) and 170(b)(1)(A)(iii)
d	☐	As a governmental unit described in section 170(c)(1).	Sections 509(a)(1) and 170(b)(1)(A)(v)
e	☐	As being operated solely for the benefit of, or in connection with, one or more of the organizations described in **a** through **d, g, h,** or **i** (MUST COMPLETE SCHEDULE D.)	Section 509(a)(3)
f	☐	As being organized and operated exclusively for testing for public safety.	Section 509(a)(4)
g	☐	As being operated for the benefit of a college or university that is owned or operated by a governmental unit.	Sections 509(a)(1) and 170(b)(1)(A)(iv)
h	☐	As receiving a substantial part of its support in the form of contributions from publicly supported organizations, from a governmental unit, or from the general public.	Sections 509(a)(1) and 170(b)(1)(A)(vi)
i	☐	As normally receiving not more than one-third of its support from gross investment income and more than one-third of its support from contributions, membership fees, and gross receipts from activities related to its exempt functions (subject to certain exceptions).	Section 509(a)(2)
j	☐	The organization is a publicly supported organization but is not sure whether it meets the public support test of **h** or **i**. The organization would like the IRS to decide the proper classification.	Sections 509(a)(1) and 170(b)(1)(A)(vi) or Section 509(a)(2)

If you checked one of the boxes a through f in question 9, go to question 14. If you checked box g in question 9, go to questions 11 and 12. If you checked box h, i, or j, in question 9, go to question 10.

Part III Technical Requirements *(Continued)*

10 If you checked box **h, i,** or **j** in question 9, has the organization completed a tax year of at least 8 months?
- ☐ **Yes**—Indicate whether you are requesting:
  - ☐ A definitive ruling. (Answer questions 11 through 14.)
  - ☐ An advance ruling. (Answer questions 11 and 14 and attach two Forms 872-C completed and signed.)
- ☐ **No—You must request an advance ruling by completing and signing two Forms 872-C and attaching them to the Form 1023.**

11 If the organization received any unusual grants during any of the tax years shown in Part IV-A, **Statement of Revenue and Expenses,** attach a list for each year showing the name of the contributor; the date and the amount of the grant; and a brief description of the nature of the grant.

12 If you are requesting a definitive ruling under section 170(b)(1)(A)(iv) or (vi), check here ▶ ☐ and:

a Enter 2% of line 8, column (e), Total, of Part IV-A . . . . _____

b Attach a list showing the name and amount contributed by each person (other than a governmental unit or "publicly supported" organization) whose total gifts, grants, contributions, etc., were more than the amount entered on line **12a** above.

13 If you are requesting a definitive ruling under section 509(a)(2), check here ▶ ☐ and:

a For each of the years included on lines 1, 2, and 9 of Part IV-A, attach a list showing the name of and amount received from each "disqualified person." (For a definition of "disqualified person," see **Specific Instructions,** Part II, Line 4d, on page 3.)

b For each of the years included on line 9 of Part IV-A, attach a list showing the name of and amount received from each payer (other than a "disqualified person") whose payments to the organization were more than $5,000. For this purpose, "payer" includes, but is not limited to, any organization described in sections 170(b)(1)(A)(i) through (vi) and any governmental agency or bureau.

14 Indicate if your organization is one of the following. If so, complete the required schedule. (Submit only those schedules that apply to your organization. **Do not submit blank schedules.**)

	Yes	No	If "Yes," complete Schedule:
Is the organization a church?			A
Is the organization, or any part of it, a school?			B
Is the organization, or any part of it, a hospital or medical research organization?			C
Is the organization a section 509(a)(3) supporting organization?			D
Is the organization a private operating foundation?			E
Is the organization, or any part of it, a home for the aged or handicapped?			F
Is the organization, or any part of it, a child care organization?			G
Does the organization provide or administer any scholarship benefits, student aid, etc.?			H
Has the organization taken over, or will it take over, the facilities of a "for profit" institution? . .			I

Part IV **Financial Data**

Complete the financial statements for the current year and for each of the 3 years immediately before it. If in existence less than 4 years, complete the statements for each year in existence. **If in existence less than 1 year, also provide proposed budgets for the 2 years following the current year.**

A. Statement of Revenue and Expenses

			Current tax year	3 prior tax years or proposed budget for 2 years			
			(a) From .... to _____	(b)	(c)	(d)	(e) TOTAL
Revenue	1	Gifts, grants, and contributions received (not including unusual grants—see page 6 of the instructions)					
	2	Membership fees received . .					
	3	Gross investment income (see instructions for definition) . .					
	4	Net income from organization's unrelated business activities not included on line 3					
	5	Tax revenues levied for and either paid to or spent on behalf of the organization					
	6	Value of services or facilities furnished by a governmental unit to the organization without charge (not including the value of services or facilities generally furnished the public without charge)					
	7	Other income (not including gain or loss from sale of capital assets) (attach schedule) . .					
	8	**Total** (add lines 1 through 7)					
	9	Gross receipts from admissions, sales of merchandise or services, or furnishing of facilities in any activity that is not an unrelated business within the meaning of section 513. Include related cost of sales on line 22					
	10	**Total** (add lines 8 and 9) . .					
	11	Gain or loss from sale of capital assets (attach schedule) . . .					
	12	Unusual grants					
	13	**Total** revenue (add lines 10 through 12)					
Expenses	14	Fundraising expenses . . .					
	15	Contributions, gifts, grants, and similar amounts paid (attach schedule)					
	16	Disbursements to or for benefit of members (attach schedule) .					
	17	Compensation of officers, directors, and trustees (attach schedule)					
	18	Other salaries and wages . .					
	19	Interest					
	20	Occupancy (rent, utilities, etc.) .					
	21	Depreciation and depletion . .					
	22	Other (attach schedule) . . .					
	23	**Total** expenses (add lines 14 through 22)					
	24	Excess of revenue over expenses (line 13 minus line 23)					

Part IV   Financial Data *(Continued)*

B. Balance Sheet (at the end of the period shown)		Current tax year Date ....
Assets		
1 Cash	1	
2 Accounts receivable, net	2	
3 Inventories	3	
4 Bonds and notes receivable (attach schedule)	4	
5 Corporate stocks (attach schedule)	5	
6 Mortgage loans (attach schedule)	6	
7 Other investments (attach schedule)	7	
8 Depreciable and depletable assets (attach schedule)	8	
9 Land	9	
10 Other assets (attach schedule)	10	
11 **Total assets** (add lines 1 through 10)	11	
Liabilities		
12 Accounts payable	12	
13 Contributions, gifts, grants, etc., payable	13	
14 Mortgages and notes payable (attach schedule)	14	
15 Other liabilities (attach schedule)	15	
16 **Total liabilities** (add lines 12 through 15)	16	
Fund Balances or Net Assets		
17 Total fund balances or net assets	17	
18 **Total liabilities and fund balances or net assets** (add line 16 and line 17)	18	

If there has been any substantial change in any aspect of the organization's financial activities since the end of the period shown above, check the box and attach a detailed explanation ▶ ☐

Form **872-C**

(Rev. September 1998)

Department of the Treasury
Internal Revenue Service

Consent Fixing Period of Limitation Upon Assessment of Tax Under Section 4940 of the Internal Revenue Code

(See instructions on reverse side.)

OMB No. 1545-0056

To be used with Form 1023. Submit in duplicate.

Under section 6501(c)(4) of the Internal Revenue Code, and as part of a request filed with Form 1023 that the organization named below be treated as a publicly supported organization under section 170(b)(1)(A)(vi) or section 509(a)(2) during an advance ruling period,

----
(Exact legal name of organization as shown in organizing document)

(Number, street, city or town, state, and ZIP code)

and the

District Director of Internal Revenue, or Assistant Commissioner (Employee Plans and Exempt Organizations)

consent and agree that the period for assessing tax (imposed under section 4940 of the Code) for any of the 5 tax years in the advance ruling period will extend 8 years, 4 months, and 15 days beyond the end of the first tax year.

However, if a notice of deficiency in tax for any of these years is sent to the organization before the period expires, the time for making an assessment will be further extended by the number of days the assessment is prohibited, plus 60 days.

Ending date of first tax year ....
(Month, day, and year)

Name of organization (as shown in organizing document)	Date
Officer or trustee having authority to sign Signature ▶	Type or print name and title

For IRS use only

District Director or Assistant Commissioner (Employee Plans and Exempt Organizations)	Date

By ▶

For Paperwork Reduction Act Notice, see page 7 of the Form 1023 Instructions.

Cat. No. 16905Q

You must complete Form 872-C and attach it to the Form 1023 if you checked box **h, i,** or **j** of Part III, question 9, and the organization has not completed a tax year of at least 8 months.

> For example: If the organization incorporated May 15 and its year ends December 31, it has completed a tax year of only 7½ months. Therefore, Form 872-C must be submitted.

(a) Enter the name of the organization. This must be entered exactly as it appears in the organizing document. Do not use abbreviations unless the organizing document does.

(b) Enter the current address.

(c) Enter the ending date of the first tax year.

> For example:

> (1) If the organization was formed on June 15 and it has chosen December 31 as its year end, enter December 31, ...

> (2) If the organization was formed June 15 and it has chosen June 30 as its year end, enter June 30, ... In this example, the organization's first tax year consists of only 15 days.

(d) The form must be signed by an authorized officer or trustee, generally the president or treasurer. The name and title of the person signing must be typed or printed in the space provided.

(e) Enter the date that the form was signed.

DO NOT MAKE ANY OTHER ENTRIES.

Schedule A. Churches

1   Provide a brief history of the development of the organization, including the reasons for its formation.

2   Does the organization have a written creed or statement of faith?. . . . ☐ **Yes**   ☐ **No**
If "Yes," attach a copy.

3   Does the organization require prospective members to renounce other religious beliefs or their membership in other churches or religious orders to become members? . . . . ☐ **Yes**   ☐ **No**

4   Does the organization have a formal code of doctrine and discipline for its members? . . . . ☐ **Yes**   ☐ **No**
If "Yes," describe.

5   Describe the form of worship and attach a schedule of worship services.

6   Are the services open to the public?. . . . . ☐ **Yes**   ☐ **No**
If "Yes," describe how the organization publicizes its services and explain the criteria for admittance.

7   Explain how the organization attracts new members.

8   **(a)** How many active members are currently enrolled in the church?

(b) What is the average attendance at the worship services?

9   In addition to worship services, what other religious services (such as baptisms, weddings, funerals, etc.) does the organization conduct?

Schedule A. Churches *(Continued)*

10 Does the organization have a school for the religious instruction of the young? . . . . □ **Yes**   □ **No**

11 Were the current deacons, minister, and/or pastor formally ordained after a prescribed course of study? . . . . □ **Yes**   □ **No**

12 Describe the organization's religious hierarchy or ecclesiastical government.

13 Does the organization have an established place of worship? . . . . . . □ **Yes**   □ **No**

If "Yes," provide the name and address of the owner or lessor of the property and the address and a description of the facility.

If the organization has no regular place of worship, state where the services are held and how the site is selected.

14 Does (or will) the organization license or otherwise ordain ministers (or their equivalent) or issue church charters? . . . . □ **Yes**   □ **No**

If "Yes," describe in detail the requirements and qualifications needed to be so licensed, ordained, or chartered.

15 Did the organization pay a fee for a church charter? . . . . □ **Yes**   □ **No**

If "Yes," state the name and address of the organization to which the fee was paid, attach a copy of the charter, and describe the circumstances surrounding the chartering.

16 Show how many hours a week the minister/pastor and officers each devote to church work and the amount of compensation paid to each of them. If the minister or pastor is otherwise employed, indicate by whom employed, the nature of the employment, and the hours devoted to that employment.

Schedule A. Churches *(Continued)*

17 Will any funds or property of the organization be used by any officer, director, employee, minister, or pastor for his or her personal needs or convenience?   ☐ **Yes**   ☐ **No**

If "Yes," describe the nature and circumstances of such use.

---

18 List any officers, directors, or trustees related by blood or marriage.

---

19 Give the name of anyone who has assigned income to the organization or made substantial contributions of money or other property. Specify the amounts involved.

Instructions

Although a church, its integrated auxiliaries, or a convention or association of churches is not required to file Form 1023 to be exempt from Federal income tax or to receive tax-deductible contributions, such an organization may find it advantageous to obtain recognition of exemption. In this event, you should submit information showing that your organization is a church, synagogue, association or convention of churches, religious order or religious organization that is an integral part of a church, and that it is carrying out the functions of a church.

In determining whether an admittedly religious organization is also a church, the IRS does not accept any and every assertion that such an organization is a church. Because beliefs and practices vary so widely, there is no single definition of the word "church" for tax purposes. The IRS considers the facts and circumstances of each organization applying for church status.

The IRS maintains two basic guidelines in determining that an organization meets the religious purposes test:

1. That the particular religious beliefs of the organization are truly and sincerely held, and

2. That the practices and rituals associated with the organization's religious beliefs or creed are not illegal or contrary to clearly defined public policy.

In order for the IRS to properly evaluate your organization's activities and religious purposes, it is important that all questions in Schedule A be answered.

The information submitted with Schedule A will be a determining factor in granting the "church" status requested by your organization. In completing the schedule, consider the following points:

1. The organization's activities in furtherance of its beliefs must be exclusively religious, and

2. An organization will not qualify for exemption if it has a substantial nonexempt purpose of serving the private interests of its founder or the founder's family.

Schedule B. Schools, Colleges, and Universities

1 Does, or will, the organization normally have: **(a)** a regularly scheduled curriculum, **(b)** a regular faculty of qualified teachers, **(c)** a regularly enrolled student body, and **(d)** facilities where its educational activities are regularly carried on? . . . . ☐ **Yes** ☐ **No**
If "No," do not complete the rest of Schedule B.

2 Is the organization an instrumentality of a state or political subdivision of a state? . . . . ☐ **Yes** ☐ **No**
If "Yes," document this in Part II and do not complete items 3 through 10 of Schedule B. (See instructions on the back of Schedule B.)

3 Does or will the organization (or any department or division within it) discriminate in any way on the basis of race with respect to:

a Admissions? . . . . ☐ **Yes** ☐ **No**
b Use of facilities or exercise of student privileges? . . . . ☐ **Yes** ☐ **No**
c Faculty or administrative staff? . . . . ☐ **Yes** ☐ **No**
d Scholarship or loan programs? . . . . ☐ **Yes** ☐ **No**
If "Yes" for any of the above, explain.

4 Does the organization include a statement in its charter, bylaws, or other governing instrument, or in a resolution of its governing body, that it has a racially nondiscriminatory policy as to students? . . . . ☐ **Yes** ☐ **No**

Attach whatever corporate resolutions or other official statements the organization has made on this subject.

5a Has the organization made its racially nondiscriminatory policies known in a manner that brings the policies to the attention of all segments of the general community that it serves? . . . . ☐ **Yes** ☐ **No**

If "Yes," describe how these policies have been publicized and how often relevant notices or announcements have been made. If no newspaper or broadcast media notices have been used, explain.

b If applicable, attach clippings of any relevant newspaper notices or advertising, or copies of tapes or scripts used for media broadcasts. Also attach copies of brochures and catalogs dealing with student admissions, programs, and scholarships, as well as representative copies of all written advertising used as a means of informing prospective students of the organization's programs.

6 Attach a numerical schedule showing the racial composition, as of the current academic year, and projected to the extent feasible for the next academic year, of: **(a)** the student body, and **(b)** the faculty and administrative staff.

7 Attach a list showing the amount of any scholarship and loan funds awarded to students enrolled and the racial composition of the students who have received the awards.

8a Attach a list of the organization's incorporators, founders, board members, and donors of land or buildings, whether individuals or organizations.

b State whether any of the organizations listed in **8a** have as an objective the maintenance of segregated public or private school education, and, if so, whether any of the individuals listed in **8a** are officers or active members of such organizations.

9a Enter the public school district and county in which the organization is located.

b Was the organization formed or substantially expanded at the time of public school desegregation in the above district or county? . . . . ☐ **Yes** ☐ **No**

10 Has the organization ever been determined by a state or Federal administrative agency or judicial body to be racially discriminatory? . . . . ☐ **Yes** ☐ **No**

If "Yes," attach a detailed explanation identifying the parties to the suit, the forum in which the case was heard, the cause of action, the holding in the case, and the citations (if any) for the case. Also describe in detail what changes in the organization's operation, if any, have occurred since then.

For more information, see back of Schedule B.

Instructions

A "school" is an organization that has the primary function of presenting formal instruction, normally maintains a regular faculty and curriculum, normally has a regularly enrolled student body, and has a place where its educational activities are carried on.

The term generally corresponds to the definition of an "educational organization" in section 170(b)(1)(A)(ii). Thus, the term includes primary, secondary, preparatory and high schools, and colleges and universities. The term does not include organizations engaged in both educational and noneducational activities unless the latter are merely incidental to the educational activities. A school for handicapped children is included within the term, but an organization merely providing handicapped children with custodial care is not.

For purposes of Schedule B, "Sunday schools" that are conducted by a church are not included in the term "schools," but separately organized schools (such as parochial schools, universities, and similar institutions) are included in the term.

A private school that otherwise meets the requirements of section 501(c)(3) as an educational institution will not qualify for exemption under section 501(a) unless it has a racially nondiscriminatory policy as to students.

This policy means that the school admits students of any race to all the rights, privileges, programs, and activities generally accorded or made available to students at that school and that the school does not discriminate on the basis of race in the administration of its educational policies, admissions policies, scholarship and loan programs, and athletic or other school-administered programs.

The IRS considers discrimination on the basis of race to include discrimination on the basis of color and national or ethnic origin. A policy of a school that favors racial minority groups in admissions, facilities, programs, and financial assistance will not constitute discrimination on the basis of race when the purpose and effect is to promote the establishment and maintenance of that school's racially nondiscriminatory policy as to students.

See Rev. Proc. 75-50, 1975-2 C.B. 587, for guidelines and recordkeeping requirements for determining whether private schools that are applying for recognition of exemption have racially nondiscriminatory policies as to students.

Line 2

An instrumentality of a state or political subdivision of a state may qualify under section 501(c)(3) if it is organized as a separate entity from the governmental unit that created it and if it otherwise meets the organizational and operational tests of section 501(c)(3). See Rev. Rul. 60-384, 1960-2 C.B. 172. Any such organization that is a school is not a private school and, therefore, is not subject to the provisions of Rev. Proc. 75-50.

Schools that incorrectly answer "Yes" to line 2 will be contacted to furnish the information called for by lines 3 through 10 in order to establish that they meet the requirements for exemption. To prevent delay in the processing of your application, be sure to answer line 2 correctly and complete lines 3 through 10, if applicable.

Schedule C. Hospitals and Medical Research Organizations

☐ Check here if claiming to be a hospital; complete the questions in Section I of this schedule; and write "N/A" in Section II.
☐ Check here if claiming to be a medical research organization operated in conjunction with a hospital; complete the questions in Section II of this schedule; and write "N/A" in Section I.

Section I   Hospitals

1a How many doctors are on the hospital's courtesy staff? . . . . _____

b Are all the doctors in the community eligible for staff privileges? . . . . ☐ Yes ☐ No
If "No," give the reasons why and explain how the courtesy staff is selected.

2a Does the hospital maintain a full-time emergency room? . . . . ☐ Yes ☐ No
b What is the hospital's policy on administering emergency services to persons without apparent means to pay?

c Does the hospital have any arrangements with police, fire, and voluntary ambulance services for the delivery or admission of emergency cases? . . . . ☐ Yes ☐ No
Explain.

3a Does or will the hospital require a deposit from persons covered by Medicare or Medicaid in its admission practices? . . . . ☐ Yes ☐ No
If "Yes," explain.

b Does the same deposit requirement, if any, apply to all other patients? . . . . ☐ Yes ☐ No
If "No," explain.

4 Does or will the hospital provide for a portion of its services and facilities to be used for charity patients? ☐ Yes ☐ No
Explain the policy regarding charity cases. Include data on the hospital's past experience in admitting charity patients and arrangements it may have with municipal or government agencies for absorbing the cost of such care.

5 Does or will the hospital carry on a formal program of medical training and research? . . . . . . ☐ Yes ☐ No
If "Yes," describe.

6 Does the hospital provide office space to physicians carrying on a medical practice? . . . . . . ☐ Yes ☐ No
If "Yes," attach a list setting forth the name of each physician, the amount of space provided, the annual rent, the expiration date of the current lease and whether the terms of the lease represent fair market value.

Section II   Medical Research Organizations

1 Name the hospitals with which the organization has a relationship and describe the relationship.

2 Attach a schedule describing the organization's present and proposed (indicate which) medical research activities; show the nature of the activities, and the amount of money that has been or will be spent in carrying them out. (Making grants to other organizations is not direct conduct of medical research.)

3 Attach a statement of assets showing their fair market value and the portion of the assets directly devoted to medical research.

For more information, see back of Schedule C.

Additional Information

Hospitals

To be entitled to status as a "hospital," an organization must have, as its principal purpose or function, the providing of medical or hospital care or medical education or research. "Medical care" includes the treatment of any physical or mental disability or condition, the cost of which may be taken as a deduction under section 213, whether the treatment is performed on an inpatient or outpatient basis. Thus, a rehabilitation institution, outpatient clinic, or community mental health or drug treatment center may be a hospital if its principal function is providing the above-described services.

On the other hand, a convalescent home or a home for children or the aged is not a hospital. Similarly, an institution whose principal purpose or function is to train handicapped individuals to pursue some vocation is not a hospital. Moreover, a medical education or medical research institution is not a hospital, unless it is also actively engaged in providing medical or hospital care to patients on its premises or in its facilities on an inpatient or outpatient basis.

Cooperative Hospital Service Organizations

Cooperative hospital service organizations (section 501(e)) should not complete Schedule C.

Medical Research Organizations

To qualify as a medical research organization, the principal function of the organization must be the direct, continuous, and active conduct of medical research in conjunction with a hospital that is described in section 501(c)(3), a Federal hospital, or an instrumentality of a governmental unit referred to in section 170(c)(1).

For purposes of section 170(b)(1)(A)(iii) only, the organization must be set up to use the funds it receives in the active conduct of medical research by January 1 of the fifth calendar year after receipt. The arrangement it has with donors to assure use of the funds within the 5-year period must be legally enforceable.

As used here, "medical research" means investigations, experiments, and studies to discover, develop, or verify knowledge relating to the causes, diagnosis, treatment, prevention, or control of human physical or mental diseases and impairments.

For further information, see Regulations section 1.170A-9(c)(2).

Schedule D. Section 509(a)(3) Supporting Organizations

1a Organizations supported by the applicant organization: Name and address of supported organization	**b** Has the supported organization received a ruling or determination letter that it is not a private foundation by reason of section 509(a)(1) or (2)?
....	☐ **Yes** ☐ **No**
....	☐ **Yes** ☐ **No**
....	☐ **Yes** ☐ **No**
....	☐ **Yes** ☐ **No**
....	☐ **Yes** ☐ **No**

   c If "No" for any of the organizations listed in **1a,** explain.

2 Does the supported organization have tax-exempt status under section 501(c)(4), 501(c)(5), or 501(c)(6)? ☐ **Yes** ☐ **No**
If "Yes," attach: **(a)** a copy of its ruling or determination letter, and **(b)** an analysis of its revenue for the current year and the preceding 3 years. (Provide the financial data using the formats in Part IV-A (lines 1–13) and Part III (lines 11, 12, and 13).)

3 Does your organization's governing document indicate that the majority of its governing board is elected or appointed by the supported organizations? . . . . ☐ **Yes** ☐ **No**
If "Yes," skip to line 9.
If "No," you must answer the questions on lines 4 through 9.

4 Does your organization's governing document indicate the common supervision or control that it and the supported organizations share? . . . . ☐ **Yes** ☐ **No**
If "Yes," give the article and paragraph numbers. If "No," explain.

5 To what extent do the supported organizations have a significant voice in your organization's investment policies, in the making and timing of grants, and in otherwise directing the use of your organization's income or assets?

6 Does the mentioning of the supported organizations in your organization's governing instrument make it a trust that the supported organizations can enforce under state law and compel to make an accounting? ☐ **Yes** ☐ **No**
If "Yes," explain.

7a What percentage of your organization's income does it pay to each supported organization?

   b What is the total annual income of each supported organization?

   c How much does your organization contribute annually to each supported organization?

For more information, see back of Schedule D.

Schedule D. Section 509(a)(3) Supporting Organizations *(Continued)*

8 To what extent does your organization conduct activities that would otherwise be carried on by the supported organizations? Explain why these activities would otherwise be carried on by the supported organizations.

9 Is the applicant organization controlled directly or indirectly by one or more "disqualified persons" (other than one who is a disqualified person solely because he or she is a manager) or by an organization that is not described in section 509(a)(1) or (2)? . . . . ☐ **Yes** ☐ **No**
If "Yes," explain.

Instructions

For an explanation of the types of organizations defined in section 509(a)(3) as being excluded from the definition of a private foundation, see Pub. 557, Chapter 3.

Line 1

List each organization that is supported by your organization and indicate in item **1b** if the supported organization has received a letter recognizing exempt status as a section 501(c)(3) public charity as defined in section 509(a)(1) or 509(a)(2). If you answer "No" in **1b** to any of the listed organizations, please explain in **1c.**

Line 3

Your organization's governing document may be articles of incorporation, articles of association, constitution, trust indenture, or trust agreement.

Line 9

For a definition of a "disqualified person," see **Specific Instructions,** Part II, Line 4d, on page 3 of the application's instructions.

Schedule E. Private Operating Foundations

Income Test		Most recent tax year
1a Adjusted net income, as defined in Regulations section 53.4942(a)-2(d)	**1a**	
b Minimum investment return, as defined in Regulations section 53.4942(a)-2(c)	**1b**	
2 Qualifying distributions:		
a Amounts (including administrative expenses) paid directly for the active conduct of the activities for which organized and operated under section 501(c)(3) (attach schedule)	**2a**	
b Amounts paid to acquire assets to be used (or held for use) directly in carrying out purposes described in section 170(c)(1) or 170(c)(2)(B) (attach schedule)	**2b**	
c Amounts set aside for specific projects that are for purposes described in section 170(c)(1) or 170(c)(2)(B) (attach schedule).	**2c**	
d **Total** qualifying distributions (add lines 2a, b, and c)	**2d**	
3 Percentages:		
a Percentage of qualifying distributions to adjusted net income (divide line 2d by line 1a)	**3a**	%
b Percentage of qualifying distributions to minimum investment return (divide line 2d by line 1b). . .	**3b**	%
(Percentage must be at least 85% for 3a or 3b)		
Assets Test		
4 Value of organization's assets used in activities that directly carry out the exempt purposes. Do not include assets held merely for investment or production of income (attach schedule)	**4**	
5 Value of any stock of a corporation that is controlled by applicant organization and carries out its exempt purposes (attach statement describing corporation)	**5**	
6 Value of all qualifying assets (add lines 4 and 5)	**6**	
7 Value of applicant organization's total assets	**7**	
8 Percentage of qualifying assets to total assets (divide line 6 by line 7—percentage must exceed 65%)	**8**	%
Endowment Test		
9 Value of assets not used (or held for use) directly in carrying out exempt purposes:		
a Monthly average of investment securities at fair market value	**9a**	
b Monthly average of cash balances	**9b**	
c Fair market value of all other investment property (attach schedule).	**9c**	
d **Total** (add lines 9a, b, and c).	**9d**	
10 Acquisition indebtedness related to line 9 items (attach schedule)	**10**	
11 Balance (subtract line 10 from line 9d)	**11**	
12 Multiply line 11 by 3⅓% (⅔ of the percentage for the minimum investment return computation under section 4942(e)). Line 2d above must equal or exceed the result of this computation	**12**	
Support Test		
13 Applicant organization's support as defined in section 509(d)	**13**	
14 Gross investment income as defined in section 509(e)	**14**	
15 Support for purposes of section 4942(j)(3)(B)(iii) (subtract line 14 from line 13)	**15**	
16 Support received from the general public, five or more exempt organizations, or a combination of these sources (attach schedule)	**16**	
17 For persons (other than exempt organizations) contributing more than 1% of line 15, enter the total amounts that are more than 1% of line 15	**17**	
18 Subtract line 17 from line 16	**18**	
19 Percentage of total support (divide line 18 by line 15—must be at least 85%)	**19**	%
20 Does line 16 include support from an exempt organization that is more than 25% of the amount of line 15?	☐ Yes ☐ No	

21 Newly created organizations with less than 1 year's experience: Attach a statement explaining how the organization is planning to satisfy the requirements of section 4942(j)(3) for the income test and one of the supplemental tests during its first year's operation. Include a description of plans and arrangements, press clippings, public announcements, solicitations for funds, etc.

22 Does the amount entered on line 2a above include any grants that the applicant organization made?   ☐ Yes ☐ No
If "Yes," attach a statement explaining how those grants satisfy the criteria for "significant involvement" grants described in section 53.4942(b)-1(b)(2) of the regulations.

For more information, see back of Schedule E.

Instructions

If the organization claims to be an operating foundation described in section 4942(j)(3) and—

a. Bases its claim to private operating foundation status on normal and regular operations over a period of years; or

b. Is newly created, set up as a private operating foundation, and has at least 1 year's experience;

provide the information under the **income test and under one of the three supplemental tests** (assets, endowment, or support). If the organization does not have at least 1 year's experience, provide the information called for on line 21. If the organization's private operating foundation status depends on its normal and regular operations as described in **a** above, attach a schedule similar to Schedule E showing the data in tabular form for the 3 years preceding the most recent tax year. (See Regulations section 53.4942(b)-1 for additional information before completing the "Income Test" section of this schedule.) Organizations claiming section 4942(j)(5) status must satisfy the income test and the endowment test.

A "private operating foundation" described in section 4942(j)(3) is a private foundation that spends substantially all of the smaller of its adjusted net income (as defined below) or its minimum investment return directly for the active conduct of the activities constituting the purpose or function for which it is organized and operated. The foundation must satisfy the income test under section 4942(j)(3)(A), as modified by Regulations section 53.4942(b)-1, and one of the following three supplemental tests: **(1)** the assets test under section 4942(j)(3)(B)(i); **(2)** the endowment test under section 4942(j)(3)(B)(ii); or **(3)** the support test under section 4942(j)(3)(B)(iii).

Certain long-term care facilities described in section 4942(j)(5) are treated as private operating foundations for purposes of section 4942 only.

"Adjusted net income" is the excess of gross income determined with the income modifications described below for the tax year over the sum of deductions determined with the deduction modifications described below. Items of gross income from any unrelated trade or business and the deductions directly connected with the unrelated trade or business are taken into account in computing the organization's adjusted net income.

Income Modifications

The following are income modifications (adjustments to gross income):

1. Section 103 (relating to interest on certain governmental obligations) does not apply. Thus, interest that otherwise would have been excluded should be included in gross income.

2. Except as provided in **3** below, capital gains and losses are taken into account only to the extent of the net short-term gain. Long-term gains and losses are disregarded.

3. The gross amount received from the sale or disposition of certain property should be included in gross income to the extent that the acquisition of the property constituted a qualifying distribution under section 4942(g)(1)(B).

4. Repayments of prior qualifying distributions (as defined in section 4942(g)(1)(A)) constitute items of gross income.

5. Any amount set aside under section 4942(g)(2) that is "not necessary for the purposes for which it was set aside" constitutes an item of gross income.

Deduction Modifications

The following are deduction modifications (adjustments to deductions):

1. Expenses for the general operation of the organization according to its charitable purposes (as contrasted with expenses for the production or collection of income and management, conservation, or maintenance of income-producing property) should not be taken as deductions. If only a portion of the property is used for production of income subject to section 4942 and the remainder is used for general charitable purposes, the expenses connected with that property should be divided according to those purposes. Only expenses related to the income-producing portion should be taken as deductions.

2. Charitable contributions, deductible under section 170 or 642(c), should not be taken into account as deductions for adjusted net income.

3. The net operating loss deduction prescribed under section 172 should not be taken into account as a deduction for adjusted net income.

4. The special deductions for corporations (such as the dividends-received deduction) allowed under sections 241 through 249 should not be taken into account as deductions for adjusted net income.

5. Depreciation and depletion should be determined in the same manner as under section 4940(c)(3)(B).

Section 265 (relating to the expenses and interest connected with tax-exempt income) should not be taken into account.

You may find it easier to figure adjusted net income by completing column (c), Part 1, Form 990-PF, according to the instructions for that form.

An organization that has been held to be a private operating foundation will continue to be such an organization only if it meets the income test and either the assets, endowment, or support test in later years. See Regulations section 53.4942(b) for additional information. No additional request for ruling will be necessary or appropriate for an organization to maintain its status as a private operating foundation. However, data related to the above tests must be submitted with the organization's annual information return, Form 990-PF.

Schedule F. Homes for the Aged or Handicapped

1 What are the requirements for admission to residency? Explain fully and attach promotional literature and application forms.

2 Does or will the home charge an entrance or founder's fee? . . . . ☐ **Yes** ☐ **No**
If "Yes," explain and specify the amount charged.

3 What periodic fees or maintenance charges are or will be required of its residents?

4a What established policy does the home have concerning residents who become unable to pay their regular charges?

b What arrangements does the home have or will it make with local and Federal welfare units, sponsoring organizations, or others to absorb all or part of the cost of maintaining those residents?

5 What arrangements does or will the home have to provide for the health needs of its residents?

6 In what way are the home's residential facilities designed to meet some combination of the physical, emotional, recreational, social, religious, and similar needs of the aged or handicapped?

7 Provide a description of the home's facilities and specify both the residential capacity of the home and the current number of residents.

8 Attach a sample copy of the contract or agreement the organization makes with or requires of its residents.

For more information, see back of Schedule F.

Instructions

Line 1

Provide the criteria for admission to the home and submit brochures, pamphlets, or other printed material used to inform the public about the home's admissions policy.

Line 2

Indicate whether the fee charged is an entrance fee or a monthly charge, etc. Also, if the fee is an entrance fee, is it payable in a lump sum or on an installment basis?

Line 4

Indicate the organization's policy regarding residents who are unable to pay. Also, indicate whether the organization is subsidized for all or part of the cost of maintaining those residents who are unable to pay.

Line 5

Indicate whether the organization provides health care to the residents, either directly or indirectly, through some continuing arrangement with other organizations, facilities, or health personnel. If no health care is provided, indicate "N/A."

Schedule G. Child Care Organizations

1 Is the organization's primary activity the providing of care for children away from their homes? . . . . ☐ **Yes**   ☐ **No**

2 How many children is the organization authorized to care for by the state (or local governmental unit), and what was the average attendance during the past 6 months, or the number of months the organization has been in existence if less than 6 months?

3 How many children are currently cared for by the organization?

4 Is substantially all (at least 85%) of the care provided for the purpose of enabling parents to be gainfully employed or to seek employment? . . . ☐ **Yes**   ☐ **No**

5 Are the services provided available to the general public? . . . . ☐ **Yes**   ☐ **No**

If "No," explain.

6 Indicate the category, or categories, of parents whose children are eligible for the child care services (check as many as apply):

☐ low-income parents

☐ any working parents (or parents looking for work)

☐ anyone with the ability to pay

☐ other (explain)

Instructions

Line 5

If your organization's services are not available to the general public, indicate the particular group or groups that may utilize the services.

REMINDER—If this organization claims to operate a school, then it must also fill out Schedule B.

Schedule H. Organizations Providing Scholarship Benefits, Student Aid, etc., to Individuals

1a Describe the nature and the amount of the scholarship benefit, student aid, etc., including the terms and conditions governing its use, whether a gift or a loan, and how the availability of the scholarship is publicized. If the organization has established or will establish several categories of scholarship benefits, identify each kind of benefit and explain how the organization determines the recipients for each category. Attach a sample copy of any application the organization requires individuals to complete to be considered for scholarship grants, loans, or similar benefits. (Private foundations that make grants for travel, study, or other similar purposes are required to obtain advance approval of scholarship procedures. See Regulations sections 53.4945-4(c) and (d).)

b If you want this application considered as a request for approval of grant procedures in the event we determine that the organization is a private foundation, check here . . . . ▶ ☐

c If you checked the box in **1b** above, check the box(es) for which you wish the organization to be considered.

☐ 4945(g)(1)   ☐ 4945(g)(2)   ☐ 4945(g)(3)

2 What limitations or restrictions are there on the class of individuals who are eligible recipients? Specifically explain whether there are, or will be, any restrictions or limitations in the selection procedures based upon race or the employment status of the prospective recipient or any relative of the prospective recipient. Also indicate the approximate number of eligible individuals.

3 Indicate the number of grants the organization anticipates making annually . . . . ▶

4 If the organization bases its selections in any way on the employment status of the applicant or any relative of the applicant, indicate whether there is or has been any direct or indirect relationship between the members of the selection committee and the employer. Also indicate whether relatives of the members of the selection committee are possible recipients or have been recipients.

5 Describe any procedures the organization has for supervising grants (such as obtaining reports or transcripts) that it awards and any procedures it has for taking action if the terms of the grant are violated.

For more information, see back of Schedule H.

Additional Information

Private foundations that make grants to individuals for travel, study, or other similar purposes are required to obtain advance approval of their grant procedures from the IRS. Such grants that are awarded under selection procedures that have not been approved by the IRS are subject to a 10% excise tax under section 4945. (See Regulations sections 53.4945-4(c) and (d).)

If you are requesting advance approval of the organization's grant procedures, the following sections apply to line **1c:**

4945(g)(1)— The grant constitutes a scholarship or fellowship grant that meets the provisions of section 117(a) prior to its amendment by the Tax Reform Act of 1986 and is to be used for study at an educational organization (school) described in section 170(b)(1)(A)(ii).

4945(g)(2)— The grant constitutes a prize or award that is subject to the provisions of section 74(b), if the recipient of such a prize or award is selected from the general public.

4945(g)(3)— The purpose of the grant is to achieve a specific objective, produce a report or other similar product, or improve or enhance a literary, artistic, musical, scientific, teaching, or other similar capacity, skill, or talent of the grantee.

Schedule I. Successors to "For Profit" Institutions

1   What was the name of the predecessor organization and the nature of its activities?

2   Who were the owners or principal stockholders of the predecessor organization? (If more space is needed, attach schedule.)

Name and address	Share or interest

3   Describe the business or family relationship between the owners or principal stockholders and principal employees of the predecessor organization and the officers, directors, and principal employees of the applicant organization.

4a Attach a copy of the agreement of sale or other contract that sets forth the terms and conditions of sale of the predecessor organization or of its assets to the applicant organization.

 b Attach an appraisal by an independent qualified expert showing the fair market value at the time of sale of the facilities or property interest sold.

5   Has any property or equipment formerly used by the predecessor organization been rented to the applicant organization or will any such property be rented? . . . .   ☐ **Yes** ☐ **No**
If "Yes," explain and attach copies of all leases and contracts.

6   Is the organization leasing or will it lease or otherwise make available any space or equipment to the owners, principal stockholders, or principal employees of the predecessor organization? . . . . . .   ☐ **Yes** ☐ **No**
If "Yes," explain and attach a list of these tenants and a copy of the lease for each such tenant.

7   Were any new operating policies initiated as a result of the transfer of assets from a profit-making organization to a nonprofit organization? . . . .   ☐ **Yes** ☐ **No**
If "Yes," explain.

Additional Information

A "for profit" institution for purposes of Schedule I includes any organization in which a person may have a proprietary or partnership interest, hold corporate stock, or otherwise exercise an ownership interest. The institution need not have operated for the purpose of making a profit.

⊛

Form **990-PF**	**Return of Private Foundation**	OMB No. 1545-0052
Department of the Treasury Internal Revenue Service	**or Section 4947(a)(1) Nonexempt Charitable Trust** **Treated as a Private Foundation** Note: *The organization may be able to use a copy of this return to satisfy state reporting requirements.*	**2001**

For calendar year 2001, or tax year beginning , 2001, **and ending** , 20

G Check all that apply: ☐ Initial return ☐ Final return ☐ Amended return ☐ Address change ☐ Name change

Use the IRS label. Otherwise, print or type. See Specific Instructions.	Name of organization	**A** Employer identification number
	Number and street (or P.O. box number if mail is not delivered to street address) | Room/suite	**B** Telephone number (see page 10 of the instructions) ( )
	City or town, state, and ZIP code	**C** If exemption application is pending, check here ► ☐ **D 1.** Foreign organizations, check here . ► ☐

H Check type of organization: ☐ Section 501(c)(3) exempt private foundation
☐ Section 4947(a)(1) nonexempt charitable trust ☐ Other taxable private foundation

2. Foreign organizations meeting the 85% test, check here and attach computation . ► ☐

I Fair market value of all assets at end of year *(from Part II, col. (c), line 16)* ► $

J Accounting method: ☐ Cash ☐ Accrual
☐ Other (specify) ----------------------------
(Part I, column (d) must be on cash basis.)

E If private foundation status was terminated under section 507(b)(1)(A), check here . ► ☐
F If the foundation is in a 60-month termination under section 507(b)(1)(B), check here . ► ☐

Part I Analysis of Revenue and Expenses *(The total of amounts in columns (b), (c), and (d) may not necessarily equal the amounts in column (a) (see page 10 of the instructions).)*

		(a) Revenue and expenses per books	(b) Net investment income	(c) Adjusted net income	(d) Disbursements for charitable purposes (cash basis only)
1	Contributions, gifts, grants, etc., received (attach schedule)				
	Check ► ☐ if the foundation is **not** required to attach Sch. B				
2	Distributions from split-interest trusts				
3	Interest on savings and temporary cash investments				
4	Dividends and interest from securities				
5a	Gross rents				
b	(Net rental income or (loss) _____)				
6a	Net gain or (loss) from sale of assets not on line 10				
b	Gross sales price for all assets on line 6a _____				
7	Capital gain net income (from Part IV, line 2) . .				
8	Net short-term capital gain				
9	Income modifications				
10a	Gross sales less returns and allowances [ ]				
b	Less: Cost of goods sold . . [ ]				
c	Gross profit or (loss) (attach schedule)				
11	Other income (attach schedule)				
12	**Total.** Add lines 1 through 11				
13	Compensation of officers, directors, trustees, etc.				
14	Other employee salaries and wages				
15	Pension plans, employee benefits				
16a	Legal fees (attach schedule)				
b	Accounting fees (attach schedule)				
c	Other professional fees (attach schedule) . . .				
17	Interest				
18	Taxes (attach schedule) (see page 14 of the instructions)				
19	Depreciation (attach schedule) and depletion .				
20	Occupancy				
21	Travel, conferences, and meetings				
22	Printing and publications				
23	Other expenses (attach schedule)				
24	**Total operating and administrative expenses.** Add lines 13 through 23				
25	Contributions, gifts, grants paid				
26	**Total expenses and disbursements.** Add lines 24 and 25				
27	Subtract line 26 from line 12:				
a	Excess of revenue over expenses and disbursements				
b	**Net investment income** (if negative, enter -0-) .				
c	**Adjusted net income** (if negative, enter -0-). .				

(Revenue / Operating and Administrative Expenses labels run vertically at left margin)

For Paperwork Reduction Act Notice, see the instructions.   Cat. No. 11289X   Form **990-PF** (2001)

Part II	**Balance Sheets** Attached schedules and amounts in the description column should be for end-of-year amounts only. (See instructions.)	Beginning of year	End of year	
		(a) Book Value	(b) Book Value	(c) Fair Market Value

Assets					
	1	Cash—non-interest-bearing			
	2	Savings and temporary cash investments			
	3	Accounts receivable ▶...			
		Less: allowance for doubtful accounts ▶.......................			
	4	Pledges receivable ▶...			
		Less: allowance for doubtful accounts ▶.......................			
	5	Grants receivable			
	6	Receivables due from officers, directors, trustees, and other disqualified persons (attach schedule) (see page 15 of the instructions)			
	7	Other notes and loans receivable (attach schedule) ▶..................			
		Less: allowance for doubtful accounts ▶...........................			
	8	Inventories for sale or use			
	9	Prepaid expenses and deferred charges			
	10a	Investments- U.S. and state government obligations (attach schedule)			
	b	Investments—corporate stock (attach schedule)			
	c	Investments—corporate bonds (attach schedule)			
	11	Investments- land, buildings, and equipment: basis ▶.................			
		Less: accumulated depreciation (attach schedule) ▶....................			
	12	Investments—mortgage loans			
	13	Investments—other (attach schedule)			
	14	Land, buildings, and equipment: basis ▶			
		Less: accumulated depreciation (attach schedule) ▶....................			
	15	Other assets (describe ▶ ....)			
	16	**Total assets** (to be completed by all filers—see page 16 of the instructions. Also, see page 1, item I)			

Liabilities				
	17	Accounts payable and accrued expenses		
	18	Grants payable		
	19	Deferred revenue		
	20	Loans from officers, directors, trustees, and other disqualified persons		
	21	Mortgages and other notes payable (attach schedule) . .		
	22	Other liabilities (describe ▶..)		
	23	**Total liabilities** (add lines 17 through 22)		

Net Assets or Fund Balances				
		Organizations that follow SFAS 117, check here ▶ ☐ **and complete lines 24 through 26 and lines 30 and 31.**		
	24	Unrestricted		
	25	Temporarily restricted		
	26	Permanently restricted		
		Organizations that do not follow SFAS 117, check here ▶ ☐ **and complete lines 27 through 31.**		
	27	Capital stock, trust principal, or current funds		
	28	Paid-in or capital surplus, or land, bldg., and equipment fund		
	29	Retained earnings, accumulated income, endowment, or other funds		
	30	**Total net assets or fund balances** (see page 17 of the instructions)		
	31	**Total liabilities and net assets/fund balances** (see page 17 of the instructions)		

Part III Analysis of Changes in Net Assets or Fund Balances

1 Total net assets or fund balances at beginning of year—Part II, column (a), line 30 (must agree with end-of-year figure reported on prior year's return)	1	
2 Enter amount from Part I, line 27a	2	
3 Other increases not included in line 2 (itemize) ▶...	3	
4 Add lines 1, 2, and 3	4	
5 Decreases not included in line 2 (itemize) ▶..	5	
6 Total net assets or fund balances at end of year (line 4 minus line 5)—Part II, column (b), line 30 . .	6	

Part IV   Capital Gains and Losses for Tax on Investment Income

(a) List and describe the kind(s) of property sold (e.g., real estate, 2-story brick warehouse; or common stock, 200 shs. MLC Co.)	(b) How acquired P—Purchase D—Donation	(c) Date acquired (mo., day, yr.)	(d) Date sold (mo., day, yr.)
1a			
b			
c			
d			
e			

(e) Gross sales price	(f) Depreciation allowed (or allowable)	(g) Cost or other basis plus expense of sale	(h) Gain or (loss) (e) plus (f) minus (g)
a			
b			
c			
d			
e			

Complete only for assets showing gain in column (h) and owned by the foundation on 12/31/69

(i) F.M.V. as of 12/31/69	(j) Adjusted basis as of 12/31/69	(k) Excess of col. (i) over col. (j), if any	(l) Gains (Col. (h) gain minus col. (k), but not less than -0-) or Losses (from col.(h))
a			
b			
c			
d			
e			

2 Capital gain net income or (net capital loss). { If gain, also enter in Part I, line 7 If (loss), enter -0- in Part I, line 7 } | **2** |

3 Net short-term capital gain or (loss) as defined in sections 1222(5) and (6):
If gain, also enter in Part I, line 8, column (c) (see pages 13 and 17 of the instructions).
If (loss), enter -0- in Part I, line 8 . . . . } | **3** |

Part V   Qualification Under Section 4940(e) for Reduced Tax on Net Investment Income

(For optional use by domestic private foundations subject to the section 4940(a) tax on net investment income.)

If section 4940(d)(2) applies, leave this part blank.

Was the organization liable for the section 4942 tax on the distributable amount of any year in the base period? ☐ Yes ☐ No
If "Yes," the organization does not qualify under section 4940(e). Do not complete this part.

1 Enter the appropriate amount in each column for each year; see page 18 of the instructions before making any entries.

(a) Base period years Calendar year (or tax year beginning in)	(b) Adjusted qualifying distributions	(c) Net value of noncharitable-use assets	(d) Distribution ratio (col. (b) divided by col. (c))
2000			
1999			
1998			
1997			
1996			

2 Total of line 1, column (d) . . . . | **2** |

3 Average distribution ratio for the 5-year base period—divide the total on line 2 by 5, or by the number of years the foundation has been in existence if less than 5 years . . . . . | **3** |

4 Enter the net value of noncharitable-use assets for 2001 from Part X, line 5 . . . . | **4** |

5 Multiply line 4 by line 3 . . . . | **5** |

6 Enter 1% of net investment income (1% of Part I, line 27b) . . . . | **6** |

7 Add lines 5 and 6 . . . . | **7** |

8 Enter qualifying distributions from Part XII, line 4 . . . . | **8** |

If line 8 is equal to or greater than line 7, check the box in Part VI, line 1b, and complete that part using a 1% tax rate. See the Part VI instructions on page 18.

Part VI   Excise Tax Based on Investment Income (Section 4940(a), 4940(b), 4940(e), or 4948—see page 18 of the instructions)

1a Exempt operating foundations described in section 4940(d)(2), check here ▶ ☐ and enter "N/A" on line 1.
  Date of ruling letter: .... **(attach copy of ruling letter if necessary–see instructions)**

b Domestic organizations that meet the section 4940(e) requirements in Part V, check here ▶ ☐ and enter 1% of Part I, line 27b . . . .

  | **1** | |

c All other domestic organizations enter 2% of line 27b. Exempt foreign organizations enter 4% of Part I, line 12, col. (b)

2 Tax under section 511 (domestic section 4947(a)(1) trusts and taxable foundations only. Others enter -0-) | **2** | |

3 Add lines 1 and 2 . . . . | **3** | |

4 Subtitle A (income) tax (domestic section 4947(a)(1) trusts and taxable foundations only. Others enter -0-) | **4** | |

5 **Tax based on investment income.** Subtract line 4 from line 3. If zero or less, enter -0- . . . | **5** | |

6 Credits/Payments:

a 2001 estimated tax payments and 2000 overpayment credited to 2001 | **6a** | |

b Exempt foreign organizations—tax withheld at source . . . . . | **6b** | |

c Tax paid with application for extension of time to file (Form 8868) . | **6c** | |

d Backup withholding erroneously withheld . . . . | **6d** | |

7 Total credits and payments. Add lines 6a through 6d . . . . | **7** | |

8 Enter any **penalty** for underpayment of estimated tax. Check here ☐ if Form 2220 is attached | **8** | |

9 **Tax due.** If the total of lines 5 and 8 is more than line 7, enter **amount owed** . . . . . ▶ | **9** | |

10 **Overpayment.** If line 7 is more than the total of lines 5 and 8, enter the **amount overpaid** . . . ▶ | **10** | |

11 Enter the amount of line 10 to be: **Credited to 2002 estimated tax** ▶ | Refunded ▶ | **11** | |

Part VII-A   Statements Regarding Activities

		Yes	No
1a During the tax year, did the organization attempt to influence any national, state, or local legislation or did it participate or intervene in any political campaign?.	1a		
b Did it spend more than $100 during the year (either directly or indirectly) for political purposes (see page 19 of the instructions for definition)?	1b		
If the answer is "Yes" to 1a or 1b, attach a detailed description of the activities and copies of any materials published or distributed by the organization in connection with the activities.			
c Did the organization file **Form 1120-POL** for this year?.	1c		
d Enter the amount (if any) of tax on political expenditures (section 4955) imposed during the year:			
(1) On the organization. ▶ $ _____ **(2)** On organization managers. ▶ $ _____			
e Enter the reimbursement (if any) paid by the organization during the year for political expenditure tax imposed on organization managers. ▶ $ _____			
2 Has the organization engaged in any activities that have not previously been reported to the IRS? . . .	2		
If "Yes," attach a detailed description of the activities.			
3 Has the organization made any changes, not previously reported to the IRS, in its governing instrument, articles of incorporation, or bylaws, or other similar instruments? *If "Yes," attach a conformed copy of the changes* . .	3		
4a Did the organization have unrelated business gross income of $1,000 or more during the year?	4a		
b If "Yes," has it filed a tax return on **Form 990-T** for this year?	4b		
5 Was there a liquidation, termination, dissolution, or substantial contraction during the year?	5		
If "Yes," attach the statement required by General Instruction T.			
6 Are the requirements of section 508(e) (relating to sections 4941 through 4945) satisfied either:			
● By language in the governing instrument or			
● By state legislation that effectively amends the governing instrument so that no mandatory directions that conflict with the state law remain in the governing instrument?.	6		
7 Did the organization have at least $5,000 in assets at any time during the year? *If "Yes," complete Part II, col. (c), and Part XV.*	7		
8a Enter the states to which the foundation reports or with which it is registered (see page 19 of the instructions) ▶			
b If the answer is "Yes" to line 7, has the organization furnished a copy of Form 990-PF to the Attorney General (or designate) of each state as required by General Instruction G? *If "No," attach explanation* .	8b		
9 Is the organization claiming status as a private operating foundation within the meaning of section 4942(j)(3) or 4942(j)(5) for calendar year 2001 or the taxable year beginning in 2001 (see instructions for Part XIV on page 25)? *If "Yes," complete Part XIV*	9		
10 Did any persons become substantial contributors during the tax year? *If "Yes," attach a schedule listing their names and addresses.*	10		
11 Did the organization comply with the public inspection requirements for its annual returns and exemption application? Web site address ▶	11		
12 The books are in care of ▶ .... Telephone no. ▶			
Located at ▶ .... ZIP+4 ▶			
13 Section 4947(a)(1) nonexempt charitable trusts filing Form 990-PF in lieu of **Form 1041**—Check here . . . . . ▶ ☐ and enter the amount of tax-exempt interest received or accrued during the year. . . . . ▶	13		

Part VII-B Statements Regarding Activities for Which Form 4720 May Be Required

File Form 4720 if any item is checked in the "Yes" column, unless an exception applies.

		Yes	No

1a During the year did the organization (either directly or indirectly):

   (1) Engage in the sale or exchange, or leasing of property with a disqualified person? ☐ **Yes** ☐ **No**

   (2) Borrow money from, lend money to, or otherwise extend credit to (or accept it from) a disqualified person? ☐ **Yes** ☐ **No**

   (3) Furnish goods, services, or facilities to (or accept them from) a disqualified person? ☐ **Yes** ☐ **No**

   (4) Pay compensation to, or pay or reimburse the expenses of, a disqualified person? ☐ **Yes** ☐ **No**

   (5) Transfer any income or assets to a disqualified person (or make any of either available for the benefit or use of a disqualified person)? ☐ **Yes** ☐ **No**

   (6) Agree to pay money or property to a government official? (**Exception.** Check "No" if the organization agreed to make a grant to or to employ the official for a period after termination of government service, if terminating within 90 days.) ☐ **Yes** ☐ **No**

  b If any answer is "Yes" to 1a(1)–(6), did **any** of the acts fail to qualify under the exceptions described in Regulations section 53.4941(d)-3 or in a current notice regarding disaster assistance (see page 19 of the instructions)? **[1b]**
Organizations relying on a current notice regarding disaster assistance check here ▶ ☐

  c Did the organization engage in a prior year in any of the acts described in 1a, other than excepted acts, that were not corrected before the first day of the tax year beginning in 2001? **[1c]**

2 Taxes on failure to distribute income (section 4942) (does not apply for years the organization was a private operating foundation defined in section 4942(j)(3) or 4942(j)(5)):

  a At the end of tax year 2001, did the organization have any undistributed income (lines 6d and 6e, Part XIII) for tax year(s) beginning before 2001? ☐ **Yes** ☐ **No**
If "Yes," list the years ▶ 20 .... , 19 .... , 19 .... , 19 .....

  b Are there any years listed in 2a for which the organization is **not** applying the provisions of section 4942(a)(2) (relating to incorrect valuation of assets) to the year's undistributed income? (If applying section 4942(a)(2) to **all** years listed, answer "No" and attach statement—see page 19 of the instructions.) **[2b]**

  c If the provisions of section 4942(a)(2) are being applied to **any** of the years listed in 2a, list the years here.
▶ 20 .... , 19 .... , 19 .... , 19 .....

3a Did the organization hold more than a 2% direct or indirect interest in any business enterprise at any time during the year? ☐ **Yes** ☐ **No**

  b If "Yes," did it have excess business holdings in 2001 as a result of **(1)** any purchase by the organization or disqualified persons after May 26, 1969; **(2)** the lapse of the 5-year period (or longer period approved by the Commissioner under section 4943(c)(7)) to dispose of holdings acquired by gift or bequest; or **(3)** the lapse of the 10-, 15-, or 20-year first phase holding period? (Use Schedule C, Form 4720, to determine if the organization had excess business holdings in 2001.). **[3b]**

4a Did the organization invest during the year any amount in a manner that would jeopardize its charitable purposes? **[4a]**

  b Did the organization make any investment in a prior year (but after December 31, 1969) that could jeopardize its charitable purpose that had not been removed from jeopardy before the first day of the tax year beginning in 2001? **[4b]**

5a During the year did the organization pay or incur any amount to:

   (1) Carry on propaganda, or otherwise attempt to influence legislation (section 4945(e))? ☐ **Yes** ☐ **No**

   (2) Influence the outcome of any specific public election (see section 4955); or to carry on, directly or indirectly, any voter registration drive? ☐ **Yes** ☐ **No**

   (3) Provide a grant to an individual for travel, study, or other similar purposes? ☐ **Yes** ☐ **No**

   (4) Provide a grant to an organization other than a charitable, etc., organization described in section 509(a)(1), (2), or (3), or section 4940(d)(2)? ☐ **Yes** ☐ **No**

   (5) Provide for any purpose other than religious, charitable, scientific, literary, or educational purposes, or for the prevention of cruelty to children or animals?. ☐ **Yes** ☐ **No**

  b If any answer is "Yes" to 5a(1)–(5), did **any** of the transactions fail to qualify under the exceptions described in Regulations section 53.4945 or in a current notice regarding disaster assistance (see page 20 of the instructions)? **[5b]**
Organizations relying on a current notice regarding disaster assistance check here ▶ ☐

  c If the answer is "Yes" to question 5a(4), does the organization claim exemption from the tax because it maintained expenditure responsibility for the grant? ☐ **Yes** ☐ **No**
If "Yes," attach the statement required by Regulations section 53.4945–5(d).

6a Did the organization, during the year, receive any funds, directly or indirectly, to pay premiums on a personal benefit contract? ☐ **Yes** ☐ **No**

  b Did the organization, during the year, pay premiums, directly or indirectly, on a personal benefit contract? **[6b]**
If you answered "Yes" to 6b, also file Form 8870.

| **Part VIII** | Information About Officers, Directors, Trustees, Foundation Managers, Highly Paid Employees, and Contractors |

1   List all officers, directors, trustees, foundation managers and their compensation (see page 20 of the instructions):

(a) Name and address	**(b)** Title, and average hours per week devoted to position	**(c)** Compensation (If not paid, enter -0-)	**(d)** Contributions to employee benefit plans and deferred compensation	**(e)** Expense account, other allowances

2   Compensation of five highest-paid employees (other than those included on line 1—see page 21 of the instructions). If none, enter "NONE."

(a) Name and address of each employee paid more than $50,000	**(b)** Title and average hours per week devoted to position	**(c)** Compensation	**(d)** Contributions to employee benefit plans and deferred compensation	**(e)** Expense account, other allowances

Total number of other employees paid over $50,000 . . . . ▶ |

3   Five highest-paid independent contractors for professional services—(see page 21 of the instructions). If none, enter "NONE."

(a) Name and address of each person paid more than $50,000	**(b)** Type of service	**(c)** Compensation

Total number of others receiving over $50,000 for professional services . . . . ▶ |

| **Part IX-A** | **Summary of Direct Charitable Activities** |

List the foundation's four largest direct charitable activities during the tax year. Include relevant statistical information such as the number of organizations and other beneficiaries served, conferences convened, research papers produced, etc.	Expenses
1	
2	
3	
4	

Part IX-B **Summary of Program-Related Investments** (see page 21 of the instructions)

Describe the two largest program-related investments made by the foundation during the tax year on lines 1 and 2.	Amount
1	
....	
....	
2	
....	
....	
All other program-related investments. See page 22 of the instructions.	
3	
....	
....	
Total. Add lines 1 through 3 . . . . ▶	

Part X **Minimum Investment Return** (All domestic foundations must complete this part. Foreign foundations, see page 22 of the instructions.)

1	Fair market value of assets not used (or held for use) directly in carrying out charitable, etc., purposes:	
a	Average monthly fair market value of securities	**1a**
b	Average of monthly cash balances	**1b**
c	Fair market value of all other assets (see page 22 of the instructions)	**1c**
d	**Total** (add lines 1a, b, and c)	**1d**
e	Reduction claimed for blockage or other factors reported on lines 1a and 1c (attach detailed explanation) **1e**	
2	Acquisition indebtedness applicable to line 1 assets	**2**
3	Subtract line 2 from line 1d	**3**
4	Cash deemed held for charitable activities. Enter 1½% of line 3 (for greater amount, see page 23 of the instructions)	**4**
5	**Net value of noncharitable-use assets.** Subtract line 4 from line 3. Enter here and on Part V, line 4	**5**
6	**Minimum investment return.** Enter 5% of line 5	**6**

Part XI **Distributable Amount** (see page 23 of the instructions) (Section 4942(j)(3) and (j)(5) private operating foundations and certain foreign organizations check here ▶ ☐ and do not complete this part.)

1	Minimum investment return from Part X, line 6	**1**
2a	Tax on investment income for 2001 from Part VI, line 5 . . . . **2a**	
b	Income tax for 2001. (This does not include the tax from Part VI.) . . . **2b**	
c	Add lines 2a and 2b	**2c**
3	Distributable amount before adjustments. Subtract line 2c from line 1	**3**
4a	Recoveries of amounts treated as qualifying distributions **4a**	
b	Income distributions from section 4947(a)(2) trusts **4b**	
c	Add lines 4a and 4b	**4c**
5	Add lines 3 and 4c	**5**
6	Deduction from distributable amount (see page 23 of the instructions)	**6**
7	**Distributable amount** as adjusted. Subtract line 6 from line 5. Enter here and on Part XIII, line 1	**7**

Part XII **Qualifying Distributions** (see page 23 of the instructions)

1	Amounts paid (including administrative expenses) to accomplish charitable, etc., purposes:	
a	Expenses, contributions, gifts, etc.—total from Part I, column (d), line 26	**1a**
b	Program-related investments—Total from Part IX-B	**1b**
2	Amounts paid to acquire assets used (or held for use) directly in carrying out charitable, etc., purposes	**2**
3	Amounts set aside for specific charitable projects that satisfy the:	
a	Suitability test (prior IRS approval required)	**3a**
b	Cash distribution test (attach the required schedule)	**3b**
4	**Qualifying distributions.** Add lines 1a through 3b. Enter here and on Part V, line 8, and Part XIII, line 4 . .	**4**
5	Organizations that qualify under section 4940(e) for the reduced rate of tax on net investment income. Enter 1% of Part I, line 27b (see page 24 of the instructions).	**5**
6	**Adjusted qualifying distributions.** Subtract line 5 from line 4	**6**
	Note: *The amount on line 6 will be used in Part V, column (b), in subsequent years when calculating whether the foundation qualifies for the section 4940(e) reduction of tax in those years.*	

Part XIII　Undistributed Income (see page 24 of the instructions)

	(a) Corpus	(b) Years prior to 2000	(c) 2000	(d) 2001
1 Distributable amount for 2001 from Part XI, line 7				
2 Undistributed income, if any, as of the end of 2000:				
a Enter amount for 2000 only				
b Total for prior years: 19___ ,19___ ,19___				
3 Excess distributions carryover, if any, to 2001:				
a From 1996				
b From 1997				
c From 1998				
d From 1999				
e From 2000				
f **Total** of lines 3a through e				
4 Qualifying distributions for 2001 from Part XII, line 4: ▶ $ _____				
a Applied to 2000, but not more than line 2a.				
b Applied to undistributed income of prior years (Election required—see page 24 of the instructions)				
c Treated as distributions out of corpus (Election required—see page 24 of the instructions)				
d Applied to 2001 distributable amount . .				
e Remaining amount distributed out of corpus				
5 Excess distributions carryover applied to 2001 *(If an amount appears in column (d), the same amount must be shown in column (a).)*				
6 **Enter the net total of each column as indicated below:**				
a Corpus. Add lines 3f, 4c, and 4e. Subtract line 5				
b Prior years' undistributed income. Subtract line 4b from line 2b				
c Enter the amount of prior years' undistributed income for which a notice of deficiency has been issued, or on which the section 4942(a) tax has been previously assessed				
d Subtract line 6c from line 6b. Taxable amount—see page 25 of the instructions .				
e Undistributed income for 2000. Subtract line 4a from line 2a. Taxable amount—see page 25 of the instructions				
f Undistributed income for 2001. Subtract lines 4d and 5 from line 1. This amount must be distributed in 2002				
7 Amounts treated as distributions out of corpus to satisfy requirements imposed by section 170(b)(1)(E) or 4942(g)(3) (see page 25 of the instructions)				
8 Excess distributions carryover from 1996 not applied on line 5 or line 7 (see page 25 of the instructions)				
9 **Excess distributions carryover to 2002.** Subtract lines 7 and 8 from line 6a . . .				
10 Analysis of line 9:				
a Excess from 1997 . . .				
b Excess from 1998 . . .				
c Excess from 1999 . . .				
d Excess from 2000 . . .				
e Excess from 2001 . . .				

Form **990-PF** (2001)

Part XIV Private Operating Foundations (see page 25 of the instructions and Part VII-A, question 9)

1a If the foundation has received a ruling or determination letter that it is a private operating foundation, and the ruling is effective for 2001, enter the date of the ruling . . . . ▶

b Check box to indicate whether the organization is a private operating foundation described in section ☐ 4942(j)(3) or ☐ 4942(j)(5)

2a Enter the lesser of the adjusted net income from Part I or the minimum investment return from Part X for each year listed	Tax year (a) 2001	Prior 3 years (b) 2000	(c) 1999	(d) 1998	(e) Total
b 85% of line 2a					
c Qualifying distributions from Part XII, line 4 for each year listed					
d Amounts included in line 2c not used directly for active conduct of exempt activities .					
e Qualifying distributions made directly for active conduct of exempt activities. Subtract line 2d from line 2c . . .					
3 Complete 3a, b, or c for the alternative test relied upon:					
a "Assets" alternative test—enter:					
(1) Value of all assets					
(2) Value of assets qualifying under section 4942(j)(3)(B)(i) .					
b "Endowment" alternative test— Enter ⅔ of minimum investment return shown in Part X, line 6 for each year listed . .					
c "Support" alternative test—enter:					
(1) Total support other than gross investment income (interest, dividends, rents, payments on securities loans (section 512(a)(5)), or royalties) . .					
(2) Support from general public and 5 or more exempt organizations as provided in section 4942(j)(3)(B)(iii) . .					
(3) Largest amount of support from an exempt organization					
(4) Gross investment income .					

Part XV Supplementary Information (Complete this part only if the organization had $5,000 or more in assets at any time during the year—see page 26 of the instructions.)

1 **Information Regarding Foundation Managers:**

a List any managers of the foundation who have contributed more than 2% of the total contributions received by the foundation before the close of any tax year (but only if they have contributed more than $5,000). (See section 507(d)(2).)

b List any managers of the foundation who own 10% or more of the stock of a corporation (or an equally large portion of the ownership of a partnership or other entity) of which the foundation has a 10% or greater interest.

2 **Information Regarding Contribution, Grant, Gift, Loan, Scholarship, etc., Programs:**

Check here ▶ ☐ if the organization only makes contributions to preselected charitable organizations and does not accept unsolicited requests for funds. If the organization makes gifts, grants, etc. (see page 26 of the instructions) to individuals or organizations under other conditions, complete items 2a, b, c, and d.

a The name, address, and telephone number of the person to whom applications should be addressed:

b The form in which applications should be submitted and information and materials they should include:

c Any submission deadlines:

d Any restrictions or limitations on awards, such as by geographical areas, charitable fields, kinds of institutions, or other factors:

Part XV Supplementary Information (continued)

3 Grants and Contributions Paid During the Year or Approved for Future Payment

Recipient		If recipient is an individual, show any relationship to any foundation manager or substantial contributor	Foundation status of recipient	Purpose of grant or contribution	Amount
Name and address (home or business)					
a Paid during the year					

Total . . . . ▶ **3a** | | | | | |

| **b** Approved for future payment | | | | | |
| | | | | | |

Total . . . . ▶ **3b** | | | | | |

Part XVI-A Analysis of Income-Producing Activities

Enter gross amounts unless otherwise indicated.

	Unrelated business income		Excluded by section 512, 513, or 514		(e)
	(a) Business code	**(b)** Amount	**(c)** Exclusion code	**(d)** Amount	Related or exempt function income (See page 26 of the instructions.)
1 Program service revenue:					
a _____					
b _____					
c _____					
d _____					
e _____					
f _____					
g Fees and contracts from government agencies					
2 Membership dues and assessments					
3 Interest on savings and temporary cash investments					
4 Dividends and interest from securities . . .					
5 Net rental income or (loss) from real estate:					
a Debt-financed property					
b Not debt-financed property					
6 Net rental income or (loss) from personal property					
7 Other investment income					
8 Gain or (loss) from sales of assets other than inventory					
9 Net income or (loss) from special events . . .					
10 Gross profit or (loss) from sales of inventory .					
11 Other revenue: **a** _____					
b _____					
c _____					
d _____					
e _____					
12 Subtotal. Add columns (b), (d), and (e) . . .					

13 Total. Add line 12, columns (b), (d), and (e) . . . . ▶ **13** _____

(See worksheet in line 13 instructions on page 26 to verify calculations.)

Part XVI-B Relationship of Activities to the Accomplishment of Exempt Purposes

Line No. ▼	Explain below how each activity for which income is reported in column (e) of Part XVI-A contributed importantly to the accomplishment of the organization's exempt purposes (other than by providing funds for such purposes). (See page 27 of the instructions.)

Part XVII Information Regarding Transfers To and Transactions and Relationships With Noncharitable Exempt Organizations

		Yes	No
1 Did the organization directly or indirectly engage in any of the following with any other organization described in section 501(c) of the Code (other than section 501(c)(3) organizations) or in section 527, relating to political organizations?			
a Transfers from the reporting organization to a noncharitable exempt organization of:			
(1) Cash	1a(1)		
(2) Other assets	1a(2)		
b Other Transactions:			
(1) Sales of assets to a noncharitable exempt organization	1b(1)		
(2) Purchases of assets from a noncharitable exempt organization	1b(2)		
(3) Rental of facilities, equipment, or other assets	1b(3)		
(4) Reimbursement arrangements	1b(4)		
(5) Loans or loan guarantees	1b(5)		
(6) Performance of services or membership or fundraising solicitations	1b(6)		
c Sharing of facilities, equipment, mailing lists, other assets, or paid employees	1c		

d If the answer to any of the above is "Yes," complete the following schedule. Column **(b)** should always show the fair market value of the goods, other assets, or services given by the reporting organization. If the organization received less than fair market value in any transaction or sharing arrangement, show in column **(d)** the value of the goods, other assets, or services received.

(a) Line no.	(b) Amount involved	(c) Name of noncharitable exempt organization	(d) Description of transfers, transactions, and sharing arrangements

2a Is the organization directly or indirectly affiliated with, or related to, one or more tax-exempt organizations described in section 501(c) of the Code (other than section 501(c)(3)) or in section 527? . . . . . . ☐ Yes ☐ No

b If "Yes," complete the following schedule.

(a) Name of organization	(b) Type of organization	(c) Description of relationship

Under penalties of perjury, I declare that I have examined this return, including accompanying schedules and statements, and to the best of my knowledge and belief, it is true, correct, and complete. Declaration of preparer (other than taxpayer or fiduciary) is based on all information of which preparer has any knowledge.

Sign Here

▶ _____ _____ ▶ _____
Signature of officer or trustee   Date   Title

Paid Preparer's Use Only

Preparer's signature ▶	Date	Check if self-employed ▶ ☐	Preparer's SSN or PTIN (See **Signature** on page 28 of the instructions.)
Firm's name (or yours if self-employed), address, and ZIP code ▶		EIN ▶	
		Phone no. ( )	

Form **990-PF** (2001)

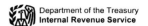
Department of the Treasury
Internal Revenue Service

Instructions for Form 990-PF

Return of Private Foundation or Section 4947(a)(1) Nonexempt Charitable Trust Treated as a Private Foundation

Section references are to the Internal Revenue Code unless otherwise noted.

Changes To Note

- **Schedule B,** Schedule of Contributors, has been revised for 2001. Instead of attaching a list of certain contributors to Form 990-PF, the foundation must now complete Schedule B and attach it to Form 990-PF. If the foundation did not have any contributors during the year or did not have any contributors required to be reported on Schedule B, the box (new for 2001) on line 1, Part I of Form 990-PF **must** be checked. See page 12 of the instructions for more information.
- If the foundation has a web site, it must now report its web site address on line 11 of Part VII-A.

Photographs of Missing Children

The Internal Revenue Service is a proud partner with the National Center for Missing and Exploited Children. Photographs of missing children selected by the Center may appear in instructions on pages that would otherwise be blank. You can help bring these children home by looking at the photographs and calling **1-800-THE-LOST** (1-800-843-5678) if you recognize a child.

Phone Help

If you have questions and/or need help completing this form, please call **1-877-829-5500**. This toll-free telephone service is available Monday through Friday from 8:00 a.m. to 9:30 p.m. Eastern time.

How To Get Forms and Publications

Personal Computer

You can access the IRS Web Site 24 hours a day, 7 days a week at **www.irs.gov** to:
- Download forms, instructions, and publications.
- See answers to frequently asked tax questions.
- Search publications on-line by topic or keyword.
- Send us comments or request help via e-mail.
- Sign up to receive local and national tax news by e-mail.

You can also reach us using file transfer protocol at **ftp.irs.gov.**

CD-ROM

Order **Pub. 1796,** Federal Tax Products on CD-ROM, and get:
- Current year forms, instructions, and publications.
- Prior year forms, instructions, and publications.

Cat. No. 11290Y

- Frequently requested tax forms that may be filled in electronically, printed out for submission, and saved for recordkeeping.
- The Internal Revenue Bulletin.

Buy the CD-ROM on the Internet at www.irs.gov/cdorders from the National Technical Information Service (NTIS) for $21 (no handling fee), or call **1-877-CDFORMS** (1-877-233-6767) toll free to buy the CD-ROM for $21 (plus a $5 handling fee).

By Phone and In Person

You can order forms and publications 24 hours a day, 7 days a week, by calling **1-800-TAX-FORM** (1-800-829-3676). You can also get most forms and publications at your local IRS office.

General Instructions

Purpose of form. Form 990-PF is used:
- To figure the tax based on investment income, and
- To report charitable distributions and activities.

Also, Form 990-PF serves as a substitute for the section 4947(a)(1) nonexempt charitable trust's income tax return, **Form 1041,** U.S. Income Tax Return for Estates and Trusts, when the trust has no taxable income.

A. Who Must File

Form 990-PF is an annual information return that must be filed by:
- Exempt private foundations (section 6033(a), (b), and (c)).
- Taxable private foundations (section 6033(d)).
- Organizations that agree to private foundation status and whose applications for exempt status are pending on the due date for filing Form 990-PF.
- Organizations that made an election under section 41(e)(6).
- Organizations that are making a section 507 termination.
- Section 4947(a)(1) nonexempt charitable trusts that **are** treated as private foundations (section 6033(d)).

Note: *Include on the foundation's return the financial and other information of any disregarded entity owned by the foundation. See Regulations sections 301.7701-1 through 3 for information on the classification of certain business organizations including an eligible entity that is disregarded as an entity separate from its owner (disregarded entity).*

Other section 4947(a)(1) nonexempt charitable trusts. Section 4947(a)(1) nonexempt charitable trusts that **are not** treated as private foundations do not file Form 990-PF. However, they may need to file **Form 990,** Return of Organization Exempt From Income Tax, or **Form 990-EZ,** Short Form Return of Organization Exempt From Income Tax. With either of these forms, the trust must also file **Schedule A (Form 990),** Organization Exempt Under Section

501(c)(3) (Except Private Foundation), and Section 501(e), 501(f), 501(k), 501(n), or Section 4947(a)(1) Nonexempt Charitable Trust Supplementary Information. (See Form 990 and Form 990-EZ instructions.)

B. Which Parts To Complete

The parts of the form listed below **do not** apply to all filers. See **How to avoid filing an incomplete return** on this page for information on what to do if a part or an item does apply.

- **Part I, column (c),** applies only to private operating foundations and to nonoperating private foundations that have income from charitable activities.
- **Part II, column (c),** with the exception of line 16, applies only to organizations having at least $5,000 in assets per books at some time during the year. Line 16, column (c), applies to all filers.
- **Part IV** does not apply to foreign organizations.
- **Parts V and VI** do not apply to organizations making an election under section 41(e).
- **Part X** does not apply to foreign foundations that check box D2 on page 1 of Form 990-PF unless they claim status as a private operating foundation.
- **Parts XI and XIII** do not apply to foreign foundations that check box D2 on page 1 of Form 990-PF. However, check the box at the top of Part XI. Part XI does not apply to private operating foundations. Also, if the organization is a private operating foundation for any of the years shown in Part XIII, do not complete the portions that apply to those years.
- **Part XIV** applies **only** to private operating foundations.
- **Part XV** applies only to organizations having assets of $5,000 or more during the year. This part does not apply to certain foreign organizations.

How to avoid filing an incomplete return.
- Complete all applicable line items,
- Answer "Yes," "No," or "N/A" (not applicable) to each question on the return,
- Make an entry (including a zero when appropriate) on all total lines, and
- Enter "None" or "N/A" if an entire part does not apply.

Sequencing Chart To Complete the Form

You may find the following chart helpful. It limits jumping from one part of the form to another to compute an amount needed to complete an earlier part. If you complete the parts in the listed order, any information you may need from another part will already be entered.

Step	Part	Step	Part
1	IV	8	XII, lines 1–4
2	I & II	9	V & VI
3	Heading	10	XII, lines 5–6
4	III	11	XI
5	VII-A	12	XIII
6	VIII	13	VII-B
7	IX-A – X	14	XIV – XVII

C. Definitions

- **A private foundation** is a domestic or foreign organization exempt from income tax under section 501(a); described in section 501(c)(3); and is **other than** an organization described in sections 509(a)(1) through (4).

  In general, churches, hospitals, schools, and broadly publicly supported organizations are excluded from private foundation status by these sections. These organizations may be required to file Form 990 (or Form 990-EZ) instead of Form 990-PF.
- **A nonexempt charitable trust** treated as a private foundation is a trust that is not exempt from tax under section 501(a) and all of the unexpired interests of which are devoted to religious, charitable, or other purposes described in section 170(c)(2)(B), and for which a deduction was allowed under a section of the Code listed in section 4947(a)(1).
- **A taxable private foundation** is an organization that is no longer exempt under section 501(a) as an organization described in section 501(c)(3). Though it may operate as a taxable entity, it will continue to be treated as a private foundation until that status is terminated under section 507.
- **A private operating foundation** is an organization that is described under section 4942(j)(3) or (5). It means any private foundation that spends at least 85% of the smaller of its adjusted net income (figured in Part I) or its minimum investment return (figured in Part X) directly for the active conduct of the exempt purpose or functions for which the foundation is organized and operated and that also meets the assets test, the endowment test, or the support test (discussed in Part XIV).
- **A nonoperating private foundation** is a private foundation that is not a private operating foundation.
- **A foundation manager** is an officer, director, or trustee of a foundation, or an individual who has powers similar to those of officers, directors, or trustees. In the case of any act or failure to act, the term "foundation manager" may also include employees of the foundation who have the authority to act.
- **A disqualified person** is:

  1. A substantial contributor (see instructions for Part VII-A, line 10, on page 19);
  2. A foundation manager;
  3. A person who owns more than 20% of a corporation, partnership, trust, or unincorporated enterprise that is itself a substantial contributor;

4. A family member of an individual described in **1, 2,** or **3** above; or

5. A corporation, partnership, trust, or estate in which persons described in **1, 2, 3,** or **4** above own a total beneficial interest of more than 35%.

6. For purposes of section 4941 (self-dealing), a disqualified person also includes certain government officials. (See section 4946(c) and the related regulations.)

7. For purposes of section 4943 (excess business holdings), a disqualified person also includes:

a. A private foundation that is effectively controlled (directly or indirectly) by the same persons who control the private foundation in question or

b. A private foundation to which substantially all of the contributions were made (directly or indirectly) by one or more of the persons described in **1, 2,** and **3** above, or members of their families, within the meaning of section 4946(d).

• **An organization is controlled** by a foundation or by one or more disqualified persons with respect to the foundation if any of these persons may, by combining their votes or positions of authority, require the organization to make an expenditure or prevent the organization from making an expenditure, regardless of the method of control. "Control" is determined regardless of how the foundation requires the contribution to be used.

D. Other Forms You May Need To File

Form W-2, Wage and Tax Statement.

Form W-3, Transmittal of Wage and Tax Statements.

Form 941, Employer's Quarterly Federal Tax Return. Used to report social security, Medicare, and income taxes withheld by an employer and social security and Medicare taxes paid by an employer.

If income, social security, and Medicare taxes that must be withheld are not withheld or are not paid to the IRS, a Trust Fund Recovery Penalty may apply. The penalty is 100% of such unpaid taxes.

This penalty may be imposed on all persons (including volunteers, see below) whom the IRS determines to be responsible for collecting, accounting for, and paying over these taxes, and who willfully did not do so.

This penalty does not apply to any volunteer, unpaid member of any board of trustees or directors of a tax-exempt organization, if this member:

1. Is solely serving in an honorary capacity,

2. Does not participate in the day-to-day or financial activities of the organization, and

3. Does not have actual knowledge of the failure to collect, account for, and pay over these taxes.

However, this exception does not apply if it results in no person being liable for the penalty.

Form 990-T, Exempt Organization Business Income Tax Return. Every organization exempt from income tax under section 501(a) that has total gross income of $1,000 or more from all trades or businesses that are unrelated to the organization's exempt purpose must file a return on Form 990-T. The form is also used by tax-exempt organizations to report other additional taxes including the additional tax figured in Part IV of **Form 8621,** Return by a Shareholder of a Passive Foreign Investment Company or Qualified Electing Fund.

Form 990-W, Estimated Tax on Unrelated Business Taxable Income for Tax-Exempt Organizations (and on Investment Income for Private Foundations).

Form 1041, U.S. Income Tax Return for Estates and Trusts. Required of section 4947(a)(1) nonexempt charitable trusts that also file Form 990-PF. However, if the trust does not have any taxable income under the income tax provisions (subtitle A of the Code), it may use the filing of Form 990-PF to satisfy its Form 1041 filing requirement under section 6012. If this condition is met, check the box for question 13, Part VII-A, of Form 990-PF and do not file Form 1041.

Form 1041-ES, Estimated Income Tax for Estates and Trusts.

Form 1096, Annual Summary and Transmittal of U.S. Information Returns.

Forms 1099-INT, MISC, OID, and R, Information returns for reporting certain interest; miscellaneous income (e.g., payments to providers of health and medical services, miscellaneous income payments, and nonemployee compensation); original issue discount; and distributions from retirement or profit-sharing plans, IRAs, SEPs or SIMPLEs, and insurance contracts.

Form 1120, U.S. Corporation Income Tax Return. Filed by nonexempt taxable private foundations that have taxable income under the income tax provisions (subtitle A of the Code). The Form 990-PF annual information return is also filed by these taxable foundations.

Form 1120-POL, U.S. Income Tax Return for Certain Political Organizations. Section 501(c) organizations must file Form 1120-POL if they are treated as having political organization taxable income under section 527(f)(1).

Form 1128, Application To Adopt, Change, or Retain a Tax Year.

Form 2220, Underpayment of Estimated Tax by Corporations, is used by corporations and trusts filing Form 990-PF to see if the foundation owes a penalty and to figure the amount of the

penalty. Generally, the foundation is not required to file this form because the IRS can figure the amount of any penalty and bill the foundation for it. However, complete and attach Form 2220 even if the foundation does not owe the penalty if:

• The annualized income or the adjusted seasonal installment method is used, or

• The foundation is a "large organization," (see General Instruction O) computing its first required installment based on the prior year's tax.

If Form 2220 is attached, check the box on line 8, Part VI, on page 4 of Form 990-PF and enter the amount of any penalty on this line.

Form 4506-A, Request for Public Inspection or Copy of Exempt or Political Organization IRS Form.

Form 4720, Return of Certain Excise Taxes on Charities and Other Persons Under Chapters 41 and 42 of the Internal Revenue Code, is primarily used to determine the excise taxes imposed on: acts of self-dealing between private foundations and disqualified persons; failure to distribute income; excess business holdings; investments that jeopardize the foundation's charitable purposes; and making political or other noncharitable expenditures. Certain excise taxes and penalties also apply to foundation managers, substantial contributors, and certain related persons and are reported on this form.

Form 5500, Annual Return/Report of Employee Benefit Plan is used to report information concerning employee benefit plans, Direct Filing Entities and fringe benefit plans.

Form 8109, Federal Tax Deposit Coupon.

Form 8282, Donee Information Return. Required of the donee of "charitable deduction property" that sells, exchanges, or otherwise disposes of the property within 2 years after the date it received the property.

Also required of any successor donee that disposes of charitable deduction property within 2 years after the date that the donor gave the property to the original donee. (It does not matter who gave the property to the successor donee. It may have been the original donee or another successor donee.) For successor donees, the form must be filed only for any property that was transferred by the original donee after July 5, 1988.

Form 8275, Disclosure Statement. Taxpayers and tax return preparers should attach this form to Form 990-PF to disclose items or positions (except those contrary to a regulation—see **Form 8275-R** below) that are not otherwise adequately disclosed on the tax return. The disclosure is made to avoid parts of the accuracy-related penalty imposed for disregard of rules or substantial understatement of tax. Form 8275 is also used for disclosures relating to preparer penalties for understatements due to unrealistic positions or for willful or reckless conduct.

Form 8275-R, Regulation Disclosure Statement. Use this form to disclose any item on a tax return for which a position has been taken that is contrary to Treasury regulations.

Form 8300, Report of Cash Payments Over $10,000 Received in a Trade or Business. Used to report cash amounts in excess of $10,000 that were received in a single transaction (or in two or more related transactions) in the course of a trade or business (as defined in section 162).

Form 8718, User Fee for Exempt Organization Determination Letter Request. Used by a private foundation that has completed a section 507 termination and seeks a determination letter that it is now a public charity.

Form 8822, Change of Address.

Form 8868, Application for Extension of Time To File an Exempt Organization Return.

Form 8870, Information Return for Transfers Associated With Certain Personal Benefit Contracts. Used to identify those personal benefit contracts for which funds were transferred to the organization, directly or indirectly, as well as the transferors and beneficiaries of those contracts.

E. Useful Publications

The following publications may be helpful in preparing Form 990-PF:

Publication 525, Taxable and Nontaxable Income.

Publication 578, Tax Information for Private Foundations and Foundation Managers.

Publication 583, Starting a Business and Keeping Records.

Publication 598, Tax on Unrelated Business Income of Exempt Organizations.

Publication 910, Guide to Free Tax Services.

Publication 1391, Deductibility of Payments Made to Charities Conducting Fund-Raising Events.

Publications and forms are available at no charge through IRS offices or by calling **1-800-TAX-FORM (1-800-829-3676).**

F. Use of Form 990-PF To Satisfy State Reporting Requirements

Some states and local government units will accept a copy of Form 990-PF and required attachments instead of all or part of their own financial report forms.

If the organization plans to use Form 990-PF to satisfy state or local filing requirements, such as those from state

charitable solicitation acts, note the following:

Determine state filing requirements. Consult the appropriate officials of all states and other jurisdictions in which the organization does business to determine their specific filing requirements. "Doing business" in a jurisdiction may include any of the following:

• Soliciting contributions or grants by mail or otherwise from individuals, businesses, or other charitable organizations,

• Conducting programs,

• Having employees within that jurisdiction, or

• Maintaining a checking account or owning or renting property there.

Monetary tests may differ. Some or all of the dollar limitations that apply to Form 990-PF when filed with the IRS may not apply when using Form 990-PF instead of state or local report forms. IRS dollar limitations that may not meet some state requirements are the $5,000 total assets minimum that requires completion of Part II, column (c), and Part XV; and the $50,000 minimum for listing the highest paid employees and for listing professional fees in Part VIII.

Additional information may be required. State and local filing requirements may require attaching to Form 990-PF one or more of the following:

• Additional financial statements, such as a complete analysis of functional expenses or a statement of changes in net assets,

• Notes to financial statements,

• Additional financial schedules,

• A report on the financial statements by an independent accountant, and

• Answers to additional questions and other information.

Each jurisdiction may require the additional material to be presented on forms they provide. The additional information does not have to be submitted with the Form 990-PF filed with the IRS.

If required information is not provided to a state, the organization may be asked by the state to provide it or to submit an amended return, even if the Form 990-PF is accepted by the IRS as complete.

Amended returns. If the organization submits supplemental information or files an amended Form 990-PF with the IRS, it must also include a copy of the information or amended return to any state with which it filed a copy of Form 990-PF.

Method of accounting. Many states require that all amounts be reported based on the accrual method of accounting.

Time for filing may differ. The time for filing Form 990-PF with the IRS may differ from the time for filing state reports.

G. Furnishing Copies of Form 990-PF to State Officials

The foundation managers must furnish a copy of the annual return Form 990-PF (and Form 4720 (if applicable)) to the attorney general of:

1. Each state required to be listed in Part VII-A, line 8a,

2. The state in which the foundation's principal office is located, and

3. The state in which the foundation was incorporated or created.

A copy of the annual return must be sent to the attorney general at the same time the annual return is filed with the IRS.

Other requirements. If the attorney general or other appropriate state official of any state requests a copy of the annual return, the foundation managers must give them a copy of the annual return.

Exceptions. These rules do not apply to any foreign foundation which, from the date of its creation, has received at least 85% of its support (excluding gross investment income) from sources outside the United States. (See Exceptions in General Instruction Q for other exceptions that affect this type of organization.)

Coordination with state reporting requirements. If the foundation managers submit a copy of Form 990-PF and Form 4720 (if applicable) to a state attorney general to satisfy a state reporting requirement, they do not have to furnish a second copy to that attorney general to comply with the Internal Revenue Code requirements discussed in this section.

If there is a state reporting requirement to file a copy of Form 990-PF with a state official other than the attorney general (such as the secretary of state), then the foundation managers must also send a copy of the Form 990-PF and Form 4720 (if applicable) to the attorney general of that state.

H. Accounting Period

1. File the 2001 return for the calendar year 2001 or fiscal year beginning in 2001. If the return is for a fiscal year, fill in the tax year space at the top of the return.

2. The return must be filed on the basis of the established annual accounting period of the organization. If the organization has no established accounting period, the return should be on the calendar-year basis.

3. For initial or final returns or a change in accounting period, the 2001 form may also be used as the return for a short period (less than 12 months) ending November 30, 2002, or earlier.

In general, to change its accounting period the organization must file Form 990-PF by the due date for the short period resulting from the change. At the top of this short period return, write "Change of Accounting Period."

If the organization changed its accounting period within the 10-calendar-year period that includes the beginning of the short period, and it had a Form 990-PF filing requirement at any time during that 10-year period, it must also attach a Form 1128 to the short-period return. See Rev. Proc. 85-58, 1985-2 C.B. 740.

I. Accounting Methods

Generally, you should report the financial information requested on the basis of the accounting method the foundation regularly uses to keep its books and records.

Exception. Complete Part I, column (d) on the cash receipts and disbursements method of accounting.

Change required by Statement of Financial Accounting Standards (SFAS) No. 116. Foundations that are changing their methods of accounting for Federal income tax purposes to comply with SFAS 116 are not required to file **Form 3115,** Application for Change in Accounting Method. Foundations may change to the methods described in SFAS 116 for Federal income tax purposes for any tax year beginning after December 15, 1994, by reflecting the change in the manner described in Notice 96-30, 1996-1 C.B. 378.

J. When and Where To File

This return must be filed by the 15th day of the 5th month following the close of the foundation's accounting period. If the regular due date falls on a Saturday, Sunday, or legal holiday, file by the next business day. If the return is filed late, see General Instruction M.

In case of a complete liquidation, dissolution, or termination, file the return by the 15th day of the 5th month following complete liquidation, dissolution, or termination.

To file the return, mail or deliver it to:
Internal Revenue Service Center
Ogden, UT 84201-0027

K. Extension of Time To File

A foundation uses Form 8868 to request an automatic or additional extension of time to file its return.

An automatic 3-month extension will be granted if you properly complete this form, file it, and pay any balance due by the due date for Form 990-PF.

If more time is needed, Form 8868 is also used to request an additional extension of up to 3 months. However, these extensions are **not** automatically granted. To obtain this additional extension of time to file, you must show

reasonable cause for the additional time requested.

L. Amended Return

To change the organization's return for any year, file an amended return, including attachments, with the correct information. The amended return must provide all the information required by the form and instructions, not just the new or corrected information. Check the "Amended Return" box in G at the top of the return.

If the organization files an amended return to claim a refund of tax paid under section 4940 or 4948, it must file the amended return within 3 years after the date the original return was due or filed, or within 2 years from the date the tax was paid, whichever date is later.

State reporting requirements. See Amended returns under General Instruction F.

Need a copy of an old return or form? Use Form 4506-A to obtain a copy of a previously filed return. You can obtain blank forms for prior years by calling 1-800-TAX-FORM (1-800-829-3676).

M. Penalty for Failure To File Timely, Completely, or Correctly

To avoid filing an incomplete return or having to respond to requests for missing information, see General Instruction B.

Against the organization. If an organization does not file timely and completely, or does not furnish the correct information, it must pay $20 for each day the failure continues ($100 a day if it is a large organization), unless it can show that the failure was due to reasonable cause. Those filing late (after the due date, including extensions) must attach an explanation to the return. The maximum penalty for each return will not exceed the smaller of $10,000 ($50,000 for a large organization) or 5% of the gross receipts of the organization for the year.

Large organization. A large organization is one that has gross receipts exceeding $1 million for the tax year.

Gross receipts. Gross receipts means the gross amount received during the foundation's annual accounting period from all sources without reduction for any costs or expenses.

To figure the foundation's gross receipts, start with Part I, line 12 column (a) then add to it lines 6b and 10b, then subtract line 6a from that amount.

Against the responsible person. The IRS will make written demand that the delinquent return be filed or the information furnished within a reasonable time after the mailing of the notice of the demand. The person failing to comply with the demand on or before the date

specified will have to pay $10 for each day the failure continues, unless there is reasonable cause. The maximum penalty imposed on all persons for any one return is $5,000. If more than one person is liable for any failures, all such persons are jointly and severally liable for such failures (see section 6652(c)).

Other penalties. Because this return also satisfies the filing requirements of a tax return under section 6011 for the tax on investment income imposed by section 4940 (or 4948 if an exempt foreign organization), the penalties imposed by section 6651 for not filing a return (without reasonable cause) also apply.

There are also penalties for willful failure to file and for filing fraudulent returns and statements. See sections 7203, 7206, and 7207.

N. Penalties for Not Paying Tax on Time

There is a penalty for not paying tax when due (section 6651). The penalty generally is $1/2$ of 1% of the unpaid tax for each month or part of a month the tax remains unpaid, not to exceed 25% of the unpaid tax. If there was reasonable cause for not paying the tax on time, the penalty can be waived. However, interest is charged on any tax not paid on time, at the rate provided by section 6621.

Estimated tax penalty. The section 6655 penalty for failure to pay estimated tax applies to the tax on net investment income of domestic private foundations and section 4947(a)(1) nonexempt charitable trusts. The penalty also applies to any tax on unrelated business income of a private foundation. Generally, if a private foundation's tax liability is $500 or more and it did not make the required payments on time, then it is subject to the penalty.

For more details, see the discussion of Form 2220 in General Instruction D.

O. Figuring and Paying Estimated Tax

A domestic exempt private foundation, a domestic taxable private foundation, or a nonexempt charitable trust treated as a private foundation must make estimated tax payments for the excise tax based on investment income if it can expect its estimated tax (section 4940 tax minus allowable credits) to be $500 or more. The number of installment payments it must make under the depository method is determined at the time during the year that it first meets this requirement. For calendar-year taxpayers, the first deposit of estimated taxes for a year generally should be made by May 15 of the year.

Although Form 990-W is used primarily to compute the installment payments of unrelated business income tax, it is also used to determine the timing and amounts of installment payments of the section 4940 tax based on investment income. Compute separately any required deposits of excise tax based on investment income and unrelated business income tax.

To figure the estimated tax for the excise tax based on investment income, apply the rules of Part VI to your tax year 2002 estimated amounts for that part. Enter the tax you figured on line 9a of Form 990-W.

The Form 990-W line items and instructions for large organizations also apply to private foundations. For purposes of paying the estimated tax on net investment income, a "large organization" is one that had net investment income of $1 million or more for any of the 3 tax years immediately preceding the tax year involved.

Penalty. A foundation that does not pay the proper estimated tax when due may be subject to the estimated tax penalty for the period of the underpayment. (See sections 6655(b) and (d) and the Form 2220 instructions.)

Special Rules

Section 4947(a)(1) nonexempt charitable trusts should use Form 1041-ES for paying any estimated tax on income subject to tax under section 1. Form 1041-ES also contains the estimated tax rules for paying the tax on that income.

Taxable private foundations should use Form 1120-W for figuring any estimated tax on income subject to tax under section 11. Form 1120-W contains the estimated tax rules for paying the tax on that income.

P. Tax Payment Methods for Domestic Private Foundations

Whether the foundation uses the depository method of tax payment or the special option for small foundations, it must pay the tax due (see Part VI) in full by the 15th day of the 5th month after the end of its tax year.

Depository Method of Tax Payment

Some foundations (described below) are required to electronically deposit all depository taxes, including their tax payments for the excise tax based on investment income.

Electronic Deposit Requirement

The foundation must make electronic deposits of **all** depository taxes (such as employment tax or the excise tax based on investment income) using the Electronic Federal Tax Payment System (EFTPS) in 2002 if:
• The total deposits of such taxes in 2000 were more than $200,000 or
• The foundation was required to use EFTPS in 2001.

If the foundation is required to use EFTPS and fails to do so, it may be subject to a 10% penalty. If the foundation is not required to use EFTPS, it may participate voluntarily. To enroll in or get more information about EFTPS, call 1-800-555-4477 or 1-800-945-8400. To enroll online, visit www.irs.gov.

Depositing on time. For deposits made by EFTPS to be on time, the foundation must initiate the transaction at least 1 business day before the date the deposit is due.

Deposits With Form 8109

If the foundation does not use EFTPS, deposit estimated tax payments and any balance due for the excise tax based on investment income with **Form 8109,** Federal Tax Deposit Coupon. If you do not have a preprinted Form 8109, use Form 8109-B to make deposits. You can get this form **only** by calling 1-800-829-1040. Be sure to have your employer identification number (EIN) ready when you call.

Do not send deposits directly to an IRS office; otherwise, the foundation may have to pay a penalty. Mail or deliver the completed Form 8109 with the payment to an authorized depositary, i.e., a commercial bank or other financial institution authorized to accept Federal tax deposits.

Make checks or money orders payable to the depositary. To help ensure proper crediting, write the foundation's EIN, the tax period to which the deposit applies, and "Form 990-PF" on the check or money order. Be sure to darken the 990-PF box on the coupon. Records of these deposits will be sent to the IRS.

For more information on deposits, see the instructions in the coupon booklet (Form 8109) and **Pub. 583,** Starting a Business and Keeping Records.

Special Payment Option for Small Foundations

A private foundation may enclose a check or money order, payable to the United States Treasury, with the Form 990-PF or Form 8868, if it meets all of the following requirements.

1. The foundation must not be required to use EFTPS.

2. The tax based on investment income shown on line 5, Part VI of Form 990-PF is less than $500.

3. If Form 8868 is used, the amount entered on line 3a of Part I or 8a of Part II of Form 8868 must be less than $500 and it must be the full balance due.

Be sure to write "2001 Form 990-PF" and the foundation's name, address, and EIN on its check or money order.

 Foreign organizations should see the instructions for Part VI, line 9.

Q. Public Inspection Requirements

A private foundation must make its annual returns and exemption application available for public inspection.

Definitions

Annual returns. An annual return is an exact copy of the Form 990-PF that was filed with the IRS including **all** schedules, attachments, and supporting documents. It also includes any amendments to the original return (amended return).

By annual returns, we mean any annual return (defined above) that is not more than 3 years old from the later of:

1. The date the return is required to be filed (including extensions) or

2. The date that the return is actually filed.

Exemption application is an application for tax exemption and includes (except as described later):
• Any prescribed application form (such as Form 1023 or Form 1024),
• All documents and statements the IRS requires an applicant to file with the form,
• Any statement or other supporting document submitted in support of the application, and
• Any letter or other document issued by the IRS concerning the application.

An application for tax exemption **does not** include:
• Any application for tax exemption filed before July 15, 1987, unless the private foundation filing the application had a copy of the application on July 15, 1987, or
• Any material that is not available for public inspection under section 6104.

Who Must Make the Annual Returns and Exemption Application Available for Public Inspection?

The foundation's annual returns and exemption application must be made available to the public by the private foundation itself and by the IRS.

How Does a Private Foundation Make Its Annual Returns and Exemption Application Available for Public Inspection?

A private foundation must make its annual returns and exemption application available in 2 ways:

1. By office visitation and

2. By providing copies or making them widely available.

Public Inspection by Office Visitation

A private foundation must make its annual returns and exemption application available for public inspection without charge at its principal, regional, and district offices during regular business hours.

Conditions that may be set for public inspection at the office. A private foundation:

• May have an employee present,
• Must allow the individual conducting the inspection to take notes freely during the inspection, and
• Must allow an individual to make photo copies of documents at no charge but only if the individual brings photocopying equipment to the place of inspection.

Determining if a site is a regional or district office. A regional or district office is any office of a private foundation, other than its principal office, that has paid employees whose total number of paid hours a week are normally 120 hours or more. Include the hours worked by part-time (as well as fulltime) employees in making that determination.

What sites are not considered a regional or district office. A site is not considered a regional or district office if:

1. The only services provided at the site further the foundations exempt purposes (e.g., day care, health care, or scientific or medical research) and

2. The site does not serve as an office for management staff, other than managers who are involved only in managing the exempt function activities at the site.

What if the private foundation does not maintain a permanent office? If the private foundation does not maintain a permanent office, it will comply with the public inspection by office visitation requirement by making the annual returns and exemption application available at a reasonable location of its choice. It must permit public inspection:

• Within a reasonable amount of time after receiving a request for inspection (normally, not more than 2 weeks) and
• At a reasonable time of day.

Optional method of complying. If a private foundation that does not have a permanent office wishes **not** to allow an inspection by office visitation, it may mail a copy of the requested documents instead of allowing an inspection. However, it must mail the documents within 2 weeks of receiving the request and may charge for copying and postage **only if the requester consents** to the charge.

Private foundations with a permanent office but limited or no hours. Even if a private foundation has a permanent office but no office hours or very limited hours during certain times of the year, it must still meet the office visitation requirement. During those periods when office hours are limited or not available, follow the rules above under **What if the private foundation does not maintain a permanent office?** to meet this requirement.

Public Inspection—Providing Copies

A private foundation must provide copies of its annual returns or exemption application to any individual who makes a request for a copy in person or in writing unless it makes these documents widely available.

In-person requests for document copies. A private foundation must provide copies to any individual who makes a request in person at the private foundation's principal, regional, or district offices during regular business hours on the **same day** that the individual makes the request.

Accepted delay in fulfilling an in-person request. If unusual circumstances exist and fulfilling a request on the same day places an unreasonable burden on the private foundation, it must provide copies by the earlier of:

• The next business day following the day that the unsusal circumstances end or
• The fifth business day after the date of the request.

Examples of unusual circumstances include:

• Receipt of a volume of requests (for document copies) that exceeds the private foundations daily capacity to make copies,
• Requests received shortly before the end of regular business hours that require an extensive amount of copying, or
• Requests received on a day when the organization's managerial staff capable of fulfilling the request is conducting official duties (e.g., student registration or attending an offsite meeting or convention) instead of its regular administrative duties.

Use of local agents for providing copies. A private foundation may use a local agent to handle in-person requests for document copies. If a private foundation uses a local agent, it must immediately provide the local agent's name, address, and telephone number to the requester.

The local agent must:

• Be located within reasonable proximity to the principal, regional, or district office where the individual makes the request and
• Provide document copies within the same time frames as the private foundation.

Written requests for document copies. If a private foundation receives a written request for a copy of its annual returns or exemption application (or parts of these documents), it must give a copy to the requester. However, this rule only applies if the request:

• Is addressed to a private foundation's principal, regional, or district office,
• Is delivered to that address by mail, electronic mail (e-mail), facsimile (fax), or a private delivery service approved by the

IRS (see **Where To File** in the Instructions for Form 990-T for a list), and
• Gives the address to which the document copies should be sent.

How and when a written request is fulfilled.
• Requested document copies must be mailed in 30 days from the date the private foundation receives the request.
• Unless other evidence exists, a request or payment that is mailed is considered to be received by the private foundation 7 days after the postmark date.
• If an advance payment is required, copies must be **provided** in 30 days from the date payment is received.
• If the private foundation requires payment in advance and it receives a request without payment or with insufficient payment, it must notify the requester of the prepayment policy and the amount due within 7 days from the date it receives the request.
• A request that is transmitted to the private foundation by e-mail or fax is considered received the day the request is transmitted successfully.
• Requested documents can be e-mailed instead of the traditional method of mailing if the requester consents to this method.

A document copy is considered as **provided** on the:
• Postmark date,
• Private delivery date,
• Registration date for certified or registered mail,
• Postmark date on the sender's receipt for certified or registered mail, or
• Day the e-mail is successfuly transmitted (if the requester agreed to this method).

Requests for parts of a document copy. A person can request all or any specific part or schedule of the annual returns or exemption application and the private foundation must fulfill their request for a copy.

Can an agent be used to provide copies? A private foundation can use an agent to provide document copies for the written requests it receives. However, the agent must provide the document copies under the same conditions that are imposed on the private foundation itself. Also, if an agent fails to provide the documents as required, the private foundation will continue to be subject to penalties.

Example. The ABC Foundation retained an agent to provide copies for all written requests for documents. However, ABC Foundation received a request for document copies before the agent did.

The deadline for providing a response is referenced by the date that the ABC Foundation received the request and not when the agent received it. If the agent received the request first, then a response would be referenced to the date that the agent received it.

Can a fee be charged for providing copies? A private foundation may charge a reasonable fee for providing copies. Also, it can require the fee to be paid before providing a copy of the requested document.

What is a reasonable fee? A fee is reasonable only if it is no more than the per-page copying fee charged by the IRS for providing copies, plus no more than the actual postage costs incurred to provide the copies.

What forms of payment must the private foundation accept? The form of payment depends on whether the request for copies is made in person or in writing.

Cash and money order must be accepted for in-person requests for document copies. The private foundation, if it wishes, may accept additional forms of payment.

Certified check, money order, and either personal check or credit card must be accepted for written requests for document copies. The private foundation, if it wishes, may accept additional forms of payment.

Other fee information. If a private foundation provides a requester with notice of a fee and the requester does not pay the fee in 30 days, it may ignore the request.

If a requester's check does not clear on deposit, it may ignore the request.

If a private foundation does not require prepayment and the requester does not prepay, the private foundation must receive consent from the requester if the copying and postage charge exceeds $20.

Private foundations subject to a harrassment campaign. If the IRS determines that a private foundation is being harrassed, it is not required to comply with any request for copies that it reasonably believes is part of the harrassment campaign.

A group of requests for a private foundation's annual returns or exemption application is indicative of a harrassment campaign if the requests are part of a single coordinated effort to disrupt the operations of the private foundation rather than to collect information about it.

See Regulations section 301.6104(d)-3 for more information.

Requests that may be disregarded without IRS approval. A private foundation may disregard any request for copies of all or part of any document beyond the first two received within any 30-day period or the first four received within any 1-year period from the same individual or the same address.

Making the Annual Returns and Exemption Application Widely Available

A private foundation does not have to provide copies of its annual returns and/or

its exemption application if it makes these documents widely available. However, it must still allow public inspection by office visitation.

How does a private foundation make its annual returns and exemption application widely available? A private foundation's annual returns and/or exemption application is widely available if it meets **all** four of the following requirements:

1. The internet posting requirement— This is met if:

• The document is posted on a World Wide Web page that the private foundation establishes and maintains or

• The document is posted as part of a database of like documents of other tax-exempt organizations on a World Wide Web page established and maintained by another entity.

2. Additional posting information requirement— This is met if:

• The World Wide Web page through which the document is available clearly informs readers that the document is available and provides instructions for downloading the document;

• After it is downloaded and viewed, the web document **exactly** reproduces the image of the annual returns or exemption application as it was originally filed with the IRS, except for any information permitted by statute to be withheld from public disclosure; and

• Any individual with access to the Internet can access, download, view, and print the document without special computer hardware or software required for that format (except software that is readily available to members of the public without payment of any fee) and without payment of a fee to the private foundation or to another entity maintaining the web page.

3. Reliability and accuracy requirements— To meet this, the entity maintaining the World Wide Web page must:

• Have procedures for ensuring the reliability and accuracy of the document that it posts on the page;

• Take reasonable precautions to prevent alteration, destruction, or accidental loss of the document when posted on its page; and

• Correct or replace the document if a posted document is altered, destroyed, or lost.

4. Notice requirement— To meet this, a private foundation must notify any individual requesting a copy of its annual returns and/or exemption application where the documents are available (including the Internet address). If the request is made in person, the private foundation must notify the individual immediately. If the request is in writing, it must notify the individual within 7 days of receiving the request.

Penalties

A penalty may be imposed on any person who does not make the annual returns (including all required attachments to each return) or the exemption application available for public inspection according to the section 6104(d) rules discussed above. If more than one person fails to comply, each person is jointly and severally liable for the full amount of the penalty. The penalty amount is $20 for each day during which a failure occurs. The maximum penalty that may be imposed on all persons for any 1 annual return is $10,000. There is no maximum penalty amount for failure to make the exemption application available for public inspection.

Any person who willfully fails to comply with the section 6104(d) public inspection requirements is subject to an additional penalty of $5,000 (section 6685).

Requirements Placed on the IRS

A private foundation's annual returns and approved exemption application may be inspected by the public at an IRS office for your area or at the IRS National Office in Washington, DC.

To request a copy or to inspect an annual return or an approved exemption application, complete Form 4506-A. Generally, there is a charge for photocopying.

Also, the IRS can provide a complete set of Form 990-PF returns filed for a year on CD-ROM. A partial set of Form 990-PF returns filed by state or by month is also available. Call 1-877-829-5500 or write to the address below for details.

Internal Revenue Service
Customer Service—TE/GE
P.O. Box 2508, Rm. 2023
Cincinnati, OH 45201

R. Disclosures Regarding Certain Information and Services Furnished

A section 501(c) organization that offers to sell or solicits money for specific information or a routine service to any individual that could be obtained by the individual from a Federal Government agency free or for a nominal charge must disclose that fact conspicuously when making such offer or solicitation.

Any organization that intentionally disregards this requirement will be subject to a penalty for each day the offers or solicitations are made. The penalty is the greater of $1,000 or 50% of the total cost of the offers and solicitations made on that day.

S. Organizations Organized or Created in a Foreign Country or U.S. Possession

If you apply any provision of any U.S. tax treaty to compute the foundation's taxable income, tax liability, or tax credits in a manner different from the 990-PF instructions, attach an explanation.

Regulations section 53.4948-1(b) states that sections 507, 508, and Chapter 42 (other than section 4948) do not apply to a foreign private foundation that from the date of its creation has received at least 85% of its support (as defined in section 509(d), other than section 509(d)(4)) from sources outside the United States.

Section 4948(a) imposes a 4% tax on the gross investment income from U.S. sources (i.e., income from dividends, interest, rents, payments received on securities loans (as defined in section 512(a)(5)), and royalties not reported on Form 990-T of an exempt foreign private foundation. This tax replaces the section 4940 tax on the net investment income of a domestic private foundation. To pay any tax due, see the instructions for Part VI, line 9.

Taxable foreign private foundations and foreign section 4947(a)(1) nonexempt charitable trusts are not subject to the excise taxes under sections 4948(a) and 4940, but are subject to income tax under subtitle A of the Code.

Certain foreign foundations are not required to send copies of annual returns to state officials, or comply with the public inspection and notice requirements of annual returns. (See General Instructions G and Q.)

T. Liquidation, Dissolution, Termination, or Substantial Contraction

If there is a liquidation, dissolution, termination, or substantial contraction (defined below) of the organization, attach:

1. A statement to the return explaining it,
2. A certified copy of the liquidation plan, resolution, etc. (if any) and all amendments or supplements that were not previously filed,
3. A schedule that lists the names and addresses of all recipients of assets, and
4. An explanation of the nature and fair market value of the assets distributed to each recipient.

Additional requirements. For a complete corporate liquidation or trust termination, attach a statement as to whether a final distribution of assets was made and the date it was made (if applicable).

Also, if the organization:
• Has ceased to exist, check the "Final Return" box in G at the top of page 1 of the return.
• Is terminating its private foundation status under section 507(b)(1)(B), see General Instructions U and V.

Relief from public inspection requirements. If the organization has terminated its private foundation status under section 507(b)(1)(A), it does not have to comply with the notice and public inspection requirements of their return for the termination year.

Filing date. See General Instruction J for the filing date.

Definitions. The term **substantial contraction** includes any partial liquidation or any other *significant disposition* of assets. However, this does not include transfers for full and adequate consideration or distributions of current income.

A **significant disposition** of assets does not include any disposition for a tax year if:

1. The total of the dispositions for the tax year is less than 25% of the fair market value of the net assets of the organization at the beginning of the tax year, and
2. The total of the related dispositions made during prior tax years (if a disposition is part of a series of related dispositions made during these prior tax years) is less than 25% of the fair market value of the net assets of the organization at the beginning of the tax year in which any of the series of related dispositions was made.

The facts and circumstances of the particular case will determine whether a significant disposition has occurred through a series of related dispositions. Ordinarily, a distribution described in section 170(b)(1)(E)(ii) (relating to private foundations making qualifying distributions out of corpus equal to 100% of contributions received during the foundation's tax year) will not be taken into account as a significant disposition of assets. See Regulations section 1.170A-9(g)(2).

U. Filing Requirements During Section 507(b)(1)(B) Termination

Although an organization terminating its private foundation status under section 507(b)(1)(B) may be regarded as a public charity for certain purposes, it is considered a private foundation for filing requirement purposes and it must file an annual return on Form 990-PF. The return must be filed for each year in the 60-month termination period, if that period has not expired before the due date of the return.

Regulations under section 507(b)(1)(B)(iii) specify that within 90 days after the

end of the termination period the organization must supply information to the IRS establishing that it has terminated its private foundation status and, therefore, qualifies as a public charity. Send the information to:

Internal Revenue Service
TE/GE Division
Centralized Files Unit
P.O. Box 2508
Cincinnati, OH 45201

If information is furnished establishing a successful termination, then, for the final year of the termination period, the organization should comply with the filing requirements for the type of public charity it has become. See the Instructions for Form 990 and Schedule A (Form 990) for details on filing requirements. This applies even if the IRS has not confirmed that the organization has terminated its private foundation status by the time the return for the final year of the termination is due (or would be due if a return were required).

The organization will be allowed a reasonable period of time to file any private foundation returns required (for the last year of the termination period) but not previously filed if it is later determined that the organization did not terminate its private foundation status. Interest on any tax due will be charged from the original due date of the Form 990-PF, but penalties under sections 6651 and 6652 will not be assessed if the Form 990-PF is filed within the period allowed by the IRS.

V. Special Rules for Section 507(b)(1)(B) Terminations

If the organization is terminating its private foundation status under the 60-month provisions of section 507(b)(1)(B), special rules apply. (See General Instructions T and U.) Under these rules, the organization may file Form 990-PF without paying the tax based on investment income if it filed a consent under section 6501(c)(4) with its notification to the TE/GE Division at the Cincinnati address given in General Instruction U of its intention to begin a section 507(b)(1)(B) termination. The consent provides that the period of limitation on the assessment of excise tax under section 4940 or 4948 based on investment income for any tax year in the 60-month period will not expire until at least 1 year after the period for assessing a deficiency for the last tax year in which the 60-month period would normally expire. Any foundation not paying the tax when it files Form 990-PF must attach a copy of the signed consent.

If the foundation did not file the consent, the tax must be paid in the normal manner as explained in General Instructions O and P. The organization may file a claim for refund after completing termination or during the termination period. The claim for refund must be filed on time and the organization must supply information establishing that it qualified as a public charity for the period for which it paid the tax.

W. Rounding, Currency, and Attachments

Rounding off to whole-dollar amounts. You may show the money items on the return and accompanying schedules as whole-dollar amounts. To do so, drop any amount less than 50 cents and increase any amount from 50 cents through 99 cents to the next higher dollar.

Currency and language requirements. Report all amounts in U.S. dollars (state conversion rate used). Report all items in total, including amounts from both U.S. and non-U.S. sources. All information must be in English.

Attachments. Use the schedules on Form 990-PF. If you need more space use attachments that are the same size as the printed forms.

On each attachment, write:
- "Form 990-PF,"
- The tax year,
- The corresponding schedule number or letter,
- The organization's name and EIN, and
- The information requested using the format and line sequence of the printed form.

Also, show totals on the printed forms.

Specific Instructions

Completing the Heading

The following instructions are keyed to items in the Form 990-PF heading.

Name and Address

If the organization received a Form 990-PF package from the IRS with a peel-off label, please use it. If the name or address on the label is wrong, make corrections on the label. The address used must be that of the principal office of the foundation.

Include the suite, room, or other unit number after the street address. If the Post Office does not deliver mail to the street address and the organization has a P.O. box, show the box number instead of the street address.

A—Employer Identification Number

The organization should have only one employer identification number. If it has more than one number, notify the Internal Revenue Service Center at the appropriate address shown under General Instruction J. Explain what numbers the organization has, the name and address to which each number was assigned, and the address of the

organization's principal office. The IRS will then advise which number to use.

B—Telephone Number

Enter a foundation telephone number (including the area code) that the public and government regulators may use to obtain information about the foundation's finances and activities. This information should be available at this telephone number during normal business hours. If the foundation does not have a telephone, enter a telephone number of a foundation official who can provide this information during normal business hours.

D2—Foreign Organizations

If the foreign organization meets the 85% test of Regulations section 53.4948-1(b), then:
  1. Check the box in D2 on page 1 of Form 990-PF,
  2. Check the box at the top of Part XI,
  3. **Do not** fill in Parts XI and XIII,
  4. **Do not** fill in Part X unless it is claiming status as a private operating foundation, and
  5. Attach the computation of the 85% test to Form 990-PF.

E—Section 507(b)(1)(A) Terminations

A private foundation that has terminated its status as such under section 507(b)(1)(A), by distributing all its net assets to one or more public charities without keeping any right, title, or interest in those assets, should check the box in E on page 1 of Form 990-PF. See General Instructions T and Q.

F—60-Month Termination Under Section 507(b)(1)(B)

Check the box in F on page 1 of Form 990-PF if the organization is terminating its private foundation status under the 60-month provisions of section 507(b)(1)(B) during the period covered by this return. To begin such a termination, a private foundation must have given advance notice to the TE/GE Division at the Cincinnati address given on page 9 and provided the information outlined in Regulations section 1.507-2(b)(3). See General Instruction U for information regarding filing requirements during a section 507(b)(1)(B) termination.

See General Instruction V for information regarding payment of the tax based on investment income (computed in Part VI) during a section 507(b)(1)(B) termination.

H—Type of Organization

Check the box for "Section 501(c)(3) exempt private foundation" if the foundation has a ruling or determination letter from the IRS in effect that recognizes its exemption from Federal income tax as an organization described in section 501(c)(3) or if the organization's exemption application is pending with the IRS.

Check the "Section 4947(a)(1) nonexempt charitable trust" box if the trust is a nonexempt charitable trust treated as a private foundation. All others, check the "Other taxable private foundation" box.

I—Fair Market Value of All Assets

In block I on page 1 of Form 990-PF, enter the fair market value of all assets the foundation held at the end of the tax year.

 This amount should be the same as the figure reported in Part II, column (c), line 16.

Part I—Analysis of Revenue and Expenses

Column Instructions

The total of amounts in columns (b), (c), and (d) **may not** necessarily equal the amounts in column (a).

The amounts entered in column (a) and on line 5b must be analyzed in Part XVI-A.

Column (a)—Revenue and Expenses per Books

Enter in column (a) all items of revenue and expense shown in the books and records that increased or decreased the net assets of the organization. However, do not include the value of services donated to the foundation, or items such as the free use of equipment or facilities, in contributions received. Also, do not include any expenses used to compute capital gains and losses on lines 6, 7, and 8 or expenses included in cost of goods sold on line 10b.

Column (b)—Net Investment Income

All domestic private foundations (including section 4947(a)(1) nonexempt charitable trusts) are required to pay an excise tax each tax year on net investment income.

Exempt foreign foundations are subject to an excise tax on gross investment income from U.S. sources. These foreign organizations should complete lines 3, 4, 5, 11, 12, and 27b of column (b) and report **only** income derived from U.S. sources. No other income should be included. No expenses are allowed as deductions.

Definitions

Gross investment income means the total amount of investment income that was received by a private foundation from all sources. However, it does not include any income subject to the unrelated business income tax. It includes interest, dividends, rents, payments with respect to securities loans (as defined in section 512(a)(5)), royalties received from assets devoted to charitable activities, income from notional principal contracts (as defined in Regulations section 1.863-7), and other substantially similar income from ordinary and routine investments excluded by section 512(b)(1). Therefore, interest received on a student loan is includible in the gross investment income of a private foundation making the loan.

Net investment income is the amount by which the sum of gross investment income and the capital gain net income exceeds the allowable deductions discussed later. Tax-exempt interest on governmental obligations and related expenses are excluded.

Investment income. Include in column (b) all or part of any amount from column (a) that applies to investment income. However, do not include in column (b) any interest, dividends, rents or royalties (and related expenses) that were reported on Form 990-T.

For example, investment income from debt-financed property unrelated to the organization's charitable purpose and certain rents (and related expenses) treated as unrelated trade or business income should be reported on Form 990-T. Income from debt-financed property that is not taxed under section 511 is taxed under section 4940. Thus, if the debt/basis percentage of a debt-financed property is 80%, only 80% of the gross income (and expenses) for that property is used to figure the section 511 tax on Form 990-T. The remaining 20% of the gross income (and expenses) of that property is used to figure the section 4940 tax on net investment income on Form 990-PF. (See Form 990-T and its instructions for more information.)

Investment expenses. Include in column (b) all ordinary and necessary expenses paid or incurred to produce or collect investment income from: interest, dividends, rents, amounts received from payments on securities loans (as defined in section 512(a)(5)), royalties, income from notional principal contracts, and other substantially similar income from ordinary and routine investments excluded by section 512(b)(1); or for the management, conservation, or maintenance of property held for the production of income that is taxable under section 4940.

If any of the expenses listed in column (a) are paid or incurred for both investment and charitable purposes, they must be allocated on a reasonable basis between the investment activities and the charitable activities so that only expenses from investment activities appear in column (b). Examples of allocation methods are given in the instructions for Part IX-A.

Limitation. The deduction for expenses paid or incurred in any tax year for producing gross investment income earned incident to a charitable function cannot be more than the amount of

income earned from the function that is includible as gross investment income for the year.

For example, if rental income is incidentally realized in 2001 from historic buildings held open to the public, deductions for amounts paid or incurred in 2001 for the production of this income may not be more than the amount of rental income includible as gross investment income in column (b) for 2001.

Expenses related to tax-exempt interest. **Do not** include on lines 13–23 of column (b) any expenses paid or incurred that are allocable to tax-exempt interest that is excluded from lines 3 and 4.

Column (c)—Adjusted Net Income

 Nonoperating private foundations should see item 1 under Nonoperating private foundations on this page to find out if they need to complete column (c).

Private operating foundations. All organizations that claim status as private operating foundations under section 4942(j)(3) or (5) must complete all lines of column (c) that apply, according to the general rules for income and expenses that apply to this column, the specific line instructions for lines 3–27c, the **Special rule,** and Examples **1** and **2** below.

General rules. In general, adjusted net income is the amount of a private foundation's gross income that is more than the expenses of earning the income. The modifications and exclusions explained below are applied to gross income and expenses in figuring adjusted net income.

For income and expenses, include on each line of column (c) only that portion of the amount from column (a) that is applicable to the adjusted net income computation.

Income. For column (c), include income from charitable functions, investment activities, short-term capital gains from investments, amounts set aside, and unrelated trade or business activities. Do not include gifts, grants, or contributions, or long-term capital gains or losses.

Expenses. Deductible expenses include the part of a private foundation's operating expenses that is paid or incurred to produce or collect gross income reported on lines 3–11 of column (c). If only part of the property produces income includible in column (c), deductions such as interest, taxes, and rent must be divided between the charitable and noncharitable uses of the property. If the deductions for property used for a charitable, educational, or other similar purpose are more than the income from the property, the excess will not be allowed as a deduction but may be treated as a qualifying distribution in Part I, column (d). See Examples **1** and **2** below.

Special rule. The expenses attributable to each specific charitable activity, limited by the amount of income from the activity, must be reported in column (c) on lines 13–26. If the expenses of any charitable activity exceed the income generated by that activity, **only** the excess of these expenses over the income should be reported in column (d).

Examples.

1. A charitable activity generated $5,000 of income and $4,000 of expenses. Report all of the income and expenses in column (c) and none in column (d).

2. A charitable activity generated $5,000 of income and $6,000 of expenses. Report $5,000 of income and $5,000 of expenses in column (c) and the excess expenses of $1,000 in column (d).

Nonoperating private foundations. The following rules apply to nonoperating private foundations.

1. If a nonoperating private foundation has no income from charitable activities that would be reportable on line 10 or line 11 of Part I, it does not have to make any entries in column (c).

2. If a nonoperating private foundation has income from charitable activities, it must report that income only on lines 10 and/or 11 in column (c). These foundations do not need to report other kinds of income and expenses (such as investment income and expenses) in column (c).

3. If a nonoperating private foundation has income that it reports on lines 10 and/or 11, report any expenses relating to this income following the general rules and the special rule. See Examples **1** and **2** above.

Column (d)—Disbursements for Charitable Purposes

Expenses entered in column (d) relate to activities that constitute the charitable purpose of the foundation.

For amounts entered in column (d):
• Use the cash receipts and disbursements method of accounting no matter what accounting method is used in keeping the books of the foundation.
• **Do not** include any amount or part of an amount that is included in column (b) or (c).
• Include on lines 13–25 all expenses, including necessary and reasonable administrative expenses, paid by the foundation for religious, charitable, scientific, literary, educational, or other public purposes, or for the prevention of cruelty to children or animals.
• Include a distribution of property at the fair market value on the date the distribution was made.
• Include only the part entered in column (a) that is allocable to the charitable purposes of the foundation.

Example. An educational seminar produced $1,000 in income that was reportable in columns (a) and (c). Expenses attributable to this charitable activity were $1,900. Only $1,000 of expense should be reported in column (c) and the remaining $900 in expense should be reported in column (d).

Qualifying distributions. Generally, gifts and grants to organizations described in section 501(c)(3), that have been determined to be publicly supported charities (i.e., organizations that are not private foundations as defined in section 509(a)), are qualifying distributions only if the granting foundation does not control the public charity.

 The total of the expenses and disbursements on line 26 is also entered on line 1a in Part XII to figure qualifying distributions.

Alternative to completing lines 13–25. If you want to provide an analysis of disbursements that is more detailed than column (d), you may attach a schedule instead of completing lines 13–25. The schedule must include all the specific items of lines 13–25, and the total from the schedule must be entered in column (d), line 26.

Line Instructions

Line 1—Contributions, gifts, grants, etc., received. Enter the total of gross contributions, gifts, grants, and similar amounts received.

Schedule B. If money, securities, or other property valued at $5,000 or more was received directly or indirectly from any one person during the year, complete Schedule B and attach it to the return. If the foundation is not required to complete Schedule B (no person contributed $5,000 or more), be sure to check the box on line 1.

To determine whether a person has contributed $5,000 or more, total only gifts of $1,000 or more from each person. Separate and independent gifts need not be totaled if less than $1,000. If a contribution is in the form of property, describe the property and include its fair market value.

The term "person" includes individuals, fiduciaries, partnerships, corporations, associations, trusts, and exempt organizations.

Split-interest trusts. Distributions from split-interest trusts should be entered on **both** line 1 of column (a) and line 2 of column (b). They are a part of the amount on line 1.

Change in accounting method to conform with SFAS 116. If the private foundation changed its accounting method for tax purposes to conform with SFAS 116 and part or all of its net asset adjustment (section 481(a) adjustment) represents contributions, then include on Schedule B any contributor of an amount that is included in the adjustment and meets the requirements above. Report

the contributors that meet these requirements in the year of the change.

Substantiation requirements. An organization must keep records, required by the regulations under section 170, for all its charitable contributions.

Generally, a donor making a charitable contribution of $250 or more will not be allowed a Federal income tax deduction unless the donor obtains a written acknowledgment from the donee organization by the earlier of the date on which the donor files a tax return for the tax year in which the contribution was made or the due date, including extensions, for filing that return. However, see section 170(f)(8) and Regulations section 1.170A-13 for exceptions to this rule.

The written acknowledgment the foundation provides to the donor must show:

1. The amount of cash contributed,
2. A description of any property contributed,
3. Whether the foundation provided any goods or services to the donor, and
4. A description and a good-faith estimate of the value of any goods or services the foundation gave in return for the contribution, unless:

   a. The goods and services have insubstantial value, or
   b. A statement is included that these goods and services consist solely of intangible religious benefits.

Generally, if a charitable organization solicits or receives a contribution of more than $75 for which it gives the donor something in return (a quid pro quo contribution), the organization must inform the donor, by written statement, that the amount of the contribution deductible for Federal income tax purposes is limited to the amount by which the contribution exceeds the value of the goods or services received by the donor. The written statement must also provide the donor with a good-faith estimate of the value of goods or services given in return for the contribution.

Penalties. An organization that does not make the required disclosure for each quid pro quo contribution will incur a penalty of $10 for each failure, not to exceed $5,000 for a particular fundraising event or mailing, unless it can show reasonable cause for not providing the disclosure.

For more information. See Regulations section 1.170A-13 for more information on charitable recordkeeping and substantiation requirements.

Line 2—Certain distributions from "split-interest" trusts described in section 4947(a)(2). The income portion of distributions from split-interest trusts that was earned on amounts placed in trust after May 26, 1969, is treated as investment income. Include only the income portion of these distributions on

line 2. That same figure is a part of line 1.

Line 3—Interest on savings and temporary cash investments.

In column (a), enter the total amount of interest income from investments of the type reportable in Balance Sheets, Part II, line 2. These include savings or other interest-bearing accounts and temporary cash investments, such as money market funds, commercial paper, certificates of deposit, and U.S. Treasury bills or other government obligations that mature in less than 1 year.

In column (b), enter the amount of interest income shown in column (a). Do not include interest on tax-exempt government obligations.

In column (c), enter the amount of interest income shown in column (a). Include interest on tax-exempt government obligations.

Line 4—Dividends and interest from securities.

In column (a), enter the amount of dividend and interest income from securities (stocks and bonds) of the type reportable in Balance Sheets, Part II, line 10. Include amounts received from payments on securities loans, as defined in section 512(a)(5). Do not include any capital gain dividends reportable on line 6. Report income from program-related investments on line 11. For debt instruments with an original issue discount, report the original issue discount ratably over the life of the bond on line 4. See section 1272 for more information.

In column (b), enter the amount of dividend and interest income, and payments on securities loans, from column (a). Do not include interest on tax-exempt government obligations.

In column (c), enter the amount of dividends and interest income, and payments on securities loans from column (a). Include interest on tax-exempt government obligations.

Line 5a—Gross rents.

In column (a), enter the gross rental income for the year from investment property reportable on line 11 of Part II.

In columns (b) and (c), enter the gross rental income from column (a).

Line 5b—Net rental income or (loss). Figure the net rental income or (loss) for the year and enter that amount on the entry line to the left of column (a).

Report rents from other sources on line 11, Other income. Enter any expenses attributable to the rental income reported on line 5, such as interest and depreciation, on lines 13–23.

Line 6a—Net gain or (loss) from sale of assets. Enter the net gain or (loss) per books from all asset sales not included on line 10.

For assets sold and not included in Part IV, attach a schedule showing:

Form 990-PF Instructions

- Date acquired,
- Manner of acquisition,
- Gross sales price,
- Cost, other basis, or value at time of acquisition (if donated) and which of these methods was used,
- Date sold,
- To whom sold,
- Expense of sale and cost of improvements made subsequent to acquisition, and
- Depreciation since acquisition (if depreciable property).

Line 6b—Gross sales price for all assets on line 6a. Enter the gross sales price from all asset sales whose net gain or loss was reported on line 6a.

Line 7—Capital gain net income. Enter the capital gain net income from Part IV, line 2. See Part IV instructions.

Line 8—Net short-term capital gain.

 Only private operating foundations report their short-term capital gains on line 8.

Include only net short-term capital gain for the year (assets sold or exchanged that were held not more than 1 year). **Do not** include a net long-term capital gain or a net loss in column (c).

Do not include on line 8 a net gain from the sale or exchange of depreciable property, or land used in a trade or business (section 1231) and held for more than 1 year. However, include a net loss from such property on line 23 as an Other expense.

In general, organizations may carry to line 8 the net short-term capital gain reported on Part IV, line 3. However, if the foundation had any short-term capital gain from sales of debt-financed property, add it to the amount reported on Part IV, line 3, to figure the amount to include on line 8. For the definition of "debt-financed property," see the instructions for Form 990-T.

Line 9—Income modifications. Include on this line:
- Amounts received or accrued as repayments of amounts taken into account as qualifying distributions (see the instructions for Part XII for an explanation of qualifying distributions) for any year.
- Amounts received or accrued from the sale or other disposition of property to the extent that the acquisition of the property was considered a qualifying distribution for any tax year.
- Any amount set aside for a specific project (see explanation in the instructions for Part XII) that was not necessary for the purposes for which it was set aside.
- Income received from an estate, but only if the estate was considered terminated for income tax purposes due to a prolonged administration period.
- Amounts treated in an earlier tax year as qualifying distributions to:

1. A nonoperating private foundation, if the amounts were not redistributed by the grantee organization by the close of its tax year following the year in which it received the funds, or

2. An organization controlled by the distributing foundation or a disqualified person if the amounts were not redistributed by the grantee organization by the close of its tax year following the year in which it received the funds.

Lines 10a, b, c—Gross profit from sales of inventory. Enter the gross sales (less returns and allowances), cost of goods sold, and gross profit or (loss) from the sale of all inventory items, including those sold in the course of special events and activities. These inventory items are the ones the organization either makes to sell to others or buys for resale.

Do not report any sales or exchanges of investments on line 10.

Do not include any profit or (loss) from the sale of capital items such as securities, land, buildings, or equipment on line 10. Enter these amounts on line 6a.

Do not include any business expenses such as salaries, taxes, rent, etc., on line 10. Include them on lines 13–23.

Attach a schedule showing the following items: Gross sales, Cost of goods sold, Gross profit or (loss). These items should be classified according to type of inventory sold (such as books, tapes, other educational or religious material, etc.). The totals from the schedule should agree with the entries on lines 10a–10c.

In column (c), enter the gross profit or (loss) from sales of inventory shown in column (a), line 10c.

Line 11—Other income. Enter the total of all the foundation's other income for the year. Attach a schedule that gives a description and the amount of the income. Include all income not reported on lines 1 through 10c. Also, see the instructions for Part XVI-A, line 11.

Include imputed interest on certain deferred payments figured under section 483 and any investment income not reportable on lines 3 through 5, including income from program-related investments (defined in the instructions for Part IX-B).

Do not include unrealized gains and losses on investments carried at market value. Report those as fund balance or net asset adjustments in Part III.

In column (b), enter the amount of investment income included in line 11, column (a). Include dividends, interest, rents, and royalties derived from assets devoted to charitable activities, such as interest on student loans.

In column (c), include all other items includible in adjusted net income not covered elsewhere in column (c).

Line 12—Total. In column (b), domestic organizations should enter the

total of lines 2–11. Exempt foreign organizations, enter the total of lines 3, 4, 5, and 11 only.

Line 13—Compensation of officers, directors, trustees, etc.

In column (a), enter the total compensation for the year of all officers, directors, and trustees. If none was paid, enter zero. Complete line 1 of Part VIII to show the compensation of officers, directors, trustees, and foundation managers.

In columns (b), (c), and (d), enter the portion of the compensation included in column (a) that is applicable to the column. For example, in column (c) enter the portion of the compensation included in column (a) that was paid or incurred to produce or collect income included in column (c).

Line 14—Other employee salaries and wages. Enter the salaries and wages of all employees other than those included on line 13.

Line 15—Contributions to employee pension plans and other benefits. Enter the employer's share of the contributions the organization paid to qualified and nonqualified pension plans and the employer's share of contributions to employee benefit programs (such as insurance, health, and welfare programs) that are not an incidental part of a pension plan. Complete the return/report of the Form 5500 series appropriate for the organization's plan. (See the Instructions for Form 5500 for information about employee welfare benefit plans required to file that form.)

Also include the amount of Federal, state, and local payroll taxes for the year, but only those that are imposed on the organization as an employer. This includes the employer's share of social security and Medicare taxes, FUTA tax, state unemployment compensation tax, and other state and local payroll taxes. **Do not** include taxes withheld from employees' salaries and paid over to the various governmental units (such as Federal and state income taxes and the employee's share of social security and Medicare taxes).

Lines 16a, b, and c—Legal, accounting, and other professional fees. On the appropriate line(s), enter the amount of legal, accounting, auditing, and other professional fees (such as fees for fundraising or investment services) charged by **outside firms and individuals** who are not employees of the foundation.

Attach a schedule for lines 16a, b, and c. Show the type of service and amount of expense for each. If the same person provided more than one of these services, include an allocation of those expenses.

Report any fines, penalties, or judgments imposed against the foundation as a result of legal proceedings on line 23, Other expenses.

Line 18—Taxes. Attach a schedule listing the type and amount of each tax reported on line 18. Do not enter any taxes included on line 15.

In column (a), enter the taxes paid (or accrued) during the year. Include all types of taxes recorded on the books, including real estate tax not reported on line 20; the tax on investment income; and any income tax.

In column (b), enter only those taxes included in column (a) that are related to investment income taxable under section 4940. **Do not** include the section 4940 tax paid or incurred on net investment income or the section 511 tax on unrelated business income. Sales taxes may not be deducted separately, but must be treated as a part of the cost of acquired property, or as a reduction of the amount realized on disposition of the property.

In column (c), enter only those taxes included in column (a) that relate to income included in column (c). **Do not** include any excise tax paid or incurred on the net investment income (as shown in Part VI), or any tax reported on Form 990-T.

In column (d), do not include any excise tax paid on net investment income (as reported in Part VI of this return or the equivalent part of a return for prior years) unless the organization is claiming status as a private operating foundation and completes Part XIV.

Line 19—Depreciation and depletion.

In column (a), enter the expense recorded in the books for the year.

For depreciation, attach a schedule showing:

1. A description of the property,
2. The date acquired,
3. The cost or other basis (exclude any land),
4. The depreciation allowed or allowable in prior years,
5. The method of computation,
6. The rate (%) or life (years), and
7. The depreciation this year.

On a separate line on the schedule, show the amount of depreciation included in cost of goods sold and not included on line 19.

In columns (b) and (c), a deduction for depreciation is allowed only for property used in the production of income reported in the column, and **only** using the straight line method of computing depreciation. A deduction for depletion is allowed but must be figured **only** using the cost depletion method.

The basis used in figuring depreciation and depletion is the basis determined under normal basis rules, without regard to the special rules for using the fair market value on December 31, 1969, that relate only to gain or loss on dispositions for purposes of the tax on net investment income.

Line 20—Occupancy. Enter the amount paid or incurred for the use of office space or other facilities. If the space is rented or leased, enter the amount of rent. If the space is owned, enter the amount of mortgage interest, real estate taxes, and similar expenses, but not depreciation (reportable on line 19). In either case, include the amount for utilities and related expenses (e.g., heat, lights, water, power, telephone, sewer, trash removal, outside janitorial services, and similar services). Do not include any salaries of the organization's own employees that are reportable on line 15.

Line 21—Travel, conferences, and meetings. Enter the expenses for officers, employees, or others during the year for travel, attending conferences, meetings, etc. Include transportation (including fares, mileage allowance, or automobile expenses), meals and lodging, and related costs whether paid on the basis of a per diem allowance or actual expenses incurred. Do not include any compensation paid to those who participate.

In column (b), only 50% of the expense for business meals, etc., paid or incurred in connection with travel, meetings, etc., relating to the production of investment income, may be deducted in figuring net investment income (section 274(n)).

In column (c), enter the total amount of expenses paid or incurred by officers, employees, or others for travel, conferences, meetings, etc., related to income included in column (c).

Line 22—Printing and publications. Enter the expenses for printing or publishing and distributing any newsletters, magazines, etc. Also include the cost of subscriptions to, or purchases of, magazines, newspapers, etc.

Line 23—Other expenses. Enter all other expenses for the year. Include all expenses not reported on lines 13–22. Attach a schedule showing the type and amount of each expense.

If a deduction is claimed for amortization, attach a schedule showing:
• Description of the amortized expenses;
• Date acquired, completed, or expended;
• Amount amortized;
• Deduction for prior years;
• Amortization period (number of months);
• Current-year amortization; and
• Total amount of amortization.

In column (c), in addition to the applicable portion of expenses from column (a), include any net loss from the sale or exchange of land or depreciable property that was held for more than 1 year and used in a trade or business.

A deduction for amortization is allowed but only for assets used for the production of income reported in column (c).

Line 25—Contributions, gifts, grants paid.

In column (a), enter the total of all contributions, gifts, grants, and similar amounts paid (or accrued) for the year. List each contribution, gift, grant, etc., in Part XV, or attach a schedule of the items included on line 25 and list:

1. Each class of activity,
2. A separate total for each activity,
3. Name and address of donee,
4. Relationship of donee if related by:
   a. Blood,
   b. Marriage,
   c. Adoption, or
   d. Employment (including children of employees) to any disqualified person (see General Instruction C for definitions), and
5. The organizational status of donee (e.g., public charity—an organization described in section 509(a)(1), (2), or (3)).

You do not have to give the name of any indigent person who received one or more gifts or grants from the foundation unless that individual is a disqualified person or one who received a total of more than $1,000 from the foundation during the year.

Activities should be classified according to purpose and in greater detail than merely classifying them as charitable, educational, religious, or scientific activities. For example, use identification such as: payments for nursing service, for fellowships, or for assistance to indigent families.

Foundations may include, as a single entry on the schedule, the total of amounts paid as grants for which the foundation exercised expenditure responsibility. Attach a separate report for each grant.

When the fair market value of the property at the time of disbursement is the measure of a contribution, the schedule must also show:

1. A description of the contributed property,
2. The book value of the contributed property,
3. The method used to determine the book value,
4. The method used to determine the fair market value, and
5. The date of the gift.

 The difference between fair market value and book value should be shown in the books of account and as a net asset adjustment in Part III.

In column (d), enter on line 25 all contributions, gifts, and grants the foundation paid during the year.
• Do not include contributions to organizations controlled by the foundation or by a disqualified person (see General Instruction C for definitions). Do not include contributions to nonoperating private foundations unless the donees are

exempt from tax under section 501(c)(3), they redistribute the contributions, and they maintain sufficient evidence of redistributions according to the regulations under section 4942(g).

• Do not reduce the amount of grants paid in the current year by the amount of grants paid in a prior year that was returned or recovered in the current year. Report those repayments in column (c), line 9, and in Part XI, line 4a.

• Do not include any payments of set-asides (see instructions for Part XII, line 3) taken into account as qualifying distributions in the current year or any prior year. All set-asides are included in qualifying distributions (Part XII, line 3) in the year of the set-aside regardless of when paid.

• Do not include current year's write-offs of prior years' program-related investments. All program-related investments are included in qualifying distributions (Part XII, line 1b) in the year the investment is made.

• Do not include any payments that are not qualifying distributions as defined in section 4942(g)(1).

Net Amounts

Line 27a—Excess of revenue over expenses. Subtract line 26, column (a), from line 12, column (a). Enter the result. Generally, the amount shown in column (a) on this line is also the amount by which net assets (or fund balances) have increased or decreased for the year. See the instructions for Part III, Analysis of Changes in Net Assets or Fund Balances.

Line 27b—Net investment income. Domestic organizations, subtract line 26 from line 12. Enter the result. Exempt foreign organizations, enter the amount shown on line 12. However, if the organization is a domestic organization and line 26 is more than line 12 (i.e., expenses exceed income), enter zero (not a negative amount).

Line 27c—Adjusted net income. Subtract line 26, column (c) from line 12, column (c) and enter the result.

Part II—Balance Sheets

For column (b), show the book value at the end of the year. For column (c), show the fair market value at the end of the year. Attached schedules must show the end-of-year value for each asset listed in columns (b) and (c).

• Foundations whose books of account included total assets of $5,000 or more at any time during the year must complete all of columns (a), (b), and (c).

• Foundations with less than $5,000 of total assets per books at all times during the year must complete all of columns (a) and (b), and only line 16 of column (c).

TIP *A foundation that is changing its method of accounting to comply with SFAS 116 should **not** restate its beginning of year statement of financial position (balance sheet) to reflect any prior period adjustments. See Part III—Analysis of Changes in Net Assets or Fund Balances to find where to show any adjustment required by section 481(a).*

Line 1—Cash—Non-interest-bearing. Enter the amount of cash on deposit in checking accounts, deposits in transit, change funds, petty cash funds, or any other non-interest-bearing account. Do not include advances to employees or officers or refundable deposits paid to suppliers or others.

Line 2—Savings and temporary cash investments. Enter the total of cash in savings or other interest-bearing accounts and temporary cash investments, such as money market funds, commercial paper, certificates of deposit, and U.S. Treasury bills or other governmental obligations that mature in less than 1 year.

Line 3—Accounts receivable. On the dashed lines to the left of column (a), enter the year-end figures for total accounts receivable and allowance for doubtful accounts from the sale of goods and/or the performance of services. In columns (a), (b), and (c), enter net amounts (total accounts receivable reduced by the corresponding allowance for doubtful accounts). Claims against vendors or refundable deposits with suppliers or others may be reported here if not significant in amount. (Otherwise, report them on line 15, Other assets.) Any receivables due from officers, directors, trustees, foundation managers, or other disqualified persons must be reported on line 6. Report receivables (including loans and advances) due from other employees on line 15.

Line 4—Pledges receivable. On the dashed lines to the left of column (a), enter the year-end figures for total pledges receivable and allowance for doubtful accounts (pledges estimated to be uncollectable). In columns (a), (b), and (c), enter net amounts (total pledges receivable reduced by the corresponding allowance for doubtful accounts).

Line 5—Grants receivable. Enter the total grants receivable from governmental agencies, foundations, and other organizations as of the beginning and end of the year.

Line 6—Receivables due from officers, directors, trustees, and other disqualified persons. Enter here (and on an attached schedule described below) all receivables due from officers, directors, trustees, foundation managers, and other disqualified persons and all secured and unsecured loans (including advances) to such persons. "Disqualified person" is defined in General Instruction C.

Attached schedules. (a) On the required schedule, report each loan separately, even if more than one loan was made to the same person, or the same terms apply to all loans made.

Salary advances and other advances for the personal use and benefit of the recipient and receivables subject to special terms or arising from transactions not functionally related to the foundation's charitable purposes must be reported as separate loans for each officer, director, etc.

(b) Receivables that are subject to the same terms and conditions (including credit limits and rate of interest) as receivables due from the general public from an activity functionally related to the foundation's charitable purposes may be reported as a single total for all the officers, directors, etc. Travel advances made for official business of the organization may also be reported as a single total.

For each outstanding loan or other receivable that must be reported separately, the attached schedule should show the following information (preferably in columnar form):

1. Borrower's name and title.
2. Original amount.
3. Balance due.
4. Date of note.
5. Maturity date.
6. Repayment terms.
7. Interest rate.
8. Security provided by the borrower.
9. Purpose of the loan.
10. Description and fair market value of the consideration furnished by the lender (e.g., cash—$1,000; or 100 shares of XYZ, Inc., common stock— $9,000).

The above detail is not required for receivables or travel advances that may be reported as a single total (see *(b)* above); however, report and identify those totals separately on the attachment.

Line 7—Other notes and loans receivable. On the dashed lines to the left of column (a), enter the combined total year-end figures for notes receivable and loans receivable and the allowance for doubtful accounts.

Notes receivable. In columns (a), (b), and (c), enter the amount of all notes receivable not listed on line 6 and not acquired as investments. Attach a schedule similar to the one for line 6. The schedule should also identify the relationship of the borrower to any officer, director, trustee, foundation manager, or other disqualified person.

For a note receivable from any section 501(c)(3) organization, list only the name of the borrower and the balance due on the required schedule.

Loans receivable. In columns (a), (b), and (c), enter the gross amount of loans receivable, minus the allowance for doubtful accounts, from the normal activities of the filing organization (such as scholarship loans). An itemized list of these loans is not required but attach a schedule showing the total amount of each type of outstanding loan. Report loans to officers, directors, trustees, foundation managers, or other disqualified persons on line 6 and loans to other employees on line 15.

Line 8—Inventories for sale or use. Enter the amount of materials, goods, and supplies purchased or manufactured by the organization and held for sale or use in some future period.

Line 9—Prepaid expenses and deferred charges. Enter the amount of short-term and long-term prepayments of expenses attributable to one or more future accounting periods. Examples include prepayments of rent, insurance, and pension costs, and expenses incurred in connection with a solicitation campaign to be conducted in a future accounting period.

Lines 10a, b, and c—Investments— government obligations, corporate stocks and bonds. Enter the book value (which may be market value) of these investments.

Attach a schedule that lists each security held at the end of the year and shows whether the security is listed at cost (including the value recorded at the time of receipt in the case of donated securities) or end-of-year market value. Do not include amounts shown on line 2. Governmental obligations reported on line 10a are those that mature in 1 year or more. Debt securities of the U.S. Government must be reported as a single total rather than itemized. Obligations of state and municipal governments may also be reported as a lump-sum total. Do not combine U.S. Government obligations with state and municipal obligations on this schedule.

Line 11—Investments—land, buildings, and equipment. On the dashed lines to the left of column (a), enter the year-end book value (cost or other basis) and accumulated depreciation of all land, buildings, and equipment held for investment purposes, such as rental property. In columns (a) and (b), enter the book value of all land, buildings, and equipment held for investment less accumulated depreciation. In column (c), enter the fair market value of these assets. Attach a schedule listing these investment fixed assets held at the end of the year and showing, for each item or category listed, the cost or other basis, accumulated depreciation, and book value.

Line 12—Investments—mortgage loans. Enter the amount of mortgage loans receivable held as investments but do not include program-related investments (see instructions for line 15).

Line 13—Investments—other. Enter the amount of all other investment holdings not reported on lines 10 through 12. Attach a schedule listing and describing each of these investments held at the end of the year. Show the book value for each and indicate whether the investment is listed at cost or end-of-year market value. Do not include

program-related investments (see instructions for line 15).

Line 14—Land, buildings, and equipment. On the dashed lines to the left of column (a), enter the year-end book value (cost or other basis) and accumulated depreciation of all land, buildings, and equipment owned by the organization and **not** held for investment. In columns (a) and (b), enter the book value of all land, buildings, and equipment **not** held for investment less accumulated depreciation. In column (c), enter the fair market value of these assets. Include any property, plant, and equipment owned and used by the organization to conduct its charitable activities. Attach a schedule listing these fixed assets held at the end of the year and showing the cost or other basis, accumulated depreciation, and book value of each item or category listed.

Line 15—Other assets. List and show the book value of each category of assets not reportable on lines 1 through 14. Attach a separate schedule if more space is needed.

One type of asset reportable on line 15 is program-related investments. These are investments made primarily to accomplish a charitable purpose of the filing organization rather than to produce income.

Line 16—Total assets. All filers must complete line 16 of columns (a), (b), and (c). These entries represent the totals of lines 1 through 15 of each column. However, organizations that have assets of less than $5,000 per books at all times during the year need not complete lines 1 through 15 of column (c).

 The column (c) amount is also entered on the entry space for I on page 1.

Line 17—Accounts payable and accrued expenses. Enter the total of accounts payable to suppliers and others and accrued expenses, such as salaries payable, accrued payroll taxes, and interest payable.

Line 18—Grants payable. Enter the unpaid portion of grants and awards that the organization has made a commitment to pay other organizations or individuals, whether or not the commitments have been communicated to the grantees.

Line 19—Deferred revenue. Include revenue that the organization has received but not yet earned as of the balance sheet date under its method of accounting.

Line 20—Loans from officers, directors, trustees, and other disqualified persons. Enter the unpaid balance of loans received from officers, directors, trustees, and other disqualified persons. For loans outstanding at the end of the year, attach a schedule that shows (for each loan) the name and title of the lender and the information listed in items

2 through 10 of the instructions for line 6 on page 15.

Line 21—Mortgages and other notes payable. Enter the amount of mortgages and other notes payable at the beginning and end of the year. Attach a schedule showing, as of the end of the year, the total amount of all mortgages payable and, for each nonmortgage note payable, the name of the lender and the other information specified in items **2** through **10** of the instructions for line 6. The schedule should also identify the relationship of the lender to any officer, director, trustee, foundation manager, or other disqualified person.

Line 22—Other liabilities. List and show the amount of each liability not reportable on lines 17 through 21. Attach a separate schedule if more space is needed.

Lines 24 Through 30—Net Assets or Fund Balances

The Financial Accounting Standards Board issued Statement of Financial Accounting Standards (SFAS) 117, Financial Statements of Not-for-Profit Organizations. SFAS 117 provides standards for external financial statements certified by an independent accountant for certain types of nonprofit organizations including private foundations.

While some states may require reporting in accordance with SFAS 117 (see General Instruction F), the IRS does not. However, a Form 990-PF return prepared in accordance with SFAS 117 will be acceptable to the IRS.

Organizations that follow SFAS 117. If the organization follows SFAS 117, check the box above line 24. Classify and report net assets in three groups—unrestricted, temporarily restricted, and permanently restricted—based on the existence or absence of donor-imposed restrictions and the nature of those restrictions. Show the sum of the three classes of net assets on line 30. On line 31, add the amounts on lines 23 and 30 to show total liabilities and net assets. This figure should be the same as the figure for Total assets on line 16.

Line 24—Unrestricted. Enter the balances per books of the unrestricted class of net assets. Unrestricted net assets are neither permanently restricted nor temporarily restricted by donor-imposed stipulations. All funds without donor-imposed restrictions must be classified as unrestricted, regardless of the existence of any board designations or appropriations.

Line 25—Temporarily restricted. Enter the balances per books of the temporarily restricted class of net assets. Donors' temporary restrictions may require that resources be used in a later period or after a specified date (time restrictions), or that resources be used for a specified purpose (purpose restrictions), or both.

Form 990-PF Instructions

Line 26—Permanently restricted.
Enter the total of the balances for the permanently restricted class of net assets. Permanently restricted net assets are **(a)** assets, such as land or works of art, donated with stipulations that they be used for a specified purpose, be preserved, and not be sold or **(b)** assets donated with stipulations that they be invested to provide a permanent source of income. The latter result from gifts and bequests that create permanent endowment funds.

Organizations that do not follow SFAS 117. If the organization does not follow SFAS 117, check the box above line 27 and report account balances on lines 27 through 29. Report net assets or fund balances on line 30. Also complete line 31 to report the sum of the total liabilities and net assets/fund balances.

Line 27—Capital stock, trust principal, or current funds. For corporations, enter the balance per books for capital stock accounts. Show par or stated value (or for stock with no par or stated value, total amount received upon issuance) of all classes of stock issued and, as yet, uncancelled. For trusts, enter the amount in the trust principal or corpus account. For organizations continuing to use the fund method of accounting, enter the fund balances for the organization's current restricted and unrestricted funds.

Line 28—Paid-in or capital surplus, or land, bldg., and equipment fund. Enter the balance per books for all paid-in capital in excess of par or stated value for all stock issued and uncancelled. If stockholders or others gave donations that the organization records as paid-in capital, include them here. Report any current-year donations you included on line 28 in Part I, line 1. The fund balance for the land, building, and equipment fund would be entered here.

Line 29—Retained earnings, accumulated income, endowment, or other funds. For corporations, enter the balance in the retained earnings, or similar account, minus the cost of any corporate treasury stock. For trusts, enter the balance per books in the accumulated income or similar account. For organizations using fund accounting, enter the total of the fund balances for the permanent and term endowment funds as well as balances of any other funds not reported on lines 27 and 28.

Line 30—Total net assets or fund balances. For organizations that follow SFAS 117, enter the total of lines 24 through 26. For all other organizations, enter the total of lines 27 through 29. Enter the beginning-of-year figure in column (a) on line 1, Part III. The end-of-year figure in column (b) must agree with the figure in Part III, line 6.

Line 31—Total liabilities and net assets/fund balances. Enter the total of lines 23 and 30. This amount must equal the amount for total assets reported on

line 16 for both the beginning and end of the year.

Part III—Analysis of Changes in Net Assets or Fund Balances

Generally, the excess of revenue over expenses accounts for the difference between the net assets at the beginning and end of the year.

On line 2, Part III, re-enter the figure from Part I, line 27(a), column (a).

On lines 3 and 5, list any changes in net assets that were not caused by the receipts or expenses shown in Part I, column (a). For example, if a foundation follows FASB Statement No. 12 and shows an asset in the ending balance sheet at a higher value than in the beginning balance sheet because of an increased market value (after a larger decrease in a prior year), include the increase in Part III, line 3.

If an organization changes its accounting method for tax purposes to conform with the method provided in SFAS 116, it should report any increase required by section 481(a) on line 3 and identify the adjustment as the effect of changing to the methods provided in SFAS 116.

If the organization uses a stepped-up basis to determine gains on sales of assets included in Part I, column (a), then include the amount of step-up in basis in Part III. If you entered a contribution, gift, or grant of property valued at fair market value on line 25 of Part I, column (a), the difference between fair market value and book value should be shown in the books of account and as a net asset adjustment in Part III.

Part IV—Capital Gains and Losses for Tax on Investment Income

Use Part IV to figure the amount of net capital gain to report on lines 7 and 8 of Part I.
• Part IV does not apply to foreign organizations.
• Nonoperating private foundations may not have to figure their short-term capital gain or loss on line 3. See the rules for **Nonoperating private foundations** on page 11.

Private foundations must report gains and losses from the sale or other disposition of property:
• Held for investment purposes or
• Used to produce unrelated business income; however, **only** include in net investment income the part of the gain or loss that is **not** included in the computation of its unrelated business taxable income.

Property held for investment purposes. Property is treated as held for investment purposes if the property is of a

type that generally produces interest, dividends, rents, or royalties, even if the foundation disposes of the property as soon as it receives it.

Charitable use property. Do not include any gain or loss from disposing of property used for the foundation's charitable purposes in the computation of tax on net investment income. If the foundation uses property for its charitable purposes, but also incidentally derives income from the property that is subject to the net investment income tax, any gain or loss from the sale or other disposition of the property is not subject to the tax.

However, if the foundation uses property both for charitable purposes and (other than incidentally) for investment purposes, include in the computation of tax on net investment income the part of the gain or loss from the sale or disposition of the property that is allocable to the investment use of the property.

***Program-related investments.* Do not** include gains or losses from the sale or exchange of program-related investments as defined in the instructions for Part IX-B.

Losses. If the disposition of investment property results in a loss, that loss may be subtracted from capital gains realized from the disposition of property during the same tax year but only to the extent of the gains. If losses are more than gains, the excess may not be subtracted from gross investment income, nor may the losses be carried back or forward to other tax years.

Basis. The basis for determining **gain** from the sale or other disposition of property is the **larger** of:

1. The fair market value of the property on December 31, 1969, plus or minus all adjustments after December 31, 1969, and before the date of disposition, if the foundation held the property on that date and continuously after that date until disposition or

2. The basis of the property on the date of disposition under normal basis rules (actual basis). See Code sections 1011–1021.

The rules that generally apply to property dispositions reported in this part are:
• Section 1011, Adjusted basis for determining gain or loss.
• Section 1012, Basis of property—cost.
• Section 1014, Basis of property acquired from a decedent.
• Section 1015, Basis of property acquired by gifts and transfers in trust.
• Section 1016, Adjustments to basis.
To figure a **loss,** basis on the date of disposition is determined under normal basis rules.

See Chapter IV of Pub. 578 for examples on how to determine gain or loss. The completed Form 990-PF in **Package 990-PF,** Returns for Private Foundations or Section 4947(a)(1)

Nonexempt Charitable Trusts Treated as Private Foundations, contains an example of a sale of investment property in which the gain was computed using the donor's basis under the rules of section 1015(a).

Part V—Qualification Under Section 4940(e) for Reduced Tax on Net Investment Income

This part is used by domestic private foundations (exempt and taxable) to determine whether they qualify for the reduced 1% tax under section 4940(e) on net investment income rather than the 2% tax on net investment income under section 4940(a).

Do not complete Part V if this is the organization's first year. A private foundation cannot qualify under section 4940(e) for its first year of existence, nor can a former public charity qualify for the first year it is treated as a private foundation.

A separate computation must be made for each year in which the foundation wants to qualify for the reduced tax.

Line 1, column (b). Enter the amount of adjusted qualifying distributions made for each year shown. The amounts in column (b) are taken from Part XII, line 6 of the Form 990-PF for 1996–2000.

Line 1, column (c). Enter the net value of noncharitable-use assets for each year. The amounts in column (c) are taken from Part X, line 5, for 1996–2000.

Part VI—Excise Tax Based on Investment Income (Section 4940(a), 4940(b), 4940(e), or 4948)

General Rules

Domestic exempt private foundations. These foundations are subject to a 2% tax on net investment income under section 4940(a). However, certain exempt operating foundations described in section 4940(d)(2) may not owe any tax, and certain private foundations that meet the requirements of section 4940(e) may qualify for a reduced tax of 1% (see the Part V instructions).

Exception. The section 4940 tax does not apply to an organization making an election under section 41(e)(6). Enter "N/A" in Part VI.

Domestic taxable private foundations and section 4947(a)(1) nonexempt charitable trusts. These organizations are subject to a modified 2% tax on net investment income under section 4940(b). (See Part V and its instructions to find out if they meet the requirements of section 4940(e) that allows them to use a modified 1% tax on net investment income.) However, they must first

compute the tax under section 4940(a) as if that tax applied to them.

Foreign organizations. Under section 4948, **exempt foreign private foundations** are subject to a 4% tax on their gross investment income derived from U.S. sources.

Taxable foreign private foundations that filed **Form 1040NR,** U.S. Nonresident Alien Income Tax Return, or **Form 1120-F,** U.S. Income Tax Return of a Foreign Corporation, enter "N/A" in Part VI.

Estimated tax. Domestic exempt and taxable private foundations and section 4947(a)(1) nonexempt charitable trusts may have to make estimated tax payments for the excise tax based on investment income. See General Instruction O for more information.

Tax Computation

 Line 1a only applies to domestic exempt operating foundations that are described in section 4940(d)(2) and that have a ruling letter from the IRS establishing exempt operating foundation status. If your organization does not have this letter, skip line 1a.

Line 1a. A domestic exempt private foundation that qualifies as an exempt operating foundation under section 4940(d)(2) is not liable for any tax on net investment income on this return.

If your organization qualifies, check the box and enter the date of the ruling letter on line 1a and enter "N/A" on line 1. Leave the rest of Part VI blank. **For the first year,** the organization must attach a copy of the ruling letter establishing exempt operating foundation status. As long as the organization retains this status, write the date of the ruling letter in the space on line 1a. If the organization no longer qualifies under section 4940(d)(2), leave the date line blank and compute the section 4940 tax in the normal manner.

Qualification. To qualify as an exempt operating foundation for a tax year, an organization must meet the following requirements of section 4940(d)(2):

1. It is an operating foundation described in section 4942(j)(3),

2. It has been publicly supported for at least 10 tax years or was a private operating foundation on January 1, 1983, or for its last tax year ending before January 1, 1983,

3. Its governing body, at all times during the tax year, consists of individuals less than 25% of whom are disqualified individuals, and is broadly representative of the general public, and

4. It has no officer who was a disqualified individual at any time during the tax year.

Line 2—Section 511 tax. Under section 4940(b), a domestic section 4947(a)(1)

nonexempt charitable trust or taxable private foundation must add to the tax figured under section 4940(a) (on line 1) the tax which would have been imposed under section 511 for the tax year if it had been exempt from tax under section 501(a). If the domestic section 4947(a)(1) nonexempt charitable trust or taxable private foundation has unrelated business taxable income that would have been subject to the tax imposed by section 511, the computation of tax must be shown in an attachment. Form 990-T may be used as the attachment. All other filers, enter zero.

Line 4—Subtitle A tax. Domestic section 4947(a)(1) nonexempt charitable trusts and taxable private foundations, enter the amount of subtitle A (income) tax for the year reported on Form 1041 or Form 1120. All other filers, enter zero.

Line 5—Tax based on investment income. Subtract line 4 from line 3 and enter the difference (but not less than zero) on line 5. Any overpayment entered on line 10 that is the result of a negative amount shown on line 5 will not be refunded. Unless the organization is a domestic section 4947(a)(1) nonexempt charitable trust or taxable private foundation, the amount on line 5 is the same as on line 1.

Line 6—Credits/Payments

 Line 6a applies only to domestic organizations.

Line 6a. Enter the amount of 2001 estimated tax payments, and any 2000 overpayment of taxes that the organization specified on its 2000 return to be credited toward payment of 2001 estimated taxes.

Trust payments treated as beneficiary payments. A trust may treat any part of estimated taxes it paid as taxes paid by the beneficiary. If the filing organization was a beneficiary that received the benefit of such a payment from a trust, include the amount on line 6a of Part VI, and write, "Includes section 643(g) payment." See section 643(g) for more information about estimated tax payments treated as paid by a beneficiary.

Line 6b. Exempt foreign foundations must enter the amount of tax withheld at the source.

Line 6d. Enter the amount of any backup withholding erroneously withheld. Recipients of interest or dividend payments must generally certify their correct tax identification number to the bank or other payer on **Form W-9,** Request for Taxpayer Identification Number and Certification. If the payer does not get this information, it must withhold part of the payments as "backup withholding." If the organization files Form 990-PF and was subject to erroneous backup withholding because the payer did not realize the payee was an exempt organization and not subject to this withholding, the organization can claim credit for the amount withheld.

 Do not claim erroneous backup withholding on line 6d if you claim it on Form 990-T.

Line 8—Penalty. Enter any penalty for underpayment of estimated tax shown on Form 2220. Form 2220 is used by both corporations and trusts.

Line 9—Tax due. Domestic foundations should see General Instruction P.

All foreign organizations should enclose a check or money order (in U.S. funds), made payable to the United States Treasury, with Form 990-PF.

Part VII-A—Statements Regarding Activities

Each question in this section must be answered "Yes," "No," or "N/A" (not applicable).

Line 1. Political purposes include, but are not limited to: directly or indirectly accepting contributions or making payments to influence the selection, nomination, election, or appointment of any individual to any Federal, state, or local public office or office in a political organization, or the election of presidential or vice presidential electors, whether or not the individual or electors are actually selected, nominated, elected, or appointed.

Line 3. A "conformed" copy of an organizational document is one that agrees with the original document and all its amendments. If copies are not signed, attach a written declaration signed by an officer authorized to sign for the organization, certifying that they are complete and accurate copies of the original documents.

Line 6. For a private foundation to be exempt from income tax, its governing instrument must include provisions that require it to act or refrain from acting so as not to engage in an act of self-dealing (section 4941), or subject the foundation to the taxes imposed by section 4942 (failure to distribute income), 4943 (excess business holdings), 4944 (investments which jeopardize charitable purpose), and 4945 (taxable expenditures). A private foundation may satisfy these section 508(e) requirements either by express language in its governing instrument or by application of state law that imposes the above requirements on the foundation or treats these requirements as being contained in the governing instrument. If an organization claims it satisfies the requirements of section 508(e) by operation of state law, the provisions of state law must effectively impose the section 508(e) requirements on the organization. See Rev. Rul. 75-38, 1975-1 C.B.161, for a list of states with legislation that satisfies the requirements of section 508(e).

However, if the state law does not apply to a governing instrument that contains mandatory directions conflicting with any of its requirements and the organization has such mandatory directions in its governing instrument, then the organization has not satisfied the requirements of section 508(e) by the operation of that legislation.

Line 8a. In the space provided list all states:

1. To which the organization reports in any way about its organization, assets, or activities and

2. With which the organization has registered (or which it has otherwise notified in any manner) that it intends to be, or is, a charitable organization or that it is, or intends to be, a holder of property devoted to a charitable purpose.

Attach a separate list if you need more space.

Line 9. If the organization claims status as a private operating foundation for 2001 and, in fact, meets the private operating foundation requirements for that year (as reflected in Part XIV), any excess distributions carryover from 2000 or prior years may not be carried over to 2001 or any year after 2001 in which it does not meet the private operating foundation requirements. See the instructions for Part XIII.

Line 10—Substantial contributors. If you answer "Yes," attach a schedule listing the names and addresses of all persons who became substantial contributors during the year.

The term **substantial contributor** means any person whose contributions or bequests during the current tax year and prior tax years total more than $5,000 and are more than 2% of the total contributions and bequests received by the foundation from its creation through the close of its tax year. In the case of a trust, the term "substantial contributor" also means the creator of the trust (section 507(d)(2)).

The term **person** includes individuals, trusts, estates, partnerships, associations, corporations, and other exempt organizations.

Each contribution or bequest must be valued at fair market value on the date it was received.

Any person who is a substantial contributor on any date will remain a substantial contributor for all later periods.

However, a person will cease to be a substantial contributor with respect to any private foundation if:

1. The person, and all related persons, made no contributions to the foundation during the 10-year period ending with the close of the taxable year;

2. The person, or any related person, was never the foundation's manager during this 10-year period; and

3. The aggregate contributions made by the person, and related persons, are determined by the IRS to be insignificant compared to the aggregate amount of contributions to the foundation by any other person and the appreciated value of contributions held by the foundation.

The term **related person** includes any other person who would be a disqualified person because of a relationship with the substantial contributor (section 4946). When the substantial contributor is a corporation, the term also includes any officer or director of a corporation. The term "substantial contributor" does not include public charities (organizations described in section 509(a)(1), (2), or (3)).

Line 11—Public inspection requirements and web site address. All domestic private foundations (including section 4947(a)(1) nonexempt charitable trusts treated as private foundations) are subject to the public inspection requirements. See General Instruction Q for information on making the foundation's annual returns and exemption application available for public inspection.

Enter the foundation's web site address if the the foundation has a web site. Otherwise, enter "N/A."

Line 13—Section 4947(a)(1) trusts. Section 4947(a)(1) nonexempt charitable trusts that file Form 990-PF instead of Form 1041 must complete this line. The trust should include exempt-interest dividends received from a mutual fund or other regulated investment company as well as tax-exempt interest received directly.

Part VII-B—Activities for Which Form 4720 May Be Required

The purpose of these questions is to determine if there is any initial excise tax due under sections 170(f)(10), 4941–4945, and section 4955. If the answer is "Yes" to question 1b, 1c, 2b, 3b, 4a, 4b, 5b, or 6b, complete and file Form 4720, unless an exception applies.

Line 1—Self-dealing. The activities listed in 1a(1)–(6) are considered self-dealing under section 4941 unless one of the exceptions applies. See Pub. 578.

The terms "disqualified person" and "foundation manager" are defined in General Instruction C.

Line 1b. If you answered "Yes" to any of the questions in **1a**, you should answer "Yes" to **1b** unless all of the acts engaged in were "excepted" acts. Excepted acts are described in Regulations sections 53.4941(d)-3 and 4 or appear in Notices published in the Internal Revenue Bulletin, relating to disaster assistance.

Line 2—Taxes on failure to distribute income. If you answer "No" to question 2b, attach a statement explaining:

1. All the facts regarding the incorrect valuation of assets and

2. The actions taken (or planned) to comply with section 4942(a)(2)(B), (C), and (D) and the related regulations.

Line 3a. A private foundation is not treated as having excess business holdings in any enterprise if, together with related foundations, it owns 2% or less of the voting stock and 2% or less in value of all outstanding shares of all classes of stock. (See "disqualified person" under General Instruction C.) A similar exception applies to a beneficial or profits interest in any business enterprise that is a trust or partnership.

For more information about excess business holdings, see Pub. 578 and the instructions for Form 4720.

Line 4—Taxes on investments that jeopardize charitable purposes. In general, an investment that jeopardizes any of the charitable purposes of a private foundation is one for which a foundation manager did not exercise ordinary business care to provide for the long- and short-term financial needs of the foundation to carry out its charitable purposes. For more details, see Pub. 578 and the regulations under section 4944.

Line 5—Taxes on taxable expenditures and political expenditures. In general, payments made for the activities described on lines 5a(1)–(5) are taxable expenditures. See Pub. 578 for exceptions.

A grant by a private foundation to a public charity is not a taxable expenditure if the private foundation does not earmark the grant for any of the activities described in lines 5a(1)–(5), and there is no oral or written agreement by which the grantor foundation may cause the grantee to engage in any such prohibited activity or to select the grant recipient.

Grants made to exempt operating foundations (as defined in section 4940(d)(2) and the instructions to Part VI) are not subject to the expenditure responsibility provisions of section 4945.

Under section 4955, a section 501(c)(3) organization must pay an excise tax for any amount paid or incurred on behalf of or opposing any candidate for public office. The organization must pay an additional excise tax if it does not correct the expenditure timely.

A manager of a section 501(c)(3) organization who knowingly agrees to a political expenditure must pay an excise tax unless the agreement is not willful and there is reasonable cause. A manager who does not agree to a correction of the political expenditure may have to pay an additional excise tax.

A section 501(c)(3) organization will lose its exempt status if it engages in political activity.

A political expenditure that is treated as an expenditure under section 4955 is

not treated as a taxable expenditure under section 4945.

For purposes of the section 4955 tax, when an organization promotes a candidate for public office (or is used or controlled by a candidate or prospective candidate), amounts paid or incurred for the following purposes are political expenditures:

1. Remuneration to the individual (or candidate or prospective candidate) for speeches or other services.

2. Travel expenses of the individual.

3. Expenses of conducting polls, surveys, or other studies, or preparing papers or other material for use by the individual.

4. Expenses of advertising, publicity, and fundraising for such individual.

5. Any other expense that has the primary effect of promoting public recognition or otherwise primarily accruing to the benefit of the individual.

See the regulations under section 4945 for more information.

Line 5b. If you answered "Yes" to any of the questions in **5a,** you should answer "Yes" to **5b** unless all of the transactions engaged in were "excepted" transactions. Excepted transactions are described in Regulations section 53.4945 or appear in Notices published in the Internal Revenue Bulletin, relating to disaster assistance.

Line 6b. Check "Yes" if, in connection with any transfer of funds to a private foundation, the foundation directly or indirectly pays premiums on any personal benefit contract, or there is an understanding or expectation that any person will directly or indirectly pay these premiums.

Report the premiums it paid and the premiums paid by others, but treated as paid by the private foundation, on Form 8870 and pay the excise tax (which is equal to premiums paid) on Form 4720.

For more information, see Form 8870 and Notice 2000-24, 2000-17 I.R.B. 952 (April 24, 2000).

Part VIII—Information About Officers, Directors, Trustees, Foundation Managers, Highly Paid Employees, and Contractors

Line 1—List of officers, directors, trustees, etc. List the names, addresses, and other information requested for those who were officers, directors, and trustees (or any person who had responsibilities or powers similar to those of officers, directors, or trustees) of the foundation at any time during the year. Each must be listed whether or not they receive any compensation from the foundation. Give the preferred address at which officers,

etc., want the Internal Revenue Service to contact them.

Also include on this list, any officers or directors (or any person who had responsibilities or powers similar to those of officers or directors) of a disregarded entity owned by the foundation who are **not** officers, directors, etc., of the foundation.

If the foundation (or disregarded entity) pays any other person, such as a management services company, for the services provided by any of the foundation's officers, directors, or trustees (or any person who had responsibilities or powers similar to those of officers, directors, or trustees), report the compensation and other items on Part VIII as if you had paid the officers, etc., directly.

Show all forms of compensation earned by each listed officer, etc. In addition to completing Part VIII, if you want to explain the compensation of one or more officers, directors, and trustees, you may provide an attachment describing the person's entire 2001 compensation package.

Enter zero in columns (c), (d), and (e) if no compensation was paid. Attach a schedule if more space is needed.

Column (b). A numerical estimate of the average hours per week devoted to the position is required for the answer to be considered complete.

 Phrases such as "as needed" or "as required" are unacceptable entries for column (b).

Column (c). Enter salary, fees, bonuses, and severance payments received by each person listed. Include current year payments of amounts reported or reportable as deferred compensation in any prior year.

Column (d). Include all forms of deferred compensation and future severance payments (whether or not funded or vested, and whether or not the deferred compensation plan is a qualified plan under section 401(a)). Include payments to welfare benefit plans (employee welfare benefit plans covered by Part I of Title 1 of ERISA, providing benefits such as medical, dental, life insurance, apprenticeship and training, scholarship funds, severance pay, disability, etc.) on behalf of the officers, etc. Reasonable estimates may be used if precise cost figures are not readily available.

Unless the amounts are reported in column (c), report, as deferred compensation in column (d), salaries and other compensation earned during the period covered by the return, but not yet paid by the date the foundation files its return.

Column (e). Enter both taxable and nontaxable fringe benefits, expense account and other allowances (other than de minimis fringe benefits described in

Form 990-PF Instructions

section 132(e)). See Pub. 525 for more information. Examples of allowances include amounts for which the recipient did not account to the organization or allowances that were more than the payee spent on serving the organization. Include payments made in connection with indemnification arrangements, the value of the personal use of housing, automobiles, or other assets owned or leased by the organization (or provided for the organization's use without charge).

Line 2—Compensation of five highest-paid employees. Fill in the information requested for the five employees (if any) of the foundation (or disregarded entity that the foundation owns) who received the greatest amount of annual compensation over $50,000. Do not include employees listed on line 1. Also enter the total number of other employees who received more than $50,000 in annual compensation.

Show each listed employee's entire compensation package for the period covered by the return. Include all forms of compensation that each listed employee received in return for his or her services. See the line 1 instructions for more details on includible compensation.

Line 3—Five highest-paid independent contractors for professional services. Fill in the information requested for the five highest-paid independent contractors (if any), whether individuals or professional service corporations or associations, to whom the organization paid more than $50,000 for the year to perform personal services of a professional nature for the organization (such as attorneys, accountants, and doctors). Also show the total number of all other independent contractors who received more than $50,000 for the year for performing professional services.

Part IX-A—Summary of Direct Charitable Activities

List the foundation's four largest programs as measured by the direct and indirect expenses attributable to each that consist of the direct active conduct of charitable activities. Whether any expenditure is for the direct active conduct of a charitable activity is determined, generally, by the definitions and special rules of section 4942(j)(3) and the related regulations, which define a private operating foundation.

Except for significant involvement grant programs, described below, do not include in Part IX-A any grants or expenses attributable to administering grant programs, such as reviewing grant applications, interviewing or testing applicants, selecting grantees, and reviewing reports relating to the use of the grant funds.

Include scholarships, grants, or other payments to individuals as part of an active program in which the foundation

maintains some **significant involvement.** Related administrative expenses should also be included. Examples of active programs and definitions of the term "significant involvement" are provided in Regulations sections 53.4942(b)-1(b)(2) and 53.4942(b)-1(d).

Do not include any program-related investments (reportable in Part IX-B) in the description and expense totals, but be sure to include qualified set-asides for direct charitable activities, reported on line 3 of Part XII. Also, include in Part IX-A, amounts paid or set aside to acquire assets used in the direct active conduct of charitable activities.

Expenditures for direct charitable activities include, among others, amounts paid or set aside to:
• Acquire or maintain the operating assets of a museum, library, or historic site or to operate the facility.
• Provide goods, shelter, or clothing to indigents or disaster victims if the foundation maintains some significant involvement in the activity rather than merely making grants to the recipients.
• Conduct educational conferences and seminars.
• Operate a home for the elderly or disabled.
• Conduct scientific, historic, public policy, or other research with significance beyond the foundation's grant program that does not constitute a prohibited attempt to influence legislation.
• Publish and disseminate the results of such research, reports of educational conferences, or similar educational material.
• Support the service of foundation staff on boards or advisory committees of other charitable organizations or on public commissions or task forces.
• Provide technical advice or assistance to a governmental body, a governmental committee, or subdivision of either, in response to a written request by the governmental body, committee, or subdivision.
• Conduct performing arts performances.
• Provide technical assistance to grantees and other charitable organizations. This assistance must have significance beyond the purposes of the grants made to the grantees and must not consist merely of monitoring or advising the grantees in their use of the grant funds. Technical assistance involves the furnishing of expert advice and related assistance regarding, for example:

1. Compliance with governmental regulations;
2. Reducing operating costs or increasing program accomplishments;
3. Fundraising methods; and
4. Maintaining complete and accurate financial records.

Report both direct and indirect expenses in the expense totals. Direct expenses are those that can be

specifically identified as connected with a particular activity. These include, among others, compensation and travel expenses of employees and officers directly engaged in an activity, the cost of materials and supplies utilized in conducting the activity, and fees paid to outside firms and individuals in connection with a specific activity.

Indirect (overhead) expenses are those that are not specifically identified as connected with a particular activity but that relate to the direct costs incurred in conducting the activity. Examples of indirect expenses include: occupancy expenses; supervisory and clerical compensation; repair, rental, and maintenance of equipment; expenses of other departments or cost centers (such as accounting, personnel, and payroll departments or units) that service the department or function that incurs the direct expenses of conducting an activity; and other applicable general and administrative expenses, including the compensation of top management, to the extent reasonably allocable to a particular activity.

No specific method of allocation is required. The method used, however, must be reasonable and must be used consistently.

Examples of acceptable allocation methods include:
• Compensation that is allocated on a time basis.
• Employee benefits that are allocated on the basis of direct salary expenses.
• Travel, conference, and meeting expenses that are charged directly to the activity that incurred the expense.
• Occupancy expenses that are allocated on a space-utilized basis.
• Other indirect expenses that are allocated on the basis of direct salary expenses or total direct expenses.

Part IX-B—Summary of Program-Related Investments

Program-related investment. Section 4944(c) and corresponding regulations define a program-related investment as one that is made primarily to accomplish a charitable purpose of the foundation and no substantial purpose of which is to produce investment income or a capital gain from the sale of the investment. Examples of program-related investments include educational loans to individuals and low-interest loans to other section 501(c)(3) organizations.

General instructions. Include only those investments that were reported in Part XII, line 1b, for the current year. **Do not** include any investments made in any prior year even if they were still held by the foundation at the end of 2001.

Investments consisting of loans to individuals (such as educational loans) are not required to be listed separately but may be grouped with other program-related investments of the same type. Loans to other section 501(c)(3) organizations and all other types of program-related investments must be listed separately on lines 1 through 3 or on an attachment.

Lines 1 and 2. List the two largest program-related investments made by the foundation in 2001, whether or not the investments were still held by the foundation at the end of the year.

Line 3. Combine all other program-related investments and enter the total on the line 3 Amount column. List the individual investments or groups of investments included (attach a schedule if necessary).

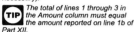 *The total of lines 1 through 3 in the Amount column must equal the amount reported on line 1b of Part XII.*

Part X—Minimum Investment Return

Who must complete this section? All domestic foundations must complete Part X.

Foreign foundations that checked box D2 on page 1 **do not** have to complete Part X unless claiming status as a private operating foundation.

Private operating foundations, described in sections 4942(j)(3) or 4942(j)(5), must complete Part X in order to complete Part XIV.

Overview. A private foundation that is not a private operating foundation must pay out, as qualifying distributions, its minimum investment return. This is generally 5% of the total fair market value of its noncharitable assets, subject to further adjustments as explained in the instructions for Part XI. The amount of this minimum investment return is figured in Part X and is used in Part XI to figure the amount that is required to be paid out (the distributable amount).

Minimum investment return. In figuring the minimum investment return, include only those assets that are not actually used or held for use by the organization for a charitable, educational, or other similar function that contributed to the charitable status of the foundation. Cash on hand and on deposit is considered used or held for use for charitable purposes **only** to the extent of the reasonable cash balances reported in Part X, line 4. See the instructions for lines 1b and 4 below.

Assets that are held for the production of income or for investment are not considered to be used directly for charitable functions even though the income from the assets is used for the charitable functions. It is a factual question whether an asset is held for the production of income or for investment

rather than used or held for use directly by the foundation for charitable purposes.

For example, an office building that is used to provide offices for employees engaged in managing endowment funds for the foundation is not considered an asset used for charitable purposes.

Dual-use property. When property is used both for charitable and other purposes, the property is considered used entirely for charitable purposes if 95% or more of its total use is for that purpose. If less than 95% of its total use is for charitable purposes, a reasonable allocation must be made between charitable and noncharitable use.

Excluded property. Certain assets are excluded entirely from the computation of the minimum investment return. These include pledges of grants and contributions to be received in the future and future interests in estates and trusts. See Pub. 578, chapter VII, for more details.

Line 1a—Average monthly fair market value of securities. If market quotations are readily available, a foundation may use any reasonable method to determine the average monthly fair market value of securities such as common and preferred stock, bonds, and mutual fund shares, as long as that method is consistently used. For example, a value for a particular month might be determined by the closing price on the first or last trading days of the month or an average of the closing prices on the first and last trading days of the month. Market quotations are considered readily available if a security is **any** of the following:

• Listed on the New York or American stock exchange or any city or regional exchange in which quotations appear on a daily basis, including foreign securities listed on a recognized foreign national or regional exchange.

• Regularly traded in the national or regional over-the-counter market for which published quotations are available.

• Locally traded, for which quotations can be readily obtained from established brokerage firms.

If securities are held in trust for, or on behalf of, a foundation by a bank or other financial institution that values those securities periodically using a computer pricing system, a foundation may use that system to determine the value of the securities. The system must be acceptable to the IRS for Federal estate tax purposes.

The foundation may reduce the fair market value of securities only to the extent that it can establish that the securities could only be liquidated in a reasonable period of time at a price less than the fair market value because of:
• The size of the block of the securities;
• The fact that the securities held are securities in a closely held corporation; or
• The fact that the sale of the securities would result in a forced or distress sale.

Any reduction in value allowed under these provisions may not be more than 10% of the fair market value (determined without regard to any reduction in value).

Also, see Regulations sections 53.4942(a)-2(c)(4)(i)(b), (c), and (iv)(a).

Line 1b—Average of monthly cash balances. Compute cash balances on a monthly basis by averaging the amount of cash on hand on the first and last days of each month. Include all cash balances and amounts that may be used for charitable purposes (see line 4 on page 23) or set aside and taken as a qualifying distribution (see Part XII).

Line 1c—Fair market value of all other assets. The fair market value of assets other than securities is determined annually except as described below. The valuation may be made by private foundation employees or by any other person even if that person is a disqualified person. If the IRS accepts the valuation, it is valid only for the tax year for which it is made. A new valuation is required for the next tax year.

5-year valuation. A written, certified, and independent appraisal of the fair market value of any real estate, including any improvements, may be determined on a 5-year basis by a **qualified person.**

The **qualified person** may not be a disqualified person (see General Instruction C) with respect to the private foundation or an employee of the foundation.

Commonly accepted valuation methods must be used in making the appraisal. A valuation based on acceptable methods of valuing property for Federal estate tax purposes will be considered acceptable.

The appraisal must include a closing statement that, in the appraiser's opinion, the appraised assets were valued according to valuation principles regularly employed in making appraisals of such property, using all reasonable valuation methods. The foundation must keep a copy of the independent appraisal for its records. If a valuation is reasonable, the foundation may use it for the tax year for which the valuation is made and for each of the 4 following tax years.

Any **valuation of real estate** by a certified independent appraisal may be replaced during the 5-year period by a subsequent 5-year certified independent appraisal or by an annual valuation as described above. The most recent valuation should be used to compute the foundation's minimum investment return.

If the valuation is made according to the above rules, the IRS will continue to accept it during the 5-year period for which it applies even if the actual fair market value of the property changes during the period.

Valuation date. An asset required to be valued annually may be valued as of any day in the private foundation's tax year, provided the foundation values the asset as of that date in all tax years. However, a valuation of real estate determined on a 5-year basis by a certified, independent appraisal may be made as of any day in the first tax year of the foundation to which the valuation applies.

Assets held for less than a tax year. To determine the value of an asset held less than 1 tax year, divide the number of days the foundation held the asset by the number of days in the tax year. Multiply the result by the fair market value of the asset.

Line 1e—Reduction claimed for blockage or other factors. If the fair market value of any securities, real estate holdings, or other assets reported on lines 1a and 1c reflects a blockage discount, marketability discount, or other reduction from full fair market value because of the size of the asset holding or any other factor, enter on line 1e the aggregate amount of the discounts claimed. Attach an explanation that includes the following information for each asset or group of assets involved:

   1. A description of the asset or asset group (e.g., 20,000 shares of XYZ, Inc., common stock);

   2. For securities, the percentage of the total issued and outstanding securities of the same class that is represented by the foundation's holding;

   3. The fair market value of the asset or asset group before any claimed blockage discount or other reduction;

   4. The amount of the discount claimed; and

   5. A statement that explains why the claimed discount is appropriate in valuing the asset or group of assets for section 4942 purposes.

In the case of securities, there are certain limitations on the size of the reduction in value that can be claimed. See the instructions for Part X, line 1a.

Line 2—Acquisition indebtedness. Enter the total acquisition indebtedness that applies to assets included on line 1. For details, see section 514(c)(1).

Line 4—Cash deemed held for charitable activities. Foundations may exclude from the assets used in the minimum investment return computation the reasonable cash balances necessary to cover current administrative expenses and other normal and current disbursements directly connected with the charitable, educational, or other similar activities. The amount of cash that may be excluded is generally 1½% of the fair market value of all assets (minus any acquisition indebtedness) as computed in Part X, line 3. However, if under the facts and circumstances an amount larger than the deemed amount is necessary to pay expenses and disbursements, then you may enter the larger amount instead of 1½% of the fair market value on line 4. If

you use a larger amount, attach an explanation.

Line 6—Short tax periods. If the foundation's tax period is less than 12 months, determine the applicable percentage by dividing the number of days in the short tax period by 365 (or 366 in a leap year). Multiply the result by 5%. Then multiply the modified percentage by the amount on line 5 and enter the result on line 6.

Part XI—Distributable Amount

If the organization is claiming status as a private operating foundation described in section 4942(j)(3) or (j)(5) or if it is a foreign foundation that checked box D2 on page 1, check the box in the heading for Part XI. You do not need to complete this part. See the Part XIV instructions for more details on private operating foundations.

Section 4942(j)(5) organizations are classified as private operating foundations for purposes of section 4942 only if they meet the requirements of Regulations section 53.4942(b)-1(a)(2).

The distributable amount for 2001 is the amount that the foundation must distribute by the end of 2002 as qualifying distributions to avoid the 15% tax on the undistributed portion.

Line 4a. Enter the total of recoveries of amounts treated as qualifying distributions for any year under section 4942(g). Include recoveries of part or all (as applicable) of grants previously made; proceeds from the sale or other disposition of property whose cost was treated as a qualifying distribution when the property was acquired; and any amount set aside under section 4942(g) to the extent it is determined that this amount is not necessary for the purposes of the set-aside.

Line 4b—Income distributions from section 4947(a)(2) trusts. The income portion of distributions from split-interest trusts on amounts placed in trust after May 26, 1969, must be **added** to the distributable amount, subject to the limitation of Regulations section 53.4942(a)-2(b)(2)(iii).

A "split-interest trust" is defined in section 4947(a)(2) as a trust that is not exempt from tax under section 501(a), not all of the unexpired interests of which are devoted to charitable, religious, educational, and like purposes, and that has amounts in trust for which a charitable contributions deduction has been allowed.

If the foundation receives distributions that include amounts placed in trust before May 27, 1969, and amounts placed in trust after May 26, 1969, these distributions must be allocated between those amounts to determine the extent to which the distributions are included in the foundation's distributable amount.

Line 6—Deduction from distributable amount. If the foundation was organized before May 27, 1969, and its governing instrument or any other instrument continues to require the accumulation of income after a judicial proceeding to reform the instrument has terminated, then the amount of the income required to be accumulated must be **subtracted** from the distributable amount beginning with the first tax year after the tax year in which the judicial proceeding was terminated. (See the instructions for Part VII-A, line 6.)

Part XII—Qualifying Distributions

"Qualifying distributions" are amounts spent or set aside for religious, educational, or similar charitable purposes. The total amount of qualifying distributions for any year is used to reduce the distributable amount for specified years to arrive at the undistributed income (if any) for those years.

Line 1a—Expenses, contributions, gifts, etc. Enter the amount from Part I, column (d), line 26. However, if the **borrowed funds** election applies, add the total of the repayments during the year to the amount from Part I, column (d), line 26, and enter it on line 1a.

Borrowed funds. If the foundation borrowed money in a tax year beginning before January 1, 1970, or later borrows money under a written commitment binding on December 31, 1969, the foundation may elect to treat any repayments of the loan principal after December 31, 1969, as qualifying distributions at the time of repayment, rather than at the earlier time that the borrowed funds were actually distributed, only if:

   1. The money is used to make expenditures for a charitable or similar purpose **and**

   2. Repayment on the loan did not start until a year beginning after 1969.

On these loans, deduct any interest payment from gross income to compute adjusted net income in the year paid.

Election. To make this election, attach a statement to Form 990-PF for the first tax year beginning after 1969 in which a repayment of loan principal is made and for each tax year after that in which any repayment of loan principal is made. The statement should show:
• The lender's name and address.
• The amount borrowed.
• The specific use of the borrowed funds.
• The private foundation's election to treat repayments of loan principal as qualifying distributions.

Line 1b—Program-related investments. Enter the total of the "Amount" column from Part IX-B. See the Part IX-B instructions for the definition of program-related investments.

Line 3—Amounts set aside. Amounts set aside may be treated as qualifying distributions only if the private foundation establishes to the satisfaction of the IRS that the amount will be paid for the specific project within 60 months from the date of the first set-aside and meets **1** or **2** below.

   1. The project can be better accomplished by a set-aside than by the immediate payment of funds (suitability test) **or**

   2. The private foundation meets the requirements of section 4942(g)(2)(B)(ii) (cash distribution test).

Set-aside under item 1. For any set-aside under **1** above, the private foundation must apply for IRS approval by the end of the tax year in which the amount is set aside. Send the **application for approval** to the Internal Revenue Service, P.O. Box 27720, McPherson Station, Washington, DC 20038.

   The application for approval must give **all** of the following information:
- The nature and purposes of the specific project and the amount of the set-aside for which approval is requested;
- The amounts and approximate dates of any planned additions to the set-aside after its initial establishment;
- The reasons why the project can be better accomplished by the set-aside than by the immediate payment of funds;
- A detailed description of the project, including estimated costs, sources of any future funds expected to be used for completion of the project, and the location(s) (general or specific) of any physical facilities to be acquired or constructed as part of the project; and
- A statement of an appropriate foundation manager that the amounts set aside will actually be paid for the specific project within a specified period of time ending within 60 months after the date of the first set-aside; or a statement explaining why the period for paying the amount set aside should be extended and indicating the extension of time requested. (Include in this statement the reason why the proposed project could not be divided into two or more projects covering periods of no more than 60 months each.)

Set-aside under item 2. For any set-aside under **2** above, the private foundation must attach a schedule to its annual information return showing how the requirements are met. A schedule is required for the year of the set-aside and for each subsequent year until the set-aside amount has been distributed. See Regulations section 53.4942(a)-3(b)(7)(ii) for specific requirements.

Line 5—Reduced tax on investment income under section 4940(e). If the organization does not qualify for the 1% tax under section 4940(e), enter zero. See Parts V and VI of the instructions.

Part XIII—Undistributed Income

If you checked box D2 on page 1, **do not** fill in this part.

   If the organization is a private operating foundation for any of the years shown in Part XIII, do not complete the portions of Part XIII that apply to those years. If there are excess qualifying distributions for any tax year, do not carry them over to a year in which the organization is a private operating foundation or to any later year. For example, if a foundation made excess qualifying distributions in 1999 and became a private operating foundation in 2001, the excess qualifying distributions from 1999 could be applied against the distributable amount for 2000 but not to any year after 2000.

   The purpose of this part is to enable the foundation to comply with the rules for applying its qualifying distributions for the year 2001. In applying the qualifying distributions, there are three basic steps.

   1. Reduce any undistributed income for 2000 (but not below zero).

   2. The organization may use any part or all remaining qualifying distributions for 2001 to satisfy elections. For example, if undistributed income remained for any year before 2000, it could be reduced to zero or, if the foundation wished, the distributions could be treated as distributions out of corpus.

   3. If no elections are involved, apply remaining qualifying distributions to the 2001 distributable amount on line 4d. If the remaining qualifying distributions are greater than the 2001 distributable amount, the excess is treated as a distribution out of corpus on line 4e.

   If for any reason the 2001 qualifying distributions do not reduce any 2000 undistributed income to zero, the amount not distributed is subject to a 15% tax. If the 2000 income remains undistributed at the end of 2002, it could be subject again to the 15% tax. Also, see section 4942(b) for the circumstances under which a second-tier tax could be imposed.

Line 1—Distributable amount. Enter the distributable amount for 2001 from Part XI, line 7.

Line 2—Undistributed income. Enter the distributable amount for 2000 and amounts for earlier years that remained undistributed at the beginning of the 2001 tax year.

Line 2b. Enter the amount of undistributed income for years before 2000.

Line 3—Excess distributions carryover to 2001. If the foundation has made excess distributions out of corpus in prior years, which have not been applied in any year, enter the amount for each year. Do not enter an amount for a particular year if the organization was a

private operating foundation for any later year.

Lines 3a through 3e. Enter the amount of any excess distribution made on the line for each year listed. Do not include any amount that was applied against the distributable amount of an earlier year or that was already used to meet pass-through distribution requirements. (See the instructions for line 7.)

Line 3f. This amount can be applied in 2001.

Line 4—Qualifying distributions. Enter the total amount of qualifying distributions made in 2001 from Part XII, line 4. The total of the amounts applied on lines 4a through 4e is equal to the qualifying distributions made in 2001.

Line 4a. The qualifying distributions for 2001 are first used to reduce any undistributed income remaining from 2000. Enter only enough of the 2001 qualifying distributions to reduce the 2000 undistributed income to zero.

Lines 4b and 4c. If there are any 2001 qualifying distributions remaining after reducing the 2000 undistributed income to zero, one or more **elections** can be made under Regulations section 53.4942(a)-3(d)(2) to apply all or part of the remaining qualifying distributions to any undistributed income remaining from years before 2000 or to apply to corpus.

   Elections. To make these elections, the organization must file a statement with the IRS or attach a statement, as described in the above regulations section, to Form 990-PF. An election made by filing a separate statement with the IRS must be made within the year for which the election is made. Otherwise, attach a statement to the Form 990-PF filed for the year the election was made.

   Where to enter. If the organization elected to apply all or part of the remaining amount to the undistributed income remaining from years before 2000, enter the amount on line 4b.

   If the organization elected to treat those qualifying distributions as a distribution out of corpus, enter the amount on line 4c.

   Entering an amount on line 4b or 4c without submitting the required statement is **not** considered a valid election.

Line 4d. Treat as a distribution of the distributable amount for 2001 any qualifying distributions for 2001 that remain after reducing the 2000 undistributed income to zero and after electing to treat any part of the remaining distributions as a distribution out of corpus or as a distribution of a prior year's undistributed income. Enter only enough of the remaining 2001 qualifying distributions to reduce the 2001 distributable amount to zero.

Line 4e. Any 2001 qualifying distributions remaining after reducing the 2001 distributable amount to zero should be treated as an excess distribution out of corpus. This amount may be carried over and applied to later years.

Line 5—Excess qualifying distributions carryover applied to 2001. Enter any excess qualifying distributions from line 3, which were applied to 2001, in both the Corpus column and the 2001 column. Apply the oldest excess qualifying distributions first. Thus, the organization will apply any excess qualifying distributions carried forward from 1996 before those from later years.

Line 6a. Add lines 3f, 4c, and 4e. Subtract line 5 from the total. Enter the net total in the Corpus column.

Line 6c. Enter only the undistributed income from 1999 and prior years for which either a notice of deficiency under section 6212(a) has been mailed for the section 4942(a) first-tier tax, or on which the first-tier tax has been assessed because the organization filed a Form 4720 for a tax year that began before 2000.

Lines 6d and 6e. These amounts are taxable under the provisions of section 4942(a), except for any part that is due solely to misvaluation of assets to which the provisions of section 4942(a)(2) are being applied (see Part VII-B, line 2b). Report the taxable amount on Form 4720. If the exception applies, attach an explanation.

Line 6f. In the 2001 column, enter the amount by which line 1 is more than the total of lines 4d and 5. This is the undistributed income for 2001. The organization must distribute the amount shown by the end of its 2002 tax year so that it will not be liable for the tax on undistributed income.

Line 7—Distributions out of corpus for 2001 pass-through distributions.

1. If the foundation is the donee and receives a contribution from another private foundation, the donor foundation may treat the contribution as a qualifying distribution only if the donee foundation makes a distribution equal to the full amount of the contribution and the distribution is a qualifying distribution that is treated as a distribution of corpus. The donee foundation must, no later than the close of the first tax year after the tax year in which it receives the contributions, distribute an amount equal in value to the contributions received in the prior tax year and have no remaining undistributed income for the prior year. For example, if private foundation X received $1,000 in tax year 2000 from foundation Y, foundation X would have to distribute the $1,000 as a qualifying distribution out of corpus by the end of 2001 and have no remaining undistributed income for 2000.

2. If a private foundation receives a contribution from an individual or a corporation and the individual is seeking the 50% contribution base limit on deductions for the tax year (or the individual or corporation is not applying the limit imposed on deductions for contributions to the foundation of capital gain property), the foundation must comply with certain distribution requirements.

By the 15th day of the 3rd month after the end of the tax year in which the foundation received the contributions, the donee foundation must distribute as qualifying distributions out of corpus:

a. An amount equal to 100% of **all** contributions received during the year in order for the individual contributor to receive the benefit of the 50% limit on deductions and

b. Distribute **all** contributions of property only so that the individual or corporation making the contribution is not subject to the section 170(e)(1)(B)(ii) limitations.

If the organization is applying excess distributions from prior years (i.e., any part of the amount in Part XIII, line 3f) to satisfy the distribution requirements of section 170(b)(1)(E) or 4942(g)(3), it must make the election under Regulations section 53.4942(a)-3(c)(2). Also, see Regulations section 1.170A-9(g)(2).

Enter on line 7 the total distributions out of corpus made to satisfy the restrictions on amounts received from donors described above.

Line 8—Outdated excess distributions carryover. Because of the 5-year carryover limitation under section 4942(i)(2), the organization must reduce any excess distributions carryover by any amounts from 1996 that were not applied in 2001.

Line 9—Excess distributions carryover to 2002. Enter the amount by which line 6a is more than the total of lines 7 and 8. This is the amount the organization may apply to 2002 and following years. Line 9 can never be less than zero.

Line 10—Analysis of line 9. In the space provided for each year, enter the amount of excess distributions carryover from that year that has not been applied as of the end of the 2001 tax year. If there is an amount on the line for 1997, it must be applied by the end of the 2002 tax year since the 5-year carryover period for 1997 ends in 2002.

Part XIV—Private Operating Foundations

All organizations that claim status as private operating foundations under section 4942(j)(3) or (5) for 2001 must complete Part XIV.

Certain elderly care facilities (section 4942(j)(5)). For purposes of section 4942 only, certain elderly care facilities may be classified as private operating foundations. To be so classified, they must be operated and maintained for the principal purpose explained in section 4942(j)(5) and also meet the **endowment test** described below.

If the foundation is a section 4942(j)(5) organization, complete only lines 1a, 1b, 2c, 2d, 2e, and 3b. Enter "N/A" on all other lines in the Total column for Part XIV.

Private operating foundation (section 4942(j)(3)). The term "private operating foundation" means any private foundation that spends at least 85% of the smaller of its adjusted net income or its minimum investment return directly for the active conduct of the exempt purpose or functions for which the foundation is organized and operated (the **Income Test**) and that also meets one of the three tests below.

1. Assets test. 65% or more of the foundation's assets are devoted directly to those activities or functionally related businesses, or both. Or 65% or more of the foundation's assets are stock of a corporation that is controlled by the foundation, and substantially all of the assets of the corporation are devoted to those activities or functionally related businesses.

2. Endowment test. The foundation normally makes qualifying distributions directly for the active conduct of the exempt purpose or functions for which it is organized and operated in an amount that is two-thirds or more of its minimum investment return.

3. Support test. The foundation normally receives 85% or more of its support (other than gross investment income as defined in section 509(e)) from the public and from five or more exempt organizations that are not described in section 4946(a)(1)(H) with respect to each other or the recipient foundation. Not more than 25% of the support (other than gross investment income) normally may be received from any one of the exempt organizations and not more than one-half of the support normally may be received from gross investment income.

See regulations under section 4942 for the meaning of "directly for the active conduct" of exempt activities for purposes of these tests.

Complying with these tests. A foundation may meet the **income test** and either the **assets, endowment,** or **support test** by satisfying the tests for any 3 years during a 4-year period consisting of the tax year in question and the 3 immediately preceding tax years. It may also meet the tests based on the total of all related amounts of income or assets held, received, or distributed during that 4-year period. A foundation may not use one method for satisfying the income test and another for satisfying one of the three alternative tests. Thus, if a foundation meets the income test on the 3-out-of-4-year basis for a particular tax year, it may not use the 4-year aggregation method for meeting one of the three alternative tests for that same year.

In completing line 3c(3) of Part XIV under the aggregation method, the largest amount of support from an exempt organization will be based on the total amount received for the 4-year period from any one exempt organization.

A new private foundation must use the aggregation method to satisfy the tests for its first tax year in order to be treated as a private operating foundation from the beginning of that year. It must continue to use the aggregation method for its 2nd and 3rd tax years to maintain its status for those years.

Part XV—Supplementary Information

● Complete this part only if the foundation had assets of $5,000 or more at any time during the year.
● This part does not apply to a foreign foundation that during its entire period of existence received substantially all (85% or more) of its support (other than gross investment income) from sources outside the United States.

Line 2. In the space provided (or in an attachment, if necessary), furnish the required information about the organization's grant, scholarship, fellowship, loan, etc., programs. In addition to restrictions or limitations on awards by geographical areas, charitable fields, and kinds of recipients, indicate any specific dollar limitations or other restrictions applicable to each type of award the organization makes. This information benefits the grant seeker and the foundation. The grant seekers will be aware of the grant eligibility requirements and the foundation should receive only applications that adhere to these grant application requirements.

If the foundation only makes contributions to preselected charitable organizations and does not accept unsolicited applications for funds, check the box on line 2.

Line 3. If necessary, attach a schedule for lines 3a and 3b that lists separately amounts given to individuals and amounts given to organizations.

Purpose of grant or contribution. Entries under this column should reflect the grant's or contribution's purpose and should be in greater detail than merely classifying them as charitable, educational, religious, or scientific activities.

For example, use an identification such as:
● Payments for nursing service,
● For fellowships, or
● For assistance to indigent families.

⚠ *Entries such as "grant" or "contribution" under the column* CAUTION *titled Purpose of grant or contribution are unacceptable. See*

Completed Example of Form 990-PF found in Package 990-PF, Returns for Private Foundations, for additional examples that describe the purpose of a grant or contribution.

Line 3a—Paid during year. List all contributions, grants, etc., actually paid during the year, including grants or contributions that are not qualifying distributions under section 4942(g). Include current year payments of set-asides treated as qualifying distributions in the current tax year or any prior year.

Line 3b—Approved for future payment. List all contributions, grants, etc., approved during the year but not paid by the end of the year, including the unpaid portion of any current year set-aside.

Part XVI-A—Analysis of Income-Producing Activities

In Part XVI-A, analyze revenue items that are also entered in Part I, column (a), lines 3–11, and on line 5b. Contributions reported on lines 1 and 2 of Part I are not entered in Part XVI-A. For information on unrelated business income, see the Instructions for Form 990-T and Pub. 598.

Columns (a) and (c). In column (a), enter a 6-digit business code, from the list in the Instructions for Form 990-T, to identify any income reported in column (b). In column (c), enter an exclusion code, from the list on page 29, to identify any income reported in column (d). If more than one exclusion code is applicable to a particular revenue item, select the lowest numbered exclusion code that applies. Also, if nontaxable revenues from several sources are reportable on the same line in column (d), use the exclusion code that applies to the largest revenue source.

Columns (b), (d), and (e). For amounts reported in Part XVI-A on lines 1–11, enter in column (b) any income earned that is unrelated business income (see section 512). In column (d), enter any income earned that is excluded from the computation of unrelated business taxable income by Code section 512, 513, or 514. In column (e), enter any related or exempt function income; that is, any income earned that is related to the organization's purpose or function which constitutes the basis for the organization's exemption.

Also enter in column (e) any income specifically excluded from gross income other than by Code section 512, 513, or

514, such as interest on state and local bonds that is excluded from tax by section 103. You must explain in Part XVI-B any amount shown in column (e).

Comparing Part XVI-A with Part I. The sum of the amounts entered on each line of lines 1–11 of columns (b), (d), and (e) of Part XVI-A should equal corresponding amounts entered in Part I, lines 3–11 of Part I, column (a), and on line 5b as shown below:

Amounts in Part XVI-A on line . . .	Correspond to Amounts in Part I, column (a), line . . .
1a–g	11
2	11
3	3
4	4
5 and 6	5b (description column)
7	11
8	6
9	11 minus any special event expenses included on lines 13 through 23 of Part I, column (a)
10	10c
11a–e	11

Line 1—Program service revenue. On lines 1a–g, list each revenue-producing program service activity of the organization. For each program service activity listed, enter the gross revenue earned for each activity, as well as identifying business and exclusion codes, in the appropriate columns. For line 1g, enter amounts that are payments for services rendered to governmental units. **Do not** include governmental grants that are reportable on line 1 of Part I. Report the total of lines 1a–g on line 11 of Part I, along with any other income reportable on line 11.

Program services are mainly those activities that the reporting organization was created to conduct and that, along with any activities begun later, form the basis of the organization's current exemption from tax.

Program services can also include the organization's unrelated trade or business activities. Program service revenue also includes income from program-related investments (such as interest earned on scholarship loans) as defined in the instructions for Part IX-B.

Line 11. On lines 11a–e, list each "Other revenue" activity not reported on lines 1 through 10. Report the sum of the amounts entered for lines 11a–e, columns (b), (d), and (e), on line 11, Part I.

Line 13. On line 13, enter the total of columns (b), (d), and (e) of line 12.

You may use the following worksheet to verify your calculations.

Line 13,	Part XVI-A	_____
Minus:	Line 5b, Part I	_____
	Note: *If line 5b, Part I, reflects a loss, add that amount here instead of subtracting.*	
Plus:	Line 1, Part I	_____
Plus:	Line 5a, Part I	_____
Plus:	Expenses of special events deducted in computing line 9 of Part XVI-A	_____
Equal:	Line 12, column (a), of Part I	_____

Part XVI-B—Relationship of Activities to the Accomplishment of Exempt Purposes

To explain how each amount in column (e) of Part XVI-A was related or exempt function income, show the line number of the amount in column (e) and give a brief description of how each activity reported in column (e) contributed importantly to the accomplishment of the organization's exempt purposes (other than by providing funds for such purposes). Activities that generate exempt-function income are activities that form the basis of the organization's exemption from tax.

Also, explain any income entered in column (e) that is specifically excluded from gross income other than by Code section 512, 513, or 514. If no amount is entered in column (e), do not complete Part XVI-B.

Example. M, a performing arts association, is primarily supported by endowment funds. It raises revenue by charging admissions to its performances. These performances are the primary means by which the organization accomplishes its cultural and educational purposes.

M reported admissions income in column (e) of Part XVI-A and explained in Part XVI-B that these performances are the primary means by which it accomplishes its cultural and educational purposes.

Because M also reported interest from state bonds in column (e) of Part XVI-A, M explained in Part XVI-B that such interest was excluded from gross income by Code section 103.

Part XVII—Information Regarding Transfers To and Transactions and Relationships With

Noncharitable Exempt Organizations

Part XVII is used to report direct and indirect transfers to (line 1a) and direct and indirect transactions with (line 1b) and relationships with (line 2) any other noncharitable exempt organization. A "noncharitable exempt organization" is an organization exempt under section 501(c) (that is not exempt under section 501(c)(3)), or a political organization described in section 527.

For purposes of these instructions, the section 501(c)(3) organization completing Part XVII is referred to as the "reporting organization."

A noncharitable exempt organization is "related to or affiliated with" the reporting organization if either:

   1. The two organizations share some element of common control **or**
   2. A historic and continuing relationship exists between the two organizations.

A noncharitable exempt organization is unrelated to the reporting organization if:

   1. The two organizations share no element of common control **and**
   2. A historic and continuing relationship does not exist between the two organizations.

An "element of common control" is present when one or more of the officers, directors, or trustees of one organization are elected or appointed by the officers, directors, trustees, or members of the other. An element of common control is also present when more than 25% of the officers, directors, or trustees of one organization serve as officers, directors, or trustees of the other organization.

A "historic and continuing relationship" exists when two organizations participate in a joint effort to achieve one or more common purposes on a continuous or recurring basis rather than on the basis of one or more isolated transactions or activities. Such a relationship also exists when two organizations share facilities, equipment, or paid personnel during the year, regardless of the length of time the arrangement is in effect.

Line 1—Reporting of certain transfers and transactions. Generally, report on line 1 any transfer to or transaction with a noncharitable exempt organization even if the transfer or transaction constitutes the only connection with the noncharitable exempt organization.

   Related organizations. If the noncharitable exempt organization is related to or affiliated with the reporting organization, report all direct and indirect transfers and transactions except for contributions and grants it received.

   Unrelated organizations. All transfers to an unrelated noncharitable exempt organization must be reported on line 1a. All transactions between the

reporting organization and an unrelated noncharitable exempt organization must be shown on line 1b unless they meet the exception in the specific instructions for line 1b.

Line 1a—Transfers. Answer "Yes" to lines 1a(1) and 1a(2) if the reporting organization made any direct or indirect transfers of any value to a noncharitable exempt organization.

A "transfer" is any transaction or arrangement whereby one organization transfers something of value (cash, other assets, services, use of property, etc.) to another organization without receiving something of more than nominal value in return. Contributions, gifts, and grants are examples of transfers.

If the only transfers between the two organizations were contributions and grants made by the noncharitable exempt organization to the reporting organization, answer "No."

Line 1b—Other transactions. Answer "Yes" for any transaction described on line 1b(1)–(6), regardless of its amount, if it is with a related or affiliated organization.

   Unrelated organizations. Answer "Yes" for any transaction between the reporting organization and an unrelated noncharitable exempt organization, regardless of its amount, if the reporting organization received less than adequate consideration. There is adequate consideration when the fair market value of the goods and other assets or services furnished by the reporting organization is not more than the fair market value of the goods and other assets or services received from the unrelated noncharitable exempt organization. The exception described below does not apply to transactions for less than adequate consideration.

Answer "Yes" for any transaction between the reporting organization and an unrelated noncharitable exempt organization if the "amount involved" is more than $500. The "amount involved" is the fair market value of the goods, services, or other assets furnished by the reporting organization.

   Exception. If a transaction with an unrelated noncharitable exempt organization was for adequate consideration and the amount involved was $500 or less, answer "No" for that transaction.

Line 1b(3). Answer "Yes" for transactions in which the reporting organization was either the lessor or the lessee.

Line 1b(4). Answer "Yes" if either organization reimbursed expenses incurred by the other.

Line 1b(5). Answer "Yes" if either organization made loans to the other or if the reporting organization guaranteed the other's loans.

Line 1b(6). Answer "Yes" if either organization performed services or membership or fundraising solicitations for the other.

Line 1c. Complete line 1c regardless of whether the noncharitable exempt organization is related to or closely affiliated with the reporting organization. For purposes of this line, "facilities" includes office space and any other land, building, or structure whether owned or leased by, or provided free of charge to, the reporting organization or the noncharitable exempt organization.

Line 1d. Use this schedule to describe the transfers and transactions for which "Yes" was entered on lines 1a–c above. You must describe each transfer or transaction for which the answer was "Yes." You may combine all of the cash transfers (line 1a(1)) to each organization into a single entry. Otherwise, make a separate entry for each transfer or transaction.

Column (a). For each entry, enter the line number from line 1a–c. For example, if the answer was "Yes" to line 1b(3), enter "b(3)" in column (a).

Column (d). If you need more space, write "see attached" in column (d) and use an attached sheet for the description. If making more than one entry on line 1d, specify on the attached sheet which transfer or transaction you are describing.

Line 2—Reporting of certain relationships. Enter on line 2 each noncharitable exempt organization that the reporting organization is related to or affiliated with, as defined above. If the control factor or the historic and continuing relationship factor (or both) is present at any time during the year, identify the organization on line 2 even if neither factor is present at the end of the year.

Do not enter unrelated noncharitable exempt organizations on line 2 even if transfers to or transactions with those organizations were entered on line 1. For example, if a one-time transfer to an unrelated noncharitable exempt organization was entered on line 1a(2), do not enter the organization on line 2.

Column (b). Enter the exempt category of the organization; for example, "501(c)(4)."

Column (c). In most cases, a simple description, such as "common directors" or "auxiliary of reporting organization" will be sufficient. If you need more space, write "see attached" in column (c) and use an attached sheet to describe the relationship. If you are entering more than one organization on line 2, identify which organization you are describing on the attached sheet.

Signature

The return must be signed by the president, vice president, treasurer, assistant treasurer, chief accounting officer, or other corporate officer (such as tax officer) who is authorized to sign. A receiver, trustee, or assignee must sign any return that he or she is required to file for a corporation. If the return is filed for a trust, it must be signed by the authorized trustee or trustees. Sign and date the form and fill in the signer's title.

If an officer or employee of the organization prepares the return, the Paid Preparer's space should remain blank. If someone prepares the return without charge, that person should not sign the return.

Generally, anyone who is paid to prepare the organization's tax return must sign the return and fill in the Paid Preparer's Use Only area.

If you have questions about whether a preparer is required to sign the return, please contact an IRS office.

The paid preparer must complete the required preparer information and:
• Sign it, by hand, in the space provided for the preparer's signature. (Signature stamps and labels are not acceptable.)
• Give the organization a copy of the return in addition to the copy to be filed with the IRS.

If the box for question 13 of Part VII-A is checked (section 4947(a)(1) nonexempt charitable trust filing Form 990-PF instead of Form 1041), the paid preparer must also enter his or her social security number or, if applicable, employer identification number in the spaces provided. Otherwise, **do not** enter the preparer's social security or employer identification number.

Paperwork Reduction Act Notice
We ask for the information on this form to carry out the Internal Revenue laws of the United States. You are required to give us the information. We need it to ensure that you are complying with these laws and to allow us to figure and collect the right amount of tax.

You are not required to provide the information requested on a form that is subject to the Paperwork Reduction Act unless the form displays a valid OMB control number. Books or records relating to a form or its instructions must be retained as long as their contents may become material in the administration of any Internal Revenue law.

The time needed to complete and file this form will vary depending on individual circumstances. The estimated average time is:

Recordkeeping . . . . 141 hr., 20 min.

Learning about the law or the form . . . . 28 hr., 7 min.

Preparing the form . . . . . . 33 hr., 27 min.

Copying, assembling, and sending the form to the IRS 32 min.

If you have comments concerning the accuracy of these time estimates or suggestions for making this form simpler, we would be happy to hear from you. You can write to the Tax Forms Committee, Western Area Distribution Center, Rancho Cordova, CA 95743-0001. **Do not** send the tax form to this address. Instead, see **When and Where To File** on page 5.

Form 990-PF Instructions

Exclusion Codes

General Exceptions

01— Income from an activity that is not regularly carried on (section 512(a)(1))

02— Income from an activity in which labor is a material income-producing factor and substantially all (at least 85%) of the work is performed with unpaid labor (section 513(a)(1))

03— Section 501(c)(3) organization— Income from an activity carried on primarily for the convenience of the organization's members, students, patients, visitors, officers, or employees (hospital parking lot or museum cafeteria, for example) (section 513(a)(2))

04— Section 501(c)(4) local association of employees organized before May 27, 1969— Income from the sale of work-related clothes or equipment and items normally sold through vending machines; food dispensing facilities; or snack bars for the convenience of association members at their usual places of employment (section 513(a)(2))

05— Income from the sale of merchandise, substantially all of which (at least 85%) was donated to the organization (section 513(a)(3))

Specific Exceptions

06— Section 501(c)(3), (4), or (5) organization conducting an agricultural or educational fair or exposition— Qualified public entertainment activity income (section 513(d)(2))

07— Section 501(c)(3), (4), (5), or (6) organization—Qualified convention and trade show activity income (section 513(d)(3))

08— Income from hospital services described in section 513(e)

09— Income from noncommercial bingo games that do not violate state or local law (section 513(f))

10— Income from games of chance conducted by an organization in North Dakota (section 311 of the Deficit Reduction Act of 1984, as amended)

11— Section 501(c)(12) organization— Qualified pole rental income (section 513(g))

12— Income from the distribution of low-cost articles in connection with the solicitation of charitable contributions (section 513(h))

13— Income from the exchange or rental of membership or donor list with an organization eligible to receive charitable contributions by a section 501(c)(3) organization; by a war veterans' organization; or an auxiliary unit or society of, or trust or foundation for, a war veterans' post or organization (section 513(h))

Modifications and Exclusions

14— Dividends, interest, payments with respect to securities loans, annuities, income from notional principal contracts, other substantially similar income from ordinary and routine investments, and loan commitment fees, excluded by section 512(b)(1)

15— Royalty income excluded by section 512(b)(2)

16— Real property rental income that does not depend on the income or profits derived by the person leasing the property and is excluded by section 512 (b)(3)

17— Rent from personal property leased with real property and incidental (10% or less) in relation to the combined income from the real and personal property (section 512(b)(3))

18— Gain or loss from the sale of investments and other non-inventory property and from certain property acquired from financial institutions that are in conservatorship or receivership (sections 512(b)(5) and (16)(A))

19— Gain or loss from the lapse or termination of options to buy or sell securities or real property, and on options and from the forfeiture of good-faith deposits for the purchase, sale, or lease of investment real estate (section 512(b)(5))

20— Income from research for the United States; its agencies or instrumentalities; or any state or political subdivision (section 512(b)(7))

21— Income from research conducted by a college, university, or hospital (section 512(b)(8))

22— Income from research conducted by an organization whose primary activity is conducting fundamental research, the results of which are freely available to the general public (section 512(b)(9))

23— Income from services provided under license issued by a federal regulatory agency and conducted by a religious order or school operated by a religious order, but only if the trade or business has been carried on by the organization since before May 27, 1959 (section 512 (b)(15))

Foreign Organizations

24— Foreign organizations only—Income from a trade or business NOT conducted in the United States and NOT derived from United States sources (patrons) (section 512(a)(2))

Social Clubs and VEBAs

25— Section 501(c)(7), (9), or (17) organization—Non-exempt function income set aside for a charitable, etc., purpose specified in section 170(c)(4) (section 512(a)(3)(B)(i))

26— Section 501(c)(7), (9), or (17) organization—Proceeds from the sale of exempt function property that was or will be timely reinvested in similar property (section 512(a)(3)(D))

27— Section 501(c)(9) or (17) organization—Non-exempt function income set aside for the payment of life, sick, accident, or other benefits (section 512(a)(3)(B)(ii))

Veterans' Organizations

28— Section 501(c)(19) organization—Payments for life, sick, accident, or health insurance for members or their dependents that are set aside for the payment of such insurance benefits or for a charitable, etc., purpose specified in section 170(c)(4) (section 512(a)(4))

29— Section 501(c)(19) organization— Income from an insurance set-aside (see code 28 above) that is set aside for payment of insurance benefits or for a charitable, etc., purpose specified in section 170(c)(4) (Regs. 1.512(a)–4(b)(2))

Debt-Financed Income

30— Income exempt from debt-financed (section 514) provisions because at least 85% of the use of the property is for the organization's exempt purposes. (**Note:** *This code is only for income from the 15% or less non-exempt purpose use.*) (section 514(b)(1)(A))

31— Gross income from mortgaged property used in research activities described in section 512(b)(7), (8), or (9) (section 514(b)(1)(C))

32— Gross income from mortgaged property used in any activity described in section 513(a)(1), (2), or (3) (section 514(b)(1)(D))

33— Income from mortgaged property (neighborhood land) acquired for exempt purpose use within 10 years (section 514(b)(3))

34— Income from mortgaged property acquired by bequest or devise (applies to income received within 10 years from the date of acquisition) (section 514(c)(2)(B))

35— Income from mortgaged property acquired by gift where the mortgage was placed on the property more than 5 years previously and the property was held by the donor for more than 5 years (applies to income received within 10 years from the date of gift (section 514(c)(2)(B))

36— Income from property received in return for the obligation to pay an annuity described in section 514(c)(5)

37— Income from mortgaged property that provides housing to low and moderate income persons, to the extent the mortgage is insured by the Federal Housing Administration (section 514(c)(6)). (**Note:** *In many cases, this would be exempt function income reportable in column (e). It would not be so in the case of a section 501(c)(5) or (6) organization, for example, that acquired the housing as an investment or as a charitable activity.*)

38— Income from mortgaged real property owned by: a school described in section 170(b)(1)(A)(ii); a section 509(a)(3) affiliated support organization of such a school; a section 501(c)(25) organization; or by a partnership in which any of the above organizations owns an interest if the requirements of section 514(c)(9)(B)(vi) are met (section 514(c)(9))

Special Rules

39— Section 501(c)(5) organization—Farm income used to finance the operation and maintenance of a retirement home, hospital, or similar facility operated by the organization for its members on property adjacent to the farm land (section 1951(b)(8)(B) of Public Law 94-455)

40— Annual dues, not exceeding $116 (subject to inflation), paid to a section 501(c)(5) agricultural or horticultural organization (section 512(d))

Trade or Business

41— Gross income from an unrelated activity that is regularly carried on but, in light of continuous losses sustained over a number of tax periods, cannot be regarded as being conducted with the motive to make a profit (not a trade or business)

Code Secs. 4942, 4945

<<FULL TEXT>>

26 CFR 601.105: Examination of returns and claims for refund, credit, or abatement; determination of correct tax liability. (Also Part I, Sections 4942, 4945; 53.4942(a)-1, 53.4945-5, 53.4945-6.)

REV. PROC. 92-94

SECTION 1. PURPOSE

Private foundations generally want their grants to foreign grantees to be treated as qualifying distributions for purposes of section 4942 of the Internal Revenue Code rather than as taxable expenditures for purposes of section 4945 of the Code. This treatment is assured if the foreign grantee has a ruling or determination letter classifying it as a public charity within the meaning of section 509(a)(1), (2), or (3), or a private operating foundation under section 4942(j)(3) of the Code. If a foreign grantee does not have such a ruling or determination letter, the Foundation Excise Tax Regulations set forth requirements that must be satisfied in order to assure that the grant will be considered a qualifying distribution.

In response to requests from private foundations, this revenue procedure provides a simplified procedure that private foundations (including nonexempt charitable trusts) may follow in making "reasonable judgments" and "good faith determinations" under sections 53.4945-6(c)(2)(ii), 53.4942(a)-3(a)(6) and 53.4945-5(a)(5) of the Foundation Excise Tax Regulations. If the requirements of this revenue procedure are met, a grant to a foreign grantee will be treated as a grant to an organization that is described in section 501(c)(3) or section 4947(a)(1) of the Internal Revenue Code, and, that is either a public charity within the meaning of section 509(a)(1), (2), or (3), or a private operating foundation under section 4942(j)(3) of the Code.

SEC. 2. BACKGROUND

.01 Section 53.4945-6(c)(2)(ii) of the regulations applies to a private foundation (grantor) making a grant for certain purposes to a foreign organization (grantee) that does not have a ruling or determination letter recognizing it as an organization described in section 501(c)(3) of the Code. ("Certain purposes" are those described in section 170(c)(2)(B) except for any transfer of assets pursuant to any liquidation, merger, redemption, recapitalization, or other adjustment, organization, or reorganization described in section 507(b)(2).) The grantor may treat such a grant as a grant to an organization described in section 501(c)(3) (other than section 509(a)(4)) if, in the reasonable judgment of the foundation manager, the grantee is an organization described in section 501(c)(3) (other than section 509(a)(4)).

.02 Sections 53.4942(a)-3(a)(6) and 53.4945-5(a)(5) of the regulations apply to a distribution (or grant) for the purposes described in section 170(c)(2)(B) of the Code to a foreign organization that has not received a ruling or determination letter that it is a public charity described in section 509(a)(1), (2), or (3), or an operating foundation described in section 4942(j)(3). In this case, the grant will be treated as a grant to a public charity (for purposes of both sections 4942 and 4945) or to an operating foundation (for purposes of section 4942 only) if the grantor has made a "good faith determination" that the grantee is described in section 509(a)(1), (2), or (3), or section 4942(j)(3).

.03 Under sections 53.4942(a)-3(a)(6) and 53.4945-5(a)(5) of the regulations, a "good faith determination" may be based on an affidavit of the grantee or an opinion of counsel of either the grantor or the grantee. The affidavit or opinion of counsel must give enough facts about the grantee's operations and support to enable the Internal Revenue Service to determine that the grantee would likely qualify as an organization described in section 509(a)(1), (2), or (3), or section 4942(j)(3) of the Code.

.04 Thus, under the regulations, a foundation that wishes to have a grant treated as a grant to a public charity must complete two steps. First, the foundation manager of the grantor must make a "reasonable judgment" that the grantee is an organization described in section 501(c)(3) (other than section 509(a)(4)). Second, the grantor must make a good faith determination, based on an affidavit of the grantee or an opinion of counsel of either the grantor or the grantee, that the grantee is described in section 509(a)(1), (2), or (3), or section 4942(j)(3).

SEC. 3. SCOPE

This revenue procedure applies to a grant made for purposes set out in section 170(c)(2)(B) of the Code, (except for any transfer of assets pursuant to any liquidation, merger, redemption, recapitalization, or other adjustment, organization, or reorganization described in section 507(b)(2)), if the grant is made by a domestic private foundation to a foreign organization that does not have an Internal Revenue Service ruling letter recognizing its exemption under section 501(c)(3), or classifying it as a public charity under section 509(a)(1), (2), or (3), or as a private operating foundation under section 4942(j)(3).

SEC. 4. PROCEDURE

.01 A private foundation will be deemed to have satisfied the requirements of sections 53.4945-6(c)(2)(ii), 53.4942(a)-3(a)(6), and 53.4945-5(a)(5) of the regulations if (1) a grant is not a transfer of assets pursuant to any liquidation, merger, redemption, recapitalization, or other adjustment, organization, or reorganization described in section 507(b)(2) of the Code, and (2) the grantor bases its "reasonable judgment" and "good faith determination" (as described in the regulations) on a "currently qualified" affidavit prepared by the grantee for the grantor or another grantor that contains the information set out in Sec. 5., below. The original affidavit, or a photocopy of the original affidavit, must be retained by the grantor and made available to the Service upon request. Whether an affidavit is "currently qualified" is discussed in .02 through .06, below. If, however, the grantor possesses information that suggests the affidavit may not be reliable, it must consider that information in determining whether the affidavit is currently qualified.

.02 An affidavit will be considered currently qualified as long as the facts it contains are up to date, as provided in either .03 or .04, below, and as long as the relevant substantive requirements of sections 501(c)(3) and 4947(a)(1) of the Code and sections 509(a)(1), (2), or (3) or section 4942(j)(3) remain unchanged.

.03 The facts in an affidavit will be considered up to date if those facts reflect the grantee organization's latest complete accounting year or the affidavit is updated to reflect the grantee organization's current data as described in .04 below.

.04 Where a grantee's status under sections 501(c)(3) and 4947(a)(1), 509(a)(1), (2), or (3) or section 4942(j)(3) of the Code does not depend on financial support, which can change from year to year, an affidavit need be updated only by asking the grantee to amend the description of any facts in the original affidavit that have changed. If the facts have not changed, an attested statement by the grantee to that effect is enough to update an affidavit. Where a grantee's status under section 509(a)(1), (2), or (3) or section 4942(j)(3) depends on financial support, the affidavit must be updated by asking the grantee to provide an attested statement containing enough financial data to establish that it continues to meet the requirements of the applicable Code section.

.05 The information required by .04, above, is not necessarily financial data from the grantee's latest accounting year. For example, financial data from years 1985, 1986, 1987, and 1988 are enough to establish that an organization is "publicly supported" within the meaning of section 509(a)(2) of the Code for years 1989 and 1990 if the granting foundation is not responsible for a substantial and material change in the grantee organization's sources of support in years 1989 and 1990. See section 1.509(a)-3(c)(1) of the regulations. A grantor will not be considered responsible for a substantial and material change in the grantee's sources of financial support as long as:

(1) The grantee's affidavit is "currently qualified" within the meaning of .04, above;

(2) The grantor neither has learned that the Internal Revenue Service is challenging the validity of the grantee's affidavit, nor has reason to doubt that the affidavit remains valid; and

(3) The grantee is not controlled directly or indirectly by the grantor. A grantee is controlled by the grantor if the grantor and disqualified persons (defined in section 4946(a)(1)(A) through (G) of the Code) with respect to the grantor, by aggregating their votes or positions of authority, may require the grantee to perform any act that significantly affects its operations or may prevent the grantee from performing such an act.

.06 Private foundations are permitted but not required to use the procedures described above in making grants to foreign organizations. The two-step procedure referred to in Section 2.04, above, is still the general mechanism for meeting the requirements of sections 53.4945-(c)(2)(ii), 53.4942(a)-3(a)(6) and 53.4945-5(a)(5) of the regulations.

SEC. 5. AFFIDAVIT REQUIREMENTS

.01 An affidavit must be written in English and contain the substantive information set out below. However, the affidavit need not strictly follow the form set forth below. An English translation must be provided for any supporting documents that are not written in English. The affidavit must be attested to by a principal officer of the grantee organization.

.02 Affidavits for grantee organizations described in section 170(b)(1)(A)(vi) of the Code must include a financial schedule as described in .04(11), below. Grantee organizations described in section 509(a)(2) must provide comparable information.

.03 Any grantee that claims to be a school described in section 170(b)(1)(A)(ii) of the Code must provide the statement set out in .03(12), concerning whether it operates pursuant to a racially nondiscriminatory policy as to students. Section 170(b)(1)(A)(ii) describes "an educational organization which normally maintains a regular faculty and curriculum and normally has a regularly enrolled body of pupils or students in attendance at the place where its educational activities are regularly carried on." In addition, the affidavit must explain any basis for the grantee school's failure to comply with one or more of the provisions of Rev. Proc. 75-50, 1975-2 C.B. 587.

.04 The affidavit must contain a declaration to the following effect: "The undersigned, to assist grant-making foundations in the United States of America determine whether [name of grantee organization] (the grantee organization) is the equivalent of a public charity described in section 509(a)(1), (2) or (3) of the United States Internal Revenue Code or a private operating foundation described in section 4942(j)(3) of the Code, makes the following statement:

"(1) I am the [title of principal officer] of the grantee organization.

"(2) The grantee organization was created by [identify statute, charter, or other document] in [year], and is operated exclusively for [check applicable box or boxes]:

[ ] charitable
[ ] religious
[ ] scientific
[ ] literary
[ ] educational
[ ] fostering national or international amateur sports competition, or
[ ] prevention of cruelty to children or animals purposes under the laws of [the country in which the grantee organization was formed].

"(3) The activities of the grantee organization have included [describe past and current activities and operations] and will include [describe future activities and operations].

"(4) Copies of the charter, bylaws, and other documents pursuant to which the grantee organization is governed are attached.

"(5) The laws and customs applicable to the grantee organization do not permit any of its income or assets to be distributed to, or applied for the benefit of, a private person or non-charitable organization other than pursuant to the conduct of the grantee organization's charitable activities, or as payment of reasonable compensation for services rendered or as payment representing the fair market value of property which the grantee organization has purchased.

"(6) The grantee organization has no shareholders or members who have a proprietary interest in the income or assets of the organization.

"(7) In the event that the grantee organization were to be liquidated or dissolved, under the laws and customs applicable, or under the governing instruments, all its assets would be distributed to another not-for-profit organization for charitable, religious, scientific, literary, or educational purposes, or to a government instrumentality. A copy of the relevant statutory law or provisions in the governing instruments controlling the distribution of the organization's assets on liquidation is attached.

"(8) The laws and customs applicable to the grantee organization do not permit the organization, other than as an insubstantial part of its activities,

(A) to engage in activities that are not for religious, charitable, scientific, literary, or educational purposes; or

(B) to attempt to influence legislation, by propaganda or otherwise.

"(9) The laws and customs applicable to the grantee organization do not permit the organization directly or indirectly to participate or intervene in any political campaign on behalf of, or in opposition to, any candidate for public office.

"(10) The grantee organization is not controlled by or operated in connection with any organization other than as follows [describe]:

"(11) (The following is required only if the grantee organization's status under sections 501(c)(3) and 4947(a)(1), 509(a)(1), (2), or (3) or section 4942(j)(3) of the Code depends on its financial support.) A schedule of support for the four most recently completed taxable years is attached showing (for each year and in total)

(A) Gifts, grants, and contributions received;

(B) Membership fees received;

(C) Gross receipts from admissions, merchandise sold or services performed, or furnishing of facilities in any activity that is not a business unrelated to the organization's exempt purposes;

(D) Gross income from interest, dividends, rents, and royalties;

(E) Net income from business activities that are unrelated to the organization's exempt purposes;

(F) The value of services or facilities furnished by a governmental unit without charge;

(G) The total of lines (A) through (F);

(H) Line (G) minus line (C);

(I) Two percent of line (H);

(J) A schedule of contributions for each donor whose support for the four-year period was greater than the amount on line (I) (a major donor), and showing the amount by which each major donor's total contributions exceeded the amount on line (I) (excess contributions);

(K) The sum of all major donors' excess contributions;

(L) The four-year total for line (H) minus the four-year totals of lines (D), (E), and (K) (the amount of public support);

(M) Line (L) divided by the four-year total for line (H) (the percentage of the organization's support that is public support).

"(12) (The following is required only if the grantee is not a public charity described in section 509(a)(1), (2), or (3) of the Code but claims to be an operating foundation described in section 4942(j)(3) of the Code.) A schedule showing that the organization satisfies (i) the income test of section 53.4942(b)-1(a) of the regulations and (ii) one of the alternative tests described in section 53.4942(b)-2.

"(13) (The following is required only if the grantee is a school described in section 170 of the Code.) The grantee organization is an organization described in section 170(b)(1)(A)(ii) of the Code that has adopted and operates pursuant to a racially nondiscriminatory policy as to students, as set forth in Rev. Rul. 71-447, 1971-2 C.B. 230, and Rev. Rul. 75-231, 1975-1 C.B. 158, and as implemented in Rev. Proc. 75-50, 1975-2 C.B. 587."

DRAFTING INFORMATION

The principal author of this revenue procedure is Thomas J. Miller of the Exempt Organizations Technical Division. For further information regarding this revenue procedure contact Mr. Miller on (202) 622-7867 (not a toll-free number).

Form **W-8EXP**	**Certificate of Foreign Government or Other Foreign Organization for United States Tax Withholding**	OMB No. 1545-1621

Form **W-8EXP**
(Rev. December 2000)

Department of the Treasury
Internal Revenue Service

Certificate of Foreign Government or Other Foreign Organization for United States Tax Withholding

(For use by foreign governments, international organizations, foreign central banks of issue, foreign tax-exempt organizations, foreign private foundations, and governments of U.S. possessions.)

▶ Section references are to the Internal Revenue Code.   ▶ See separate instructions.
▶ Give this form to the withholding agent or payer. Do not send to the IRS.

OMB No. 1545-1621

Do not use this form for:	Instead, use Form:
● Any foreign government or other foreign organization that is not claiming the applicability of section(s) 115(2), 501(c), 892, 895, or 1443(b).	W-8BEN or W-8ECI
● A beneficial owner solely claiming foreign status or treaty benefits	W-8BEN
● A foreign partnership or a foreign trust	W-8BEN or W-8IMY
● A person claiming an exemption from U.S. withholding on income effectively connected with the conduct of a trade or business in the United States	W-8ECI
● A person acting as an intermediary	W-8IMY

Part I   **Identification of Beneficial Owner** (See instructions.)

1 Name of organization	2 Country of incorporation or organization

3 Type of entity	☐ Foreign government ☐ International organization ☐ Foreign central bank of issue (not wholly owned by the foreign sovereign)	☐ Foreign tax-exempt organization
	☐ Government of a U.S. possession	☐ Foreign private foundation

4 Permanent address (street, apt. or suite no., or rural route). **Do not use a P.O. box.**

City or town, state or province. Include postal code where appropriate.	Country (do not abbreviate)

5 Mailing address (if different from above)

City or town, state or province. Include postal or ZIP code where appropriate.	Country (do not abbreviate)

6 U.S. taxpayer identification number, if required (see instructions)	7 Foreign tax identifying number, if any (optional)

8 Reference number(s) (see instructions)

Part II   **Qualification Statement**

9   For a foreign government:
a ☐ I certify that the entity identified in Part I is a foreign government within the meaning of section 892 and the payments are within the scope of the exemption granted by section 892.
  Check box 9b or box 9c, whichever applies:
b ☐ The entity identified in Part I is an integral part of the government of ....
c ☐ The entity identified in Part I is a controlled entity of the government of ....
10   For an international organization:
  ☐ I certify that:
   ● The entity identified in Part I is an international organization within the meaning of section 7701(a)(18) **and**
   ● The payments are within the scope of the exemption granted by section 892.
11   For a foreign central bank of issue (not wholly owned by the foreign sovereign):
  ☐ I certify that:
   ● The entity identified in Part I is a foreign central bank of issue,
   ● The entity identified in Part I does not hold obligations or bank deposits to which this form relates for use in connection with the conduct of a commercial banking function or other commercial activity, **and**
   ● The payments are within the scope of the exemption granted by section 895.

(Part II and required certification continued on page 2)

For Paperwork Reduction Act Notice, see separate instructions.   Cat. No. 25401F   Form **W-8EXP** (Rev. 12-2000)

Part II   **Qualification Statement** *(continued)*

12 **For a foreign tax-exempt organization, including foreign private foundations:**

If any of the income to which this certification relates constitutes income includible under section 512 in computing the entity's unrelated business taxable income, attach a statement identifying the amounts.

Check either box 12a or box 12b:

a ☐ I certify that the entity identified in Part I has been issued a determination letter by the IRS dated ....
that is currently in effect and that concludes that it is an exempt organization described in section 501(c).

b ☐ I have attached to this form an opinion from U.S. counsel concluding that the entity identified in Part I is described in section 501(c).

For section 501(c)(3) organizations only, check either box 12c or box 12d:

c ☐ If the determination letter or opinion of counsel concludes that the entity identified in Part I is described in section 501(c)(3), I certify that the organization is not a private foundation described in section 509. I have attached an affidavit of the organization setting forth sufficient facts for the IRS to determine that the organization is not a private foundation because it meets one of the exceptions described in section 509(a)(1), (2), (3), or (4).

d ☐ If the determination letter or opinion of counsel concludes that the entity identified in Part I is described in section 501(c)(3), I certify that the organization is a private foundation described in section 509.

13 **For a government of a U.S. possession:**

☐ I certify that the entity identified in Part I is a government of a possession of the United States, or is a political subdivision thereof, and is claiming the exemption granted by section 115(2).

Part III   **Certification**

Under penalties of perjury, I declare that I have examined the information on this form and to the best of my knowledge and belief it is true, correct, and complete. I further certify under penalties of perjury that:

- The organization for which I am signing is the beneficial owner of the income to which this form relates,
- The beneficial owner is not a U.S. person,
- For a beneficial owner that is a controlled entity of a foreign sovereign (other than a central bank of issue wholly owned by a foreign sovereign), the beneficial owner is not engaged in commercial activities within or outside the United States, **and**
- For a beneficial owner that is a central bank of issue wholly owned by a foreign sovereign, the beneficial owner is not engaged in commercial activities within the United States.

Furthermore, I authorize this form to be provided to any withholding agent that has control, receipt, or custody of the income of which I am the beneficial owner or any withholding agent that can disburse or make payments of the income of which I am the beneficial owner.

Sign
Here

| Signature of authorized official | Date (MM-DD-YYYY) | Capacity in which acting |

⊕

Instructions for Form W-8EXP

(Rev. August 2001)

Department of the Treasury
Internal Revenue Service

(Use with the December 2000 revision of Form W-8EXP.)

Certificate of Foreign Government or Other Foreign Organization for United States Tax Withholding

Section references are to the Internal Revenue Code unless otherwise noted.

General Instructions

Note: *For definitions of terms used throughout these instructions, see* **Definitions** *on pages 2 and 3.*

Purpose of form. Foreign persons are subject to U.S. tax at a 30% rate on income they receive from U.S. sources that consists of interest (including certain original issue discount (OID)), dividends, rents, premiums, annuities, compensation for, or in expectation of, services performed, or other fixed or determinable annual or periodical gains, profits, or income. This tax is imposed on the gross amount paid and is generally collected by withholding on that amount. A payment is considered to have been made whether it is made directly to the beneficial owner or to another person for the benefit of the beneficial owner.

If you receive certain types of income, you must provide Form W-8EXP to:
• Establish that you are not a U.S. person,
• Claim that you are the beneficial owner of the income for which Form W-8EXP is given, and
• Claim a reduced rate of, or exemption from, withholding as a foreign government, international organization, foreign central bank of issue, foreign tax-exempt organization, foreign private foundation, or government of a U.S. possession.

In general, payments to a foreign government (including a foreign central bank of issue wholly-owned by a foreign sovereign) from investments in the United States in stocks, bonds, other domestic securities, financial instruments held in the execution of governmental financial or monetary policy, and interest on deposits in banks in the United States are exempt from tax under section 892 and exempt from withholding under sections 1441 and 1442. Payments other than those described above, including income derived in the U.S. from the conduct of a commercial activity, income received from a controlled commercial entity (including gain from the disposition of any interest in a controlled commercial entity), and income received by a controlled commercial entity, do not qualify for exemption from tax under section 892 or exemption from withholding under sections 1441 and 1442. See Temporary Regulations section 1.892-3T. In addition, certain distributions to a foreign government from a real estate investment trust (REIT) may not be eligible for relief from withholding and may be subject to withholding at 35% of the gain realized. For the definition of "commercial activities," see Temporary Regulations section 1.892-4T.

In general, payments to an international organization from investment in the United States in stocks, bonds and other domestic securities, interest on deposits in banks in the United States, and payments from any other source within the United States are exempt from tax under section 892 and exempt from withholding under sections 1441 and 1442. See Temporary Regulations section 1.892-6T. Payments to a foreign central bank of issue (whether or not wholly owned by a foreign sovereign) or to the Bank for International Settlements from obligations of the United States or of any agency or instrumentality thereof, or from interest on deposits with persons carrying on the banking business, are also generally exempt from tax under section 895 and exempt from withholding under sections 1441 and 1442. In addition, payments to a foreign central bank of issue from bankers' acceptances are exempt from tax under section 871(i)(2)(C) and exempt from withholding under sections 1441 and 1442.

Payments to a foreign tax-exempt organization of certain types of U.S. source income are also generally exempt from tax and exempt from withholding. Gross investment income of a foreign private foundation, however, is subject to withholding under section 1443(b) at a rate of 4%.

Payments to a government of a possession of the United States are generally exempt from tax and withholding under section 115(2).

To establish eligibility for exemption from 30% tax and withholding, a foreign government, international organization, foreign central bank of issue, foreign tax-exempt organization, foreign private foundation, or government of a U.S. possession must provide a Form W-8EXP to a withholding agent or payer with all necessary documentation. The withholding agent or payer of the income may rely on a properly completed Form W-8EXP to treat the payment associated with the Form W-8EXP as a payment to a foreign government, international organization, foreign central bank of issue, foreign tax-exempt organization, foreign private foundation, or government of a U.S. possession exempt from withholding at source (or, where appropriate, subject to withholding at a 4% rate).

Provide Form W-8EXP to the withholding agent or payer before income is paid or credited to you. Failure by a beneficial owner to provide a Form W-8EXP when requested may lead to withholding at a 30% rate (foreign-person withholding) or the backup withholding rate.

Cat. No. 25903G

Note: *For additional information and instructions for the withholding agent, see the **Instructions for the Requester of Forms W-8BEN, W-8ECI, W-8EXP, and W-8IMY.***

Who must file. You must give Form W-8EXP to the withholding agent or payer if you are a foreign government, international organization, foreign central bank of issue, foreign tax-exempt organization, foreign private foundation, or government of a U.S. possession. Submit Form W-8EXP whether or not you are claiming a reduced rate of, or exemption from, U.S. tax withholding.

Do not use Form W-8EXP if:
• You are not a foreign government, international organization, foreign central bank of issue, foreign tax-exempt organization, foreign private foundation, or government of a U.S. possession claiming the applicability of section 115(2), 501(c), 892, 895, or 1443(b). Instead, provide **Form W-8BEN,** Certificate of Foreign Status of Beneficial Owner for United States Tax Withholding, or **Form W-8ECI,** Certificate of Foreign Person's Claim for Exemption From Withholding on Income Effectively Connected With the Conduct of a Trade or Business in the United States. For example, if you are a foreign tax-exempt organization claiming a benefit under an income tax treaty, provide Form W-8BEN.
• You are receiving income that is effectively connected with the conduct of a trade or business in the United States. Instead, provide Form W-8ECI.
• You are a tax-exempt organization receiving unrelated business taxable income subject to withholding under section 1443(a). Instead, provide Form W-8BEN or Form W-8ECI for this portion of your income.
• You are a foreign partnership, a foreign simple trust, or a foreign grantor trust. Instead, provide Form W-8ECI or **Form W-8IMY,** Certificate of Foreign Intermediary, Foreign Flow-Through Entity, or Certain U.S. Branches for United States Tax Withholding.
• You are acting as an intermediary (that is, acting not for your own account, but for the account of others as an agent, nominee, or custodian). Instead, provide Form W-8IMY.

Giving Form W-8EXP to the withholding agent. Do not send Form W-8EXP to the IRS. Instead, give it to the person who is requesting it from you. Generally, this person will be the one from whom you receive the payment or who credits your account. Generally, a separate Form W-8EXP must be given to each withholding agent.

Give Form W-8EXP to the person requesting it before the payment is made to you or credited to your account. If you do not provide this form, the withholding agent may have to withhold tax at a 30% rate (foreign-person withholding) or the backup withholding rate. If you receive more than one type of income from a single withholding agent, the withholding agent may require you to submit a Form W-8EXP for each different type of income.

Change in circumstances. If a change in circumstances makes any information on the Form W-8EXP you have submitted incorrect, you must notify the withholding agent within 30 days of the change in circumstances and you **must** file a new Form W-8EXP or other appropriate form.

Expiration of Form W-8EXP. Generally, a Form W-8EXP filed without a U.S. taxpayer identification number (TIN) will remain in effect for a period starting on the date the form is signed and ending on the last day of the third succeeding calendar year. However, in the case of an integral part of a foreign government (within the meaning of Temporary Regulations section 1.892-2T(a)(2)) or a foreign central bank of issue, a Form W-8EXP filed without a U.S. TIN will remain in effect until a change in circumstances makes any of the information on the form incorrect. A Form W-8EXP furnished with a U.S. TIN will remain in effect until a change in circumstances makes any information on the form incorrect provided that the withholding agent reports on **Form 1042-S,** Foreign Person's U.S. Source Income Subject to Withholding, at least one payment annually to the beneficial owner.

Definitions

Beneficial owner. For payments other than those for which a reduced rate of withholding is claimed under an income tax treaty, the beneficial owner of income is generally the person who is required under U.S. tax principles to include the income in gross income on a tax return. A person is not a beneficial owner of income, however, to the extent that person is receiving the income as a nominee, agent, or custodian, or to the extent the person is a conduit whose participation in a transaction is disregarded. In the case of amounts paid that do not constitute income, beneficial ownership is determined as if the payment were income.

Foreign partnerships, foreign simple trusts, and foreign grantor trusts are not the beneficial owners of income paid to the partnership or trust. The beneficial owners of income paid to a foreign partnership are generally the partners in the partnership, provided that the partner is not itself a partnership, foreign simple or grantor trust, nominee or other agent. The beneficial owners of income paid to a foreign simple trust (that is, a foreign trust that is described in section 651(a)) are generally the beneficiaries of the trust, if the beneficiary is not a foreign partnership, foreign simple or grantor trust, nominee or other agent. The beneficial owners of a foreign grantor trust (that is, a foreign trust to the extent that all or a portion of the income of the trust is treated as owned by the grantor or another person under sections 671 through 679) are the persons treated as the owners of the trust. The beneficial owners of income paid to a foreign complex trust (that is, a foreign trust that is not a foreign simple trust or foreign grantor trust) is the trust itself.

The beneficial owner of income paid to a foreign estate is the estate itself.

Foreign person. A foreign person includes a nonresident alien individual, foreign corporation, foreign partnership, foreign trust, foreign estate, foreign government, international organization, foreign central bank of issue, foreign tax-exempt organization, foreign private foundation, or government of a U.S. possession, and any other person that is not a U.S. person. It also includes a foreign branch or office of a U.S. financial institution or U.S. clearing organization if the foreign branch is a qualified intermediary. Generally, a payment to a U.S. branch of a foreign person is a payment to a foreign person.

Foreign government. A foreign government includes only the integral parts or controlled entities of a foreign

-2-

sovereign as defined in Temporary Regulations section 1.892-2T.

An **integral part** of a foreign sovereign, in general, is any person, body of persons, organization, agency, bureau, fund, instrumentality, or other body, however designated, that constitutes a governing authority of a foreign country. The net earnings of the governing authority must be credited to its own account or to other accounts of the foreign sovereign, with no portion benefiting any private person.

A **controlled entity** of a foreign sovereign is an entity that is separate in form from the foreign sovereign or otherwise constitutes a separate juridical entity only if:

1. It is wholly owned and controlled by the foreign sovereign directly or indirectly through one or more controlled entities;

2. It is organized under the laws of the foreign sovereign by which it is owned;

3. Its net earnings are credited to its own account or to other accounts of the foreign sovereign, with no portion of its income benefiting any private person; and

4. Its assets vest in the foreign sovereign upon dissolution.

A controlled entity also includes a **pension trust** defined in Temporary Regulations section 1.892-2T(c) and may include a **foreign central bank of issue** to the extent that it is wholly owned by a foreign sovereign.

A foreign government must provide Form W-8EXP to establish eligibility for exemption from withholding for payments exempt from tax under section 892.

International organization. An international organization is any public international organization entitled to enjoy privileges, exemptions, and immunities as an international organization under the International Organizations Immunities Act (22 U.S.C. 288-288(f)). In general, to qualify as an international organization, the United States must participate in the organization pursuant to a treaty or under the authority of an Act of Congress authorizing such participation.

Amounts exempt from tax under section 892. Only a foreign government or an international organization as defined above qualifies for exemption from taxation under section 892. Section 892 generally excludes from gross income and exempts from U.S. taxation income a foreign government receives from investments in the United States in stocks, bonds, or other domestic securities; financial instruments held in the execution of governmental financial or monetary policy; and interest on deposits in banks in the United States of monies belonging to the foreign government. Income of a foreign government from sources other than those enumerated above or that is **(a)** derived from the conduct of any commercial activity, **(b)** received directly or indirectly from a controlled commercial entity, or **(c)** derived from the disposition of any interest in a controlled commercial entity is not exempt from U.S. taxation. For the definition of "commercial activity," see Temporary Regulations section 1.892-4T.

Section 892 also generally excludes from gross income and exempts from U.S. taxation income of an international organization received from investments in

the United States in stocks, bonds, or other domestic securities and interest on deposits in banks in the United States of monies belonging to the international organization or from any other source within the United States.

Controlled commercial entity. A controlled commercial entity is an entity engaged in commercial activities (whether within or outside the United States) if the foreign government **(a)** holds any interest in the entity that is 50% or more of the total of all interests in the entity **or (b)** holds a sufficient interest or any other interest in the entity which provides the foreign government with effective practical control of the entity.

Note: *A foreign central bank of issue will be treated as a controlled commercial entity only if it engages in commercial activities within the United States.*

Foreign central bank of issue. A foreign central bank of issue is a bank that is by law or government sanction the principal authority, other than the government itself, to issue instruments intended to circulate as currency. Such a bank is generally the custodian of the banking reserves of the country under whose law it is organized. For purposes of section 895, the Bank of International Settlements is treated as though it were a foreign central bank of issue.

A foreign central bank of issue must provide Form W-8EXP to establish eligibility for exemption from withholding for payments exempt from tax under either section 892 or section 895.

Amounts exempt from tax under section 895. Section 895 generally excludes from gross income and exempts from U.S. taxation income a foreign central bank of issue receives from obligations of the United States (or of any agency or instrumentality thereof) or from interest on deposits with persons carrying on the banking business unless such obligations or deposits are held for, or used in connection with, the conduct of commercial banking functions or other commercial activities of the foreign central bank of issue.

Amounts subject to withholding. Generally, an amount subject to withholding is an amount from sources within the United States that is fixed or determinable annual or periodical (FDAP) income. FDAP income is all income included in gross income, including interest (as well as original issue discount (OID)), dividends, rents, royalties, and compensation. FDAP income does not include most gains from the sale of property (including market discount and option premiums).

Withholding agent. Any person, U.S. or foreign, that has control, receipt, or custody of an amount subject to withholding or who can disburse or make payments of an amount subject to withholding is a withholding agent. The withholding agent may be an individual, corporation, partnership, trust, association, or any other entity including (but not limited to) any foreign intermediary, foreign partnership, and U.S. branches of certain foreign banks and insurance companies. Generally, the person who pays (or causes to be paid) an amount subject to withholding to the foreign person (or to its agent) must withhold.

-3-

Specific Instructions

Part I

Note: *Before completing Part I, complete the **Worksheet for Foreign Governments, International Organizations, and Foreign Central Banks of Issue** on page 5 to determine whether amounts received are or will be exempt from U.S. tax under section 892 or 895 and exempt from withholding under sections 1441 and 1442. Use the results of this worksheet to check the appropriate box in Part II. **Do not** give the worksheet to the withholding agent. Instead, keep it for your records.*

Line 1. Enter the full name of the organization.

Line 2. Enter the country under the laws of which the foreign government or other foreign organization was created, incorporated, organized, or governed.

Line 3. Check the **one** box that applies. A foreign central bank of issue (wholly owned by a foreign sovereign) should check the "Foreign government" box.

Line 4. The permanent address of a foreign government, international organization, or foreign central bank of issue is where it maintains its principal office. For all other organizations, the permanent address is the address in the country where the organization claims to be a resident for tax purposes. **Do not** show the address of a financial institution, a post office box, or an address used solely for mailing purposes.

Line 5. Enter the mailing address only if it is different from the address shown on line 4.

Line 6. A U.S. taxpayer identification number (TIN) means an employer identification number (EIN). A U.S. TIN is generally required if you are claiming an exemption or reduced rate of withholding based solely on your claim of tax-exempt status under section 501(c) or private foundation status. Use **Form SS-4,** Application for Employer Identification Number, to obtain an EIN.

Line 7. If the country of residence for tax purposes has issued the organization a tax identifying number, enter it here.

Line 8. This line may be used by the filer of Form W-8EXP or by the withholding agent to whom it is provided to include any referencing information that is useful to the withholding agent in carrying out its obligations. A filer may use line 8 to include the name and number of the account for which the filer is providing the form.

Part II

Line 9. Check box 9a **and** box 9b or box 9c, whichever applies. Enter the name of the foreign sovereign's country on line 9b (if the entity is an integral part of a foreign government) or on line 9c (if the entity is a controlled entity). A central bank of issue (wholly owned by a foreign sovereign) should check box 9c.

Line 10. Check this box if you are an international organization. By checking this box, you are certifying to all the statements made in line 10.

Line 11. Check this box if you are a foreign central bank of issue not wholly owned by a foreign sovereign. By checking this box, you are certifying to all the statements made in line 11.

Line 12. Check the appropriate box if you are a foreign tax-exempt organization.

 If you are a foreign tax-exempt organization, you must attach a statement setting forth any income that is includible under section 512 in computing your unrelated business taxable income.

Box 12a. Check this box if you have been issued a determination letter by the IRS. Enter the date of the IRS determination letter.

Box 12b. Check this box if you do not have an IRS determination letter, but are providing an opinion of U.S. counsel concluding that you are an organization described in section 501(c).

Box 12c. If you are a section 501(c)(3) organization, check this box if you are **not** a private foundation. You must attach to the withholding certificate an affidavit setting forth sufficient facts concerning your operations and support to enable the IRS to determine that you would be likely to qualify as an organization described in section 509(a)(1), (2), (3), or (4).

Box 12d. Check this box if you are a section 501(c)(3) organization and you are a private foundation described in section 509.

Part III

Form W-8EXP must be signed and dated by an authorized official of the foreign government, international organization, foreign central bank of issue, foreign tax-exempt organization, foreign private foundation, or government of a U.S. possession, as appropriate.

Paperwork Reduction Act Notice. We ask for the information on this form to carry out the Internal Revenue laws of the United States. You are required to provide the information. We need it to ensure that you are complying with these laws and to allow us to figure and collect the right amount of tax.

You are not required to provide the information requested on a form that is subject to the Paperwork Reduction Act unless the form displays a valid OMB control number. Books or records relating to a form or its instructions must be retained as long as their contents may become material in the administration of any Internal Revenue law. Generally, tax returns and return information are confidential, as required by section 6103.

The time needed to complete and file this form will vary depending on individual circumstances. The estimated average time is: **Recordkeeping,** 7 hr., 10 min.; **Learning about the law or the form,** 5 hr., 28 min.; **Preparing and sending the form to IRS,** 5 hr., 49 min.

If you have comments concerning the accuracy of these time estimates or suggestions for making this form simpler, we would be happy to hear from you. You can write to the Tax Forms Committee, Western Area Distribution Center, Rancho Cordova, CA 95743-0001. **Do not** send Form W-8EXP to this office. Instead, give it to your withholding agent.

WORKSHEET FOR FOREIGN GOVERNMENTS, INTERNATIONAL ORGANIZATIONS, AND FOREIGN CENTRAL BANKS OF ISSUE
(Do not give to the withholding agent. Keep for your records.)

Complete this worksheet to determine whether amounts received are or will be exempt from United States tax under section 892 or section 895 and exempt from withholding under sections 1441 and 1442.
- *Foreign governments and foreign central banks of issue, start with question 1.*
- *International organizations, go directly to question 6.*

FOREIGN GOVERNMENT	Yes	No
1 a Is the foreign government an integral part of a foreign sovereign (see **Definitions**)?	❏	❏
(If "Yes," go to question **4**. If "No," answer question **1b**.)		
b Is the foreign government a controlled entity of a foreign sovereign (see **Definitions**)?	❏	❏
(If "Yes," answer question **2a**. If "No," go to question **7a**.)		
2 a Is the controlled entity a foreign central bank of issue (see **Definitions**)?	❏	❏
(If "Yes," answer question **2b**. If "No," go to question **3**.)		
b Is the foreign central bank of issue engaged in commercial activities within the United States?	❏	❏
(If "Yes," answer question **7a**. If "No," go to question **4**.)		
3 Is the controlled entity engaged in commercial activities anywhere in the world?	❏	❏
(If "Yes," income is **not** exempt from tax under section 892 and may be subject to withholding. **Do not** complete Form W-8EXP for such income. Instead, complete Form W-8BEN or W-8ECI. If "No," answer question **4**.)		
4 Does the foreign government or foreign central bank of issue (wholly owned by the foreign sovereign) receive income directly or indirectly from any controlled commercial entities or income derived from the disposition of any interest in a controlled commercial entity (see **Definitions**)?	❏	❏
(If "Yes," income is **not** exempt from tax under section 892 and may be subject to withholding. **Do not** complete Form W-8EXP for such income. Instead, complete Form W-8BEN or W-8ECI. If "No," answer question **5**.)		
5 Is any of the income received by the foreign government or foreign central bank of issue (wholly owned by the foreign sovereign) from sources other than investments in the United States in stocks, bonds, other domestic securities (as defined in Temporary Regulations section 1.892-3T(a)(3)), financial instruments held in the execution of governmental financial or monetary policy (as defined in Temporary Regulations section 1.892-3T(a)(4) and (a)(5)), or interest on deposits in banks in the United States?	❏	❏
(If "Yes," income is **not** exempt from tax under section 892 and may be subject to withholding. **Do not** complete Form W-8EXP for such income. Instead, complete Form W-8BEN or W-8ECI. If "No," check the appropriate box on **line 9** of Form W-8EXP.)		

INTERNATIONAL ORGANIZATION	Yes	No
6 Is the international organization an organization in which the United States participates pursuant to any treaty or under an Act of Congress authorizing such participation and to which the President of the United States has issued an Executive Order entitling the organization to enjoy the privileges, exemptions, and immunities provided under the International Organization Immunities Act (22 U.S.C. 288, 288e, 288f)?	❏	❏
(If "Yes," check the box on **line 10** of Form W-8EXP. If "No," income may be subject to withholding. **Do not** complete this form for such income. Instead, complete Form W-8BEN or W-8ECI.)		

FOREIGN CENTRAL BANK OF ISSUE	Yes	No
7 a Is the entity, whether wholly or partially owned by the foreign sovereign, a foreign central bank of issue?	❏	❏
(If "Yes," answer question **7b**. If "No," income is **not** exempt from tax under section 895 and may be subject to withholding. **Do not** complete Form W-8EXP for such income. Instead, complete Form W-8BEN or W-8ECI.)		
b Is the income received by the foreign central bank of issue from sources other than obligations of the United States (or any agency or instrumentality thereof) or from interest on deposits with persons carrying on the banking business?	❏	❏
(If "Yes," income is **not** exempt from tax under section 895 and may be subject to withholding. **Do not** complete Form W-8EXP for such income. Instead, complete Form W-8BEN or W-8ECI. If "No," answer question **7c**.)		
c Are the obligations of the United States (or any agency or instrumentality thereof) or bank deposits owned by the foreign central bank of issue held for, or used in connection with, the conduct of commercial banking functions or other commercial activities by the foreign central bank of issue?	❏	❏
(If "Yes," income is **not** exempt from tax under section 895 and may be subject to withholding. **Do not** complete Form W-8EXP for such income. Instead, complete Form W-8BEN or W-8ECI. If "No," check the box on **line 11** of Form W-8EXP.)		

DATE:

DECLARATION   OF   TRUST

constituting

THE ABC FOUNDATION

A BERMUDA CHARITABLE TRUST

THE ABC FOUNDATION

Table of contents

DECLARATION OF TRUST

THIS DECLARATION OF TRUST is made the _____ day of   , 200_ by THE HEMISPHERE TRUST COMPANY LIMITED, a company incorporated under the laws of Bermuda and having its registered office at Hemisphere House, 9 Church Street, P.O. Box HM 951, Hamilton, Bermuda (the "Original Trustee").

RECITALS

(A)   The Trustee has agreed to make this Declaration of Trust, and has received the property specified in the Schedule to be held by it on the trusts specified below. It intends to accept donations, subscriptions, covenants, sponsorships, legacies and other gifts to be held on the same trusts.

(B)   This trust shall be irrevocable.

PART 1—OPERATIVE PROVISIONS

1   Title

The charity constituted by this Deed shall be called **THE ABC FOUNDATION** or such other name as the Trustee may from time to time determine in accordance with the power contained in this Deed.

2   Definitions and construction

In this Deed, where the context admits, the following definitions and rules of construction shall apply.

2.1   The **'Charity'** shall mean the charity constituted by this Deed.

2.2   The **'Committee'** shall mean the Committee of Trust Advisors as constituted in Part 2, clause 26 of this Deed.

2.3   The **'Trust Fund'** shall mean:

(a)   the property specified in the Schedule;

(b) all money, investments or other property paid or transferred by any person to, or so as to be under the control of, and in either case, accepted by the Trustee;

(c) all accumulations (if any) of income; and

(d) the money, investments and property from time to time representing the above.

2.4 **'charitable'** means charitable according to the law of Bermuda.

2.5 The **'Commission'** shall mean the Charity Commissioners for Bermuda.

2.6 The expression **'the Trustee'** shall, where the context admits, include the Original Trustee or other trustee or trustees for the time being of this Trust.

2.7 Words denoting the singular shall include the plural and vice versa.

2.8 Words denoting any gender shall include both the other genders.

2.9 References to any statutory provision shall include any statutory modification or re-enactment of such provision.

2.10 The table of contents and clause headings are included for reference only and shall not affect the interpretation of this Deed.

3 **Objects**

3.1 The Trustee shall hold the capital and income of the Trust Fund upon trust to apply the income and all or such part or parts of the capital, at such times and in such manner, as the Trustee may in its discretion think fit for:

(a) _____;

(b) _____; and

(c) the benefit of such other exclusively charitable objects and purposes in any part of the world as the Trustee may in its discretion think fit.

3.2 The Trustee shall not apply any part of the Trust Fund directly in relief of public funds, but may apply the whole or any part of the Trust Fund in supplementing public funds.

3.3   The Trustee may, in its discretion, instead of applying the income of the Charity in any year, accumulate all or any part of such income at compound interest by investing the same, and the resulting income, in any authorised investments and shall hold the same as an accretion to and as part of the capital of the Charity, without prejudice to their right to apply the whole or any part of such accumulated income in any subsequent year as if the same were income of the Charity arising in the then current year.

4   Conduct of charity and general management powers

The Trustee shall conduct the affairs of the Charity in such manner as it may consider appropriate, and may make such arrangements in relation to the administration of the Charity as it considers advisable.

5   Accounts, reports and returns

The Trustees shall maintain financial records, and prepare and submit accounts and returns, in accordance with the requirements of the Charities Act 1978.

6   Exercise of trustees' powers and discretions

6.1   The Trustee shall, in addition and without prejudice to clause 4 and all statutory powers, have the powers and immunities set out in Part 2 of this Deed.

6.2   No power or discretion conferred on the Trustee shall be exercised except in furtherance of the charitable objects.   No portion of the Trust Fund shall be distributed as a private inurement or benefit in contravention of the objects of the charity as set forth in clause 3 hereof.

7   Appointment of new trustees

7.1   A new trustee or new trustees may be appointed at any time (either by way of replacement or addition) by the Committee but so that the total number of Trustees shall at no time exceed five.

7.2   A trustee may be appointed or discharged by a resolution of a meeting of the Committee, provided that a memorandum declaring such appointment or discharge shall be signed as a deed, either at the meeting by the person presiding, or in some other manner directed by the meeting, and attested by two other persons present at the meeting.

8   Meetings

8.1   The Trustees shall hold at least one meeting in each calendar year.

8.2   One half of the number (for the time being) of the Trustees will form a quorum at any meeting.

8.3   Trustees shall attend meetings in person unless the Trustees shall agree another appropriate means of communication between those taking part.

9   Voting

9.1   Save in exercise of the powers in clauses 24 (to vary the terms of this Deed) and 25 (to wind up the Charity) and set out in Part 2 of this Deed, which shall be exercisable only by unanimous decision of the Trustees, a decision of the majority of the Trustees present and voting at any duly constituted meeting shall be valid and binding on all the Trustees.

9.2   Any of the Trustees who shall dissent from such a decision shall nevertheless concur in executing or signing any document or doing any act necessary for giving effect to such decision without being responsible for any resulting loss.

10   Written resolutions

A resolution in writing signed by all the Trustees shall be as valid as a resolution passed at a meeting.

11   Ratification

The Trustees may implement decisions reached by them informally, provided that such decisions are ratified at the next or subsequent meeting of the Trustees.

12   Notices

Notices to be given to the Trustees shall be in writing and shall be sufficiently given if delivered to any one of the Trustees either personally, or sent by registered post to the usual or last known address of such Trustee.

13   Trustee benefit

13.1   Subject to the provisions of clause 19 (power to take out trustee indemnity insurance) and clause 21 (professional trustees' charging) in Part 2 of this Deed, no Trustee may

(a)   receive any benefit in money or kind from the Charity (other than reasonable out of pocket expenses); or

(b)   have a financial interest in the supply of goods or services to the Charity; or

(c)   acquire or hold any interest in property of the Charity (except in order to hold it as Trustee of the Charity).

13.2   Notwithstanding the provisions of sub-clause 13.1, the Trustees shall not, nor shall any of them, be accountable for any remuneration or other benefit received by the Trustees, or any of them (whether as director, auditor or other officer or otherwise), from any company in which shares, stock, debentures or other securities are for the time being held by the Trustees as trustees, except to the extent (if any) to which such remuneration or other benefit is received by the Trustees or any of them by reason of such shares, stock, debentures or other securities being in the name of the Trustees or held on their behalf. None of the Trustees shall concur in exercising any voting rights in respect of any shares, stock, debentures or other securities comprised in the Trust Fund in such a way that a personal benefit is thereby secured to the Trustees or any of them.

PART 2—ADMINISTRATIVE PROVISIONS

1   General

1.1   The Trustees shall have power to do all such lawful acts or things as shall further the attainment of the objects of the Charity.

1.2   Subject to such restrictions as may be imposed by law, or such consents as may be required by law, the Trustees shall have all the powers of an absolute beneficial owner in relation to the management and administration of the Trust Fund.

2 Publicity

The Trustees may print, publish, circulate, and broadcast or cause to be printed, published, circulated or broadcast (whether gratuitously or not) any newspapers, periodicals, magazines, books, pamphlets, leaflets and any programmes or other publicity material of any kind that may be deemed desirable for the promotion of the objects of the Charity or for the informing of contributors and others of the needs and progress of the Charity.

3 Collaboration

The Trustees may act in collaboration with any person, body, institution or authority.

4 Assistance to and support of other charities

The Trustees may make contributions, as they may think fit, towards, or otherwise to assist (and whether out of capital or income), the objects or expenses of any charitable trust, institution or body having objects similar to those declared in this Deed.

5 Appeals, acceptance of gifts, etc

5.1 The Trustees may accept any devises, gifts, subscriptions (whether or not under Deed of Covenant), donations or bequests of land, money, securities or other real or personal property, offered or made for the objects of the Charity, and utilise or employ the same (whether in its original form or converted into another appropriate form of investment as the Trustees shall think fit) for such objects.

5.2 The Trustees may take such lawful steps, by personal or written appeals (whether periodical or occasional), public meetings, or otherwise, as may from time to time be deemed expedient for the purpose of procuring contributions to the Charity in the form of donations, annual subscriptions, covenants or in any other form whatever.

5.3 The Trustees may accept any funds or donations on any special trusts or conditions within the objects of the Charity, so that each fund or donation so accepted shall be held, subject to the trusts or conditions on which it is transferred or given, and may undertake any special trust or trusts falling within the objects of the Charity, and may hold and apply any particular or designated funds upon and subject to any such special trust or trusts.

6   Investment power

The Trustees may apply any money to be invested in the purchase of or at interest upon the security of such shares, stocks, funds, securities, land, buildings, chattels or other investments or property of whatever nature and wherever situate, and whether involving liabilities or producing income or not, as it think fit, so that it shall have the same powers to apply money to be invested as if they were an absolute beneficial owner.

7   Trustees' responsibility as shareholder

The Trustees shall not be bound to interfere in the management or conduct of the business of any company the shares or securities of which comprise the whole or any part of the Trust Fund. Where the Trustees' holding of such shares is sufficient to confer voting control of the company concerned, the Trustees shall nevertheless from time to time obtain such information from the company as would be made available to a non-executive director, to satisfy themselves (so far as may be possible from such information) that the affairs of the company are being properly managed and, in the absence of any notice to the contrary, the Trustees shall be at liberty to leave the conduct of their business (including the payment or non-payment of dividends) wholly to the directors.

8   Powers in relation to land

8.1   Subject to such restrictions imposed on them, and with such consents as may be required by law, the Trustees shall have all the powers of an absolute beneficial owner in relation to the disposition, development and improvement of any land comprised in the Trust Fund.

8.2   The Trustees shall not be bound to maintain any building or other structure on land comprised in the Trust Fund or to preserve or repair any chattels comprised in the Trust Fund.

8.3   The Trustees may transfer land comprised in the Trust Fund to such other charitable body or bodies, having objects the same as or similar to the Charity, on such terms as the Trustees shall in their discretion think fit.

9   **Borrowing**

Subject to such restrictions imposed on them, and such consents as may be required by law, the Trustees may borrow on the security of all or any part of the Trust Fund or otherwise for any purpose.

10   **Reserves**

The Trustees shall have power to establish funds for particular purposes or to maintain reserves.

11   **Delegation**

11.1   The Trustees may delegate such of their powers of management and administration as the Trustees may from time to time decide to committees, consisting of not less than one of their number and such other persons as the Trustees may appoint, and may make regulations for the conduct of such committees and from time to time amend regulations. All acts and proceedings of any such committee shall be reported as soon as possible to the Trustees and no such committee shall incur expenditure on behalf of the Charity except in accordance with a budget that has been approved by the Trustees.

11.2   The Trustees may delegate, upon such terms and at such reasonable remuneration as the Trustees may think fit, to any person who is, in the opinion of the Trustees, qualified for that purpose, the management of any land comprised in the Trust Fund. All acts and proceedings of any such person must be reported to the Trustees as soon as possible.

11.3   The Trustees may delegate, upon such terms and at such reasonable remuneration as the Trustees may think fit, to professional investment managers (the **'Managers'**) the exercise of all or any of their powers of investment on condition that:

(a)   the Managers shall be persons who are entitled to carry on investment business under the provisions of any Financial Services legislation from time to time in force within Bermuda;

<table>
<tr><td>(b)</td><td>the delegated powers shall be exercisable only within clear policy guidelines drawn up in advance by the Trustees and within the powers of investment conferred by this Deed;</td></tr>
<tr><td>(c)</td><td>the Managers shall be under a duty to report promptly to the Trustees any exercise of the delegated powers, and in particular to report every transaction carried out by the Managers to the Trustees within 14 days, and to report on the performance of investments managed by them at least every three months;</td></tr>
<tr><td>(d)</td><td>the Trustees shall be entitled at any time and without notice to review, alter or determine the delegation or their terms;</td></tr>
<tr><td>(e)</td><td>the Trustees shall be bound to review the arrangements for delegation at intervals not (in the absence of special reasons) exceeding 12 months, but so that any failure by the Trustees to undertake such reviews within the period of 12 months shall not invalidate the delegation;</td></tr>
<tr><td>(f)</td><td>the Trustees shall be liable for any failure to take reasonable care in choosing the Managers, fixing or enforcing the terms upon which the Managers are employed, requiring the remedying of any breaches of those terms and otherwise supervising the Managers, but otherwise shall not be liable for the acts and defaults of the Managers.</td></tr>
</table>

12 Custodians and nominees

12.1 The Trustees may hold all or any part of the Trust Fund in the name of any corporation or any other person (being, if individuals, at least two in number, whether or not including one or more of the Trustees) as nominee for the Trustees and on such terms as the Trustees think fit.

12.2 The Trustees shall have power to appoint as custodian trustee any corporation empowered so to act, upon such terms as it shall think fit, and may transfer the whole or any part of the Trust Fund to or so as to be under the control of such custodian trustee, provided that the remuneration payable to such corporation shall in no case exceed what is provided for in sub-clause 21.3.

13   Power to employ staff and pay for services, appoint a chairman and officers, etc

13.1   The Trustees may:

(a)   employ any person or firm, not being a trustee, to manage or assist in managing the grant-making activities of the Charity or the day-to-day running of the Charity or the Trust Fund; and

(b)   employ a secretary and other such officials or staff, not being a trustee, as the Trustees may in their discretion from time to time determine;

And in either case upon such terms and at such remuneration as the Trustees think fit.

13.2   The Trustees may from time to time:

(a)   appoint one of their number to be the Chairman of Trustees (the **'Chairman'**) for the time being;

(b)   authorise the Chairman, between meetings of the Trustees, to act on their behalf and to report such actions at the next or any subsequent meeting; and

(c)   appoint the Chairman to be an ex officio member of any committee set up by the Trustees under their powers under this Deed;

PROVIDED ALWAYS that the Trustees reserve the right at any time to remove the Chairman from the office of Chairman.

13.3   The Trustees may from time to time:

(a)   appoint any one or more from among their number to be officers of the Charity (the **'Officers'**) to act in such capacity and with such title as the Trustees deem expedient for a fixed period or for the time being;

(b)   authorise the Officers to act on their behalf in any matter or to undertake or be responsible for any activity of the Charity and to report such actions at the next or any subsequent meeting of the Trustees; and

(c)   appoint any one or more of the Officers to be an ex officio member of any committee set up by the Trustees under their powers under this Deed;

PROVIDED ALWAYS that the Trustees reserve the right at any time and from time to time to remove the Officers (or any one or more of them) from their office.

14   Regulations

The Trustees may make regulations for the management of the Charity and for the conduct of the business of the Trustees and may, from time to time, amend such regulations.

15   Bank accounts

15.1   The Trustees may open and maintain in the name of the Charity, or in such other name as the Trustees may think fit, bank accounts at such banks as the Trustees may from time to time decide, and at any time may pay any money forming part of the Trust Fund or its income to the credit of any such account or place the same on deposit with any bank.

15.2   The Trustees may from time to time make such arrangements as it shall think fit for the operation of any bank account in the name of the Charity or under the control of the Trustees.

16   Power to pay for audit

The Trustees may arrange for the accounts of the Charity to be audited annually by a qualified accountant at the expense of the Trust Fund even if not so required by law.

17   Receipts

When making grants of any funds to any charitable organisation or charitable institution, the Trustees may accept as a good discharge in respect of any such funds the receipt of the treasurer, secretary or other authorised officer for the time being of such charitable organisation or charitable institution.

18   Power to insure

The Trustees may insure any fund raising activities of the Charity and all or any part of the Trust Fund against any risk, for any amount and on such terms as it think fit.

14

19   Indemnity insurance

19.1   The Trustees may pay out of the Trust Fund the cost of any premium in respect of insurance or indemnity (notwithstanding the Trustees' interest in such insurance or indemnity) to cover all personal liabilities which may be incurred by the Trustees, or any of them, in connection with the Charity or its fund raising activities. No Trustee shall be accountable for any money paid to a Trustee under the terms of any such insurance or indemnity unless such Trustee shall otherwise have been fully indemnified in respect of the liability to which such payment relates.

19.2   Any such insurance or indemnity shall not extend to any claim by a Trustee arising from any act or omission which the Trustee in question commits, either knowing it to be a breach of trust, or breach of duty, or in reckless disregard of whether it was a breach of trust or breach of duty or not.

20   Trustees liability

In the professed execution of these trusts and powers, no Trustee, being an individual shall be liable for any loss to the Trust Fund arising by reason of any improper investment made in good faith (so long as he shall have sought professional advice before making such investment), or for the negligence or fraud of any agent employed by him, or by any other Trustee in good faith, although the employment of such agent was not strictly necessary or expedient (provided reasonable supervision shall have been exercised), or by reason of any mistake or omission made in good faith by any Trustee or by reason of any other matter or thing except the deliberate, reckless or negligent breach of an equitable duty on the part of the Trustee who is sought to be made liable.

21   Professional charging clause

21.1   Subject to sub-clause 21.2 any Trustee, being a person who possesses specialist skill or knowledge, shall be entitled to charge and be paid all usual professional or other charges for work done by him, or his firm, when instructed by his co-Trustees so to act in that capacity on behalf of the Charity.

21.2   At no time shall a majority of the Trustees benefit under the provisions of sub-clause 22.1 and a Trustee shall withdraw from any meeting of the Trustees while his or her own instruction or remuneration, or that of his or her firm, is being discussed.

21.3   Any Trustee, being a corporation appointed to act as a custodian trustee, may act on its published terms and conditions in force from time to time, provided that this shall not authorise payment for any act done or services rendered by any director or other officer of such corporation in a personal capacity.

22   Costs

22.1   The Trustees shall have power to pay out of the capital or income of the Trust Fund all costs of and incidental to:

(a)   the creation of the Charity; and

(b)   the management and administration of the same, including the costs of appeals for funds, expenses and fees for fund raising and the services of financial consultants, professional managers and advisers in connection with any such appeal.

22.2   Subject to clauses 13 of Part 1 of this Deed (Trustee benefit clause) and 21 of Part 2 of this Deed (professional charging clause), no Trustee shall receive any such remuneration.

23   Change of name

Subject to the prior written approval of the Commission (if required), the Trustees may at any time or times alter the name of the Charity by deed.

24   Power of variation

24.1   Subject to the provisions of sub-clause 24.2, the Trustees shall have power to vary this Deed in any particular by any deed which shall be expressed to be supplemental to this Deed. From and after the date of any such supplemental deed, this Deed shall be read and construed as if the provisions of such supplemental deed were incorporated in this Deed.

24.2 (a) No such variation shall be made that shall cause the trusts declared by this Deed to cease to be charitable; and

(b) no variation shall be made to clauses 3 (objects), 13 (Trustee benefit), 20 (Trustees' indemnity insurance), 21 (Trustees' charging clause) or 26 (winding-up of charity) without the prior written approval of the Commission (if required by law).

25 Power to wind up charity

If at any time the Trustees are of the opinion that the purposes of the Charity can no longer be effectively carried out by them or can be more effectively carried out by others, it shall wind up the Charity. After discharging the debts of the Charity out of the Trust Fund, the Trustees shall transfer the remainder of the Trust Fund to such other charitable body or bodies, having objects the same as or similar to the Charity, in such proportions and on such terms as the Trustees shall in their discretion decide.

26 Committee of Trust Advisors

26.1 A Committee of Trust Advisors is hereby constituted to provide advice to the Trustees as the Committee deems it appropriate to give. The Committee shall have any and all powers provided to it hereunder, and should the Committee deem it desirable for any reason otherwise to diminish their powers, it shall promptly notify the Trustees in writing.

26.2 The Committee shall be comprised of no more than five (5) members and no fewer than one member. The first Chairman of the Committee shall be irrevocably appointed by the Original Trustee and shall hold office until such time as he shall respectively die, resign or become incapacitated. The remaining members of the Committee shall be appointed by the Board of Directors of StarCapital Corp., a Bahamian International Business Corporation.

26.3 The first Chairman may appoint a first Vice-Chairman to serve for a term to be designated by the First Chairman, which Vice-Chairman shall also be designated as successor Chairman to serve in that capacity in the event that the first Chairman shall resign or for any reason cease or be unable to act as first Chairman. The first Chairman may, if he so chooses, appoint and designate subsequent Vice Chairmen and successor Chairmen. Subsequent Vice-Chairmen and other members shall be appointed by the then-acting Chairman so far as such action is not precluded by the above and shall serve for a term designated by him. Subsequent Chairmen so far as not precluded from the above may designate a successor Chairman. The Vice-Chairman may also serve as successor Chairman. All appointments and designations shall be made by an instrument in writing duly signed and acknowledged by the persons so making the appointment of designation and delivered to the Trustees. In the event that a successor Chairman has not been designated and the Chairman ceases or is unable or unwilling to act as Chairman, then the then-acting Vice-Chairman shall succeed to the position of Chairman. The person appointing a first Vice-Chairman, successor Chairman and subsequent Vice-Chairman shall have the power to terminate any such appointment.

26.4   For so long as the first Chairman shall serve in that position, all actions taken and advice rendered by the Committee shall require his approval only. Thereafter, all actions taken and advice rendered by the Committee shall require the written approval of a majority of the members (should there be more than one) either in the form of approval of the Minutes of meetings or unanimous consent to actions by proxy or otherwise. Approvals signed in counterpart shall be as valid as if signed on the same document.

26.5   In the event that the office of Chairman shall become vacant and no successor shall be named in accordance with clause 26.2 or 26.3, the Committee shall appoint one of its members to be Chairman who shall serve as such until he shall die, resign, or become incapacitated. If at any time there shall be no Chairman acting hereunder for a period of ninety (90) days, then the Trustees are empowered to appoint a successor Chairman to act hereunder.

26.6   A Trustee who in the opinion of the Committee is in any way interested otherwise than as a Trustee in any trust business proposed to be transacted at any meeting of the Trustees or who is otherwise subject or likely to be subject to any such extraneous constraint or influence as would in the opinion of the Committee preclude him from transacting any such trust business or exercising or refraining from exercising any power or discretion conferred upon him by this Settlement (whether alone or jointly with any others) or for any other reason determined in the sole discretion of the Committee shall not be entitled to participate in any such trust business or vote in regard to any decision to be made in connection therewith and may be removed as a Trustee as the Committee may direct. In the case of removal, the decision of the Committee shall be approved by the other Trustees not being removed, and the Committee may thereafter appoint a successor Trustee who must be an independent trustee. A certificate in writing signed by the Chairman of the Committee to the effect that the contents thereof represent the opinion of the Committee shall be conclusive evidence thereof, and neither the Trustees nor any other person entitled or interested or claiming to be entitled or interested under the trusts, powers and provisions contained in this Settlement shall be concerned or entitled to inquire into or question the propriety or validity of such opinion or the reasons therefor.

IN WITNESS WHEREOF the Original Trustee has hereunto set its hand and seal to be hereunto affixed as of the date and year first above written.

THE COMMON SEAL OF HEMISPHERE TRUST COMPANY LIMITED
was hereunto affixed in the presence of:

_____

SCHEDULE

APPOINTMENT OF FIRST CHAIRMAN

OF THE

COMMITTEE OF TRUST ADVISORS

OF

THE ABC FOUNDATION

The Trustee of the ABC Foundation hereby appoints _____ as the first Chairman of the Committee of Trust Advisors, effective immediately.

Date: _____   _____

Duly Authorized Trustee

The COMMON SEAL of HEMISPHERE   )
TRUST COMPANY LIMITED   )
was affixed in the presence of:)

_____

XYZ FOUNDATION

This irrevocable trust agreement made and entered into by and between _____, herein referred to as Settlor" and _____ of _____ and _____ of Bridgetown, Barbados, herein referred to as "Trustees," on this __th day of _____, 200_.

ARTICLE I

NAME

This trust shall be known as the XYZ FOUNDATION.

ARTICLE 11

TRUST PROPERTY

The trust property shall consist of any and all property listed on SCHEDULE A attached hereto and made a part hereof, and the Settlor hereby transfers and agrees to do all acts necessary to complete the transfer of such property to the Trustees.

The Settlor reserves the right to add property to the trust.

The Trustees may receive and accept property, whether real, personal, or mixed, by way of gift, bequest, legacy or devise, from any person, firm, trust, or corporation, to be held, administered, and disposed of in accordance with and pursuant to the provisions of this trust; but no gift, bequest, legacy or devise of any such property shall be received and accepted if it is conditioned or limited in such manner as to require the disposition of the income or its principal to any person or organization other than a "Charitable Organization" or for other than "Charitable Purposes" within the meaning of such terms as defined in Article VI of this trust, or as shall in the opinion of the Trustees, jeopardize either (i) the United States federal income tax exemption of this trust pursuant to Section 501(c)(3) of the United States Internal Revenue Code of 1986, as now in force or afterwards amended (such Code as may be amended from time to time and any successor provisions thereto shall be referred to herein as "Code"); (ii) the status of this trust as an organization described in Section 2055(a) of the Code at the time of the Settlor's death; or (iii) the status of this trust as an institution entitled to be treated as a charity under applicable Barbados law, as now in force or afterwards amended (such law as may be amended from time to time and any successor provisions thereto shall be referred to herein as "Barbados Law").

All of the property listed in SCHEDULE A and all property subsequently coming into the possession of the Trustees shall be held in trust according to the terms and conditions hereinafter set forth.

ARTICLE III

ACCEPTANCE OF TRUST

The Trustees hereby accept all of the trust property listed in SCHEDULE A attached hereto, and all other property coming into the possession of the Trustees, and Trustees agree to administer and distribute the trust property and the income therefrom according to the terms and conditions hereinafter set forth.

ARTICLE IV

AMENDMENT, ALTERNATION OR REVOCATION

(a)   This trust is irrevocable. This trust agreement may be amended at any time by a written document signed by the Settlor prior to issuance of a ruling or determination letter by the United States Internal Revenue Service recognizing that the trust is exempt under the Code ("IRS Tax Exempt Status Determination") and accepted by the Trustees, or after Settlor's death, by a written document signed by the Trustees and consented to, in writing, by the Advisory Committee in accordance with the requirements of Article XI; provided, however, that no such amendment made after issuance of an IRS Tax Exempt Status Determination shall be inconsistent with Sections 501(c)(3) or 2055(a) of the Code or any applicable provisions of the Barbados Law (unless in the case of amendments inconsistent with any applicable provisions of the Barbados Law such amendments are made pursuant to the exercise of the power given to the Trustees by Article IX(c)). An amendment to this Article IV (or any amendment to it) shall be valid only if and to the extent that such amendment further restricts the Settlor's and/or the Trustees' amending power. All documents or instruments amending this trust shall be noted upon or kept attached to the executed original (or executed counterpart) of this trust agreement held by the Trustees.

(b)   The Settlor authorizes and empowers, but does not direct, the Trustees to form one or more corporations, at any time, to contain within its or their name the words "XYZ Foundation Limited" (or a name similar thereto) to carry out the purposes and exercise the powers provided by this agreement. Upon the organization of such corporation(s), the Trustees are authorized and empowered to transfer to the corporation(s) all or a portion of the property and income held by the trust. Any such corporation(s) shall be organized in Barbados or such other jurisdiction(s) as the Trustees shall determine and operated in a manner consistent with Sections 501(c)(3) and 2055(c) of the Code and all applicable provisions of Barbados Law. In addition,

2

the Settlor authorizes and empowers, but does not direct, the Trustees at any time, to transfer all or a portion of the trust property and income to, merge, consolidate, combine, or otherwise join with such Charitable Organizations (within the meaning of Article VI(b)) as the Settlor has or may hereafter create or organize during his lifetime or at death; provided, however for that any such Charitable Organization is organized and operated for Charitable Purposes within the meaning of Article VI(c).

ARTICLE V

TERM, PERIOD FOR COMMENCING OPERATIONS; TIME FOR FILING FOR TAX EXEMPTION

(a)　　This trust, including any successor, unless the trust shall have sooner terminated in accordance with Article IV, shall continue forever, provided, however, that at any time after twenty-five (25) years after the date of the Settlor's death, the Trustees may terminate this trust with the written consent of the Advisory Committee in accordance with the requirements of Article XI. On such termination, the trust property and income as then constituted shall be distributed to or for the use of such Charitable Organizations, in such amounts and for such Charitable Purposes as the Trustees shall then select and determine.

(b)　　For purposes of complying with Barbados Law, it is hereby stated that this trust in all events shall commence operations prior to the greater of 21 years after the death of the Settlor or 80 years from the date hereof or such other date as the Trustees may determine is required under any applicable Barbados Law.

(c)　　It is anticipated that this trust may file an application to be recognized as an exempt organization under United States tax law and that this filing might be made at a time when the Settlor's family's interest in Optimay Corporation is less than twenty (20) percent.

ARTICLE VI

CHARITABLE PURPOSES

(a)　　(1) The principal and income of all property received and accepted by the Trustees to be administered under this trust shall be held in trust by it, and the Trustees may make payments or distributions from income or principal, or both, to or for the use of such Charitable Organizations, within the meaning of that term as defined in paragraph (b) of this Article, in such amounts and for such Charitable Purposes of the trust as the Trustees shall from time to time select and determine; and the Trustees may make payments or distributions from income or principal, or both, directly for such Charitable Purposes, within the meaning of that term as defined in paragraph (c), in such amounts as the Trustees shall from time to time select and determine without making use of any other Charitable Organization. The Trustees may also make payments or distributions of all or any part of the income or principal to states, territories, or possessions of the United States, any political subdivision of any of the foregoing, or to the United States or the District of Columbia but only for Charitable Purposes within the meaning of that term as defined in paragraph (c). No part of the net earnings of this trust shall inure or be payable to or for the benefit of any private shareholder or individual and no substantial part of the activities of this trust shall be the carrying on of propaganda, or otherwise attempting, to influence legislation in any jurisdiction. No part of the activities of this trust in any jurisdiction shall be the participation in, or intervention in (including the publishing or distributing of statements) any political campaign on behalf of any candidate for public office.

      (2)   The trust shall distribute its income for each taxable year at such time and in such manner as not to become subject to the tax on undistributed income imposed by Section 4942 of the Code.

      (3)   The trust shall not engage in any act of self-dealing as defined in Section 4941(d) of the Code.

      (4)   The trust shall not retain any excess business holdings as defined in Section 4943(c) of the Code which would subject the trust to tax under Section 4943 of the Code.

      (5)   The trust shall not make any investments in such manner as to subject it to tax under Section 4944 of the Code.

      (6)   The trust shall not make any taxable expenditures as defined in Section 4945(d) of the Code.

      (7)   Notwithstanding any other provisions of this trust agreement, the trust shall not conduct or carry on any activities not permitted to be conducted or carried on by an organization exempt under Section 501(c)(3) of the Code and its regulations as they now exist or as they may hereafter be amended, or by an organization to which bequests, legacies, devises, or transfers are deductible under Section 2055(a) of such Code and its regulations as they now exist or as they may hereafter be amended.

      (b)   In this trust agreement and in any amendments to it, references to "Charitable Organizations" or "Charitable Organization" mean corporations, trusts, funds, foundations, or community chests created or organized and operated exclusively for Charitable Purposes, no part of the net earnings of which inures or is payable to or for the benefit of any private shareholder or individual, and no substantial part of the activities of which is carrying on propaganda, or otherwise attempting, to influence legislation, and which do not participate in or intervene in (including the publishing or distributing of statements) any political campaign on behalf of any candidate for public office. It is intended that the organization(s) described in this paragraph (b) shall be entitled to exemption from United States federal income tax under Section 501(c)(3) of the Code and shall be organization(s) to which bequests, legacies, devises or transfers are deductible for United States federal estate tax purposes under Section 2055(a) of such Code.

Such organization(s) may include registered charities in Barbados, as defined in applicable Barbados Law.

(c)   In this trust agreement and in any amendments to it, the term "Charitable Purposes" shall be limited to and shall include only religious, charitable, scientific, literary, or educational purposes within the meaning of those terms as used in Sections 501(c)(3) and 2055(a) of the Code and Barbados Law.

(d)   The trust shall maintain a substantial and genuine connection with Barbados as defined in Barbados Law for the purposes of safeguarding the status of the Trust as a Barbados qualified charity.

(e)   For as long as this trust shall be a Barbados qualified charity the Trustees shall distribute in priority and before any other payment or distribution pursuant to subparagraph Article (a)(1) of this Article, whether out of income or out of principal, the sum of US$1,000 (One Thousand U.S. Dollars) per annum for such one or more Charitable Purposes which in the opinion of the Trustees shall be beneficial to the communities or inhabitants of Barbados and upon this trust ceasing to be a Barbados qualified charity the Trustees may make such distribution as it deems appropriate and the absolute entitlement conferred by this subparagraph (e) shall cease. This provision shall not take effect until such time as this trust disposes of some or all of the Optimay Corporation shares transferred to it upon its establishment.

ARTICLE VII

DEATH TAX CLAIMS

The principal and income of this trust shall not be subject to claim for any taxing jurisdiction's estate, inheritance or succession taxes or duties which may be assessed against the estate of the Settlor or due because of the Settlor's death provided that the Settlor, at the date of his death, is not a resident or domiciliary of Barbados and no assets included in his estate are located in Barbados.

ARTICLE VIII

TRUSTEES' POWERS

Except as limited by Article VI hereof, the Trustees shall have all the usual powers conferred by law upon Trustees in every jurisdiction in which the Trustees may act. Subject to Article VI and in extension and not in limitation of law and statutory powers of Trustees and other powers granted in this agreement, the Trustees shall have the following additional powers:

(a)   To invest and reinvest the principal and income of the trust in such property, real, personal, or mixed, and in such manner as it shall deem proper, and from time to time to change investments as it shall deem advisable; to invest in or retain any stocks, shares, bonds, notes, obligations, or personal or real property (including without limitation any interests in or obligations of any corporation, association business trust, investment trust, common trust fund, or investment company) although some or all of the property so acquired or retained is of a kind or size which but for this express authority would not be considered proper and although all of the trust funds are invested in the securities of one company. No principal or income, however, shall be loaned, directly or indirectly, to any Trustees or to anyone else, corporate or otherwise, who has at any time made a contribution to this trust, nor to anyone except on the basis of an adequate interest charge and with adequate security.

(b)   To sell, lease, or exchange any personal, mixed, or real property, at public auction or by private contract, for such consideration and on such terms as to credit or otherwise, and to make such contracts and enter into such undertakings relating to the trust property, as it considers advisable, whether or not such leases or contracts may extend beyond the duration of the trust.

(c)   To borrow money for such periods, at such rates of interest, and upon such terms as the Trustees considers advisable, and as security for such loans to mortgage or pledge any real or personal property with or without power of sale; to acquire or hold any real or personal property, subject to any mortgage or pledge on or of property acquired or held by this trust.

(d)   To execute and deliver deeds, assignments, transfers, mortgages, pledges, leases, covenants, contracts, promissory notes, releases, and other instruments, sealed or unsealed, incident to any transaction in which it engages.

(e)   To vote, to give proxies to participate in the reorganization, merger or consolidation of any concern, or in the sale, lease, disposition, or distribution of its assets; to join with other security holders in acting through a committee, depository, voting trustees, or otherwise, and in this connection to delegate authority to such committee, depository, or trustees and to deposit securities with them or transfer securities to them; to pay assessments levied on securities or to exercise subscription rights in respect of securities.

(f)   To employ a bank or trust company as custodian of any funds or securities and to delegate to it such powers as it deems appropriate; to hold trust property without indication of fiduciary capacity but only in the name of a registered nominee, provided the trust property is at all times identified as such on the books of the trust; to keep any or all of the trust property or funds in any place or places in the world; to employ clerks, accountants, investment counsel, investment agents, and any special services, and to pay the reasonable compensation and expenses of all such services in addition to the compensation of the Trustees and the Advisory Committee.

The Trustees' powers are exercisable solely in their fiduciary capacity consistent with and in furtherance of the Charitable Purposes of this trust as specified in Article VI and not otherwise. In this trust agreement and in any amendment to it, references to "Trustees" means the one or more trustees, whether original or successor, for the time being in office. Any person may rely upon a copy, certified by a notary public or an officer of a court, of the executed original (or executed counterpart) of this trust agreement held by the Trustees, and of any of the notations on it and writings attached to it, as fully as he might rely on the original documents themselves. Any such person may rely fully upon any statements of facts certified by anyone who appears from such documents or from such certified copy to be a trustee under this trust agreement. No one dealing with the Trustees need inquire concerning the validity of anything the Trustees purport to do. No one dealing with the Trustees needs to see the application of anything paid or transferred to or upon the order of the Trustees or the trust.

ARTICLE IX

GOVERNING LAW; SITUS OF ADMINISTRATION
POWER TO CREATE SEPARATE TRUSTS-, POWER TO CHANGE GOVERNING
LAW AND/OR SITUS OF ADMINISTRATION

(a)   This trust is established under the laws of Barbados (unless either a different law is selected, or a change of place of management and control of the trust property and income is made, by the Trustees under paragraph (b) of this Article) and the rights of all parties and the construction and effect of each provision hereof, subject only as herein appears, shall be subject to the exclusive jurisdiction of and construed only according to the said laws of Barbados which, subject as aforesaid, shall be the forum for the administration hereof. Notwithstanding the foregoing, this trust and the provisions hereof shall be construed in a manner consistent with (i) the Charitable Purposes and limitations as set forth in Article VI hereof and (ii) the Code provisions referenced in this trust agreement. It is the Settlor's intention that this trust shall be qualified as an organization described in Section 2055(a) of such Code at the time of his death and at all other relevant times so as to ensure that all bequests, legacies, devises and transfers to this trust received by it on account of Settlor's death, if any, shall be deductible for United States federal estate tax purposes under Section 2055(a) of such Code.

(b)   Subject as hereinabove provided in Articles IV, V, VI, and VII the Trustees may pay or transfer any trust property and income to the Trustees of any trust (whether or not governed by the law of Barbados), the charitable purposes of which are the same as those of this trust. The receipt of a recipient Trustees shall be a complete and absolute discharge to the Trustees paying or transferring for such payment or transfer and all and any liability of the latter Trustees in relation to the money property or investments so paid or transferred shall thereupon cease.

(c)   The Trustees may by any deed revocable or irrevocable declare that this trust shall from the date of such declaration take effect in accordance with the laws of any other place in any part of the world or have the administration of this trust including the situs of the trust property and income removed to any other place in any other part of the world with full effects regarding the jurisdiction and the forum for the administration and with the rights for the Trustees to make

7

in its absolute discretion such alterations in the trust provisions as it considers necessary to secure that this trust be rendered as valid and effective under the laws of the country named in such declaration as it is under the laws of Barbados, PROVIDED THAT no such deed shall take effect unless and until a copy thereof shall have been endorsed on or annexed to this trust agreement and that no such alteration be inconsistent, in any material respect, with the Charitable Purposes and limitations of Article VI hereof

ARTICLE X

ADDITIONAL TRUSTEES PROVISIONS

(a)   Number of Trustees.

The number of Trustees shall be not less than one and not more than three at least one of whom shall be resident in Barbados so long as this trust is governed by the laws of Barbados.

(b)   Meetings of Trustees.

The Trustees shall meet together for the conduct of trust business and otherwise regulate their meetings in such manner as they shall in heir absolute discretion think fit.

(c)   Calling of Meetings of Trustees.

Any Trustees or the Chairman of the Advisory Committee shall be entitled to convene a meeting of the Trustees by giving to the other Trustees and to the Chairman of the Advisory Committee seven days notice in writing thereof specifying the date, time and place at which such meeting is to be held and the business to be transacted thereat.

(d)   Conduct of Meetings of Trustees.

If within half an hour from the time appointed for the holding of the meeting any two or more Trustees (if more than one trustees is then serving) shall be present, the trustees present shall constitute a quorum. The Trustees present shall elect one of their number to be the Chairman of the meeting and shall proceed to business. Decisions taken and business transacted at such meeting shall be valid for all the purposes of this trust agreement and shall be binding on any dissenting Trustee and any Trustee absent from the meeting.

(e)   Conduct of Meeting Attended By One Trustee.

If within half an hour from the time appointed for the holding of the meeting one Trustee only shall be present, such Trustee shall constitute the meeting and the Chairman thereof and shall proceed to business. Decisions taken and business transacted by such Trustee shall be valid for all the purposes of this trust agreement and shall be binding on any Trustees absent from the meeting.

(f)   Representative of Corporate Trustees.

A Trustee which is a corporation may by resolution of its directors or other governing body authorize such individual as it thinks fit to act as its representative at any meeting of the Trustees and any person so authorized shall be entitled to exercise the same powers on behalf of the corporation which he represents as the corporation could have exercised if it were an individual.

(g)   Voting of Trustees.

Decisions of the Trustees shall be taken by majority vote. In the event of an equality of votes, the trustee acting as Chairman shall have a casting vote. A declaration by the Chairman that a particular resolution proposed has been carried or lost and an entry to that effect in the minutes of the meeting signed by the Chairman shall be conclusive evidence thereof and no Charitable Organization or other person entitled or interested or claiming to be entitled or interested under the trusts powers and provisions contained in this trust agreement shall be concerned or entitled to inquire into or question the proprietary or validity of the passing or otherwise of such resolution.

(h)   Minutes of Meetings.

The Trustees shall keep minutes of their meetings and such minutes if signed by the Chairman shall be conclusive evidence of the proceedings thereof and of any decisions taken at the meeting to which the minutes relate and no Charitable Organization or other person entitled or interested or claiming to be entitled or interested under the trusts powers and provisions contained in this trust agreement shall be concerned or entitled to inquire into or question the propriety or validity of any such proceedings or decision.

(i)   Resolutions at Meetings.

A resolution in writing signed by or on behalf of all the Trustees for the time being hereof shall be as valid and effective as a resolution passed at a meeting of the Trustees duly convened and held and may consist of one or more documents signed as aforesaid.

(j) <u>Removal and Appointment of Trustees.</u>

(1)	The Settlor shall have the right, during his lifetime, to terminate the appointment of any Trustee or any member of the Advisory Committee, with or without cause.

(2)	A Trustee who, in the opinion of the Advisory Committee, is in any way interested otherwise than as a trustee in any trust business proposed to be transacted at any meeting of the Trustees or who is otherwise subject or likely to be subject to any such extraneous constraint or influence as would in the opinion of the Advisory Committee preclude them from transacting any such trust business or exercising or refraining from exercising any power or discretion conferred upon him by this trust agreement whether alone or jointly with any other or others solely in the best interests of this trust or any Charitable Organization or other person entitled or interested under the trusts powers and provisions in this trust agreement contained shall not be entitled to participate in any such trust business or vote in regard to any decision to be made in connection therewith and may be removed as a Trustee as the Advisory Committee may direct or by the Settlor as provided by the preceding subparagraph (1) hereof. In the case of removal of any Trustee by the Advisory Committee, the decision of the Advisory Committee shall be approved by the other Trustees not being removed. In the case of removal of any Trustee by the Advisory Committee or by the Settlor as aforesaid, then the Advisory Committee may thereafter appoint a successor Trustee who must be an independent trustee. A certificate in writing signed by the Chairman of the Advisory Committee to the effect that the contents thereof represent the opinion of the Advisory Committee shall be conclusive evidence thereof and neither the Trustees nor any Charitable Organization nor other person entitled or interested or claiming to be entitled or interested under the trusts powers and provisions in this trust agreement contained shall be concerned or entitled to inquire into or question the propriety or validity of such opinion or the reasons therefor PROVIDED THAT nothing herein shall in any way preclude any Trustee excluded hereunder from participation in any trust business or from voting in connection therewith from executing any deed or document whether alone or jointly with the other Trustees or from otherwise giving effect to any decision of the other Trustees or shall in any way invalidate the execution of any deed or document by the Trustee whether by the Trustee itself or by a duly appointed attorney.

(k)	<u>Trustees to Act Without Interference But With Advice of The Committee.</u>

Notwithstanding anything to the contrary in this trust agreement expressed or implied, the Advisory Committee shall in no circumstances transact any trust business, make any decisions, or exercise or refrain from exercising any powers or discretions to be transacted, made or exercised under this trust agreement by the Trustees or, subject as hereinabove provided in Article X(j) hereof, in any way participate or interfere in the transaction of any such business making or in any such decisions or the exercise or otherwise of any such discretion PROVIDED THAT the Trustees shall be entitled at all times to consider and have regard to the advice of the Advisory Committee in transacting trust business, making decisions, or exercising or refraining from exercising powers and discretions as aforesaid.

ARTICLE XI

ADVISORY COMMITTEE

(a)   Constitution.

An Advisory Committee (the "Committee") is hereby constituted to provide advice to the Trustees as the Committee deems it appropriate to give and such consent to the Trustees as this trust agreement may require. The Committee shall have any and all powers provided to it hereunder. Should the Committee deem it desirable for any reason to otherwise diminish its powers it shall promptly notify the Trustees in writing.

(b)   Membership.

The Advisory Committee shall be comprised of no fewer than one and no more than three members. The original members of the Committee shall be [the Settlor] and one or two other individuals that may be selected by him and shall hold office until such time as they shall respectively die, resign or be removed as provided in this Article XI or Article X(j)(1). The first Chairman shall be [the Settlor] who shall serve as such until he shall die, resign or be removed from office as hereinafter provided in this Article XI.

(c)   Vice-Chairman And Successor Chairman.

(1)   During his lifetime, the first Chairman shall have the sole and absolute right to select and appoint the Vice-Chairman of the Committee and his successor Chairman. The successor Chairman need not be a member of the Committee at the time of his designation and appointment, but shall be an individual who meets the qualifications set out at paragraph (f) of this Article. The Vice-Chairman shall have such duties and serve for such term as determined by the first Chairman. All designations and appointments by the first Chairman may be made by will or a written instrument duly signed and acknowledged by him and delivered to the Trustees.

(2)   Upon the death of the first Chairman, or should the first Chairman become unable or unwilling to act as Chairman, then his successor Chairman shall be the individual duly designated and appointed by the first Chairman as provided by the preceding subparagraph. In the event that a successor Chairman has not been so designated and the first Chairman ceases or is unable or unwilling to act as Chairman, then the then-acting Vice-Chairman shall succeed to the position of Chairman and should the Vice-Chairman cease or be unable to serve in the capacity of Chairman, then the Trustees are empowered and directed to appoint one of the remaining members of the Committee to act as a successor Chairman hereunder for a term of no more than three (3) years. Thereafter, any other successor Chairman shall be designated and appointed by the Trustees from the members of the Committee, on a rotating basis and for such term as the Trustees shall determine. The person(s) appointing a first Vice-Chairman, successor Chairman, and subsequent Vice-Chairman shall have the power to terminate any such appointment.

(d) Voting.

For so long as the first Chairman shall serve in that position all actions taken and advice rendered by the Committee shall require his approval only. Thereafter, except as hereinbelow specifically provided otherwise, all actions taken and advice rendered by the Committee shall require the written approval of a majority of the members should there be more than one either in the form of approval of the minutes of meetings, unanimous consent to actions by proxy or otherwise. Approvals signed in counterpart shall be as valid as if signed on the same document. After the first Chairman's death, resignation or removal from office as provided in this Article XI, the following Committee actions shall require the written approval of at least two (2) of the members of the Committee (or if less than two (2) members of the Committee are then serving or entitled to vote hereunder, such actions will require the unanimous written approval of such members).

(1) Any written consent to any amendment to this trust agreement by the Trustees;

(2) Removal of any Trustee and appointment of its successor;

(3) Removal of any member of the Committee (in which even, the member who is the subject of removal shall not vote with respect to the same);

(4) Designation and appointment of a new member of the Committee; and

(5) Diminution of the powers of the Committee as provided herein.

(e) Removal for Incapacity of Chairman Or Vice-Chairman Or Members.

If the Chairman or Vice-Chairman of the Committee or any member thereof shall in the opinion of the Committee (as determined pursuant to paragraph (d) of this Article) be unable or unwilling to act as such, the Committee, by notice in writing to the Trustees and such non-acting member, may remove him from office.   In so removing a Chairman, Vice-Chairman or Committee Member from office, the Committee may consider any relevant evidence, including medical evidence. No member of the Committee, Charitable Organization or any other person entitled or interested or claiming to be entitled or interested under the trusts powers and provisions in this trust agreement shall be in any way concerned or entitled to inquire into or question the removal by the Committee of any such Chairman, Vice-Chairman or member. Upon such removal, the Committee shall designate and appoint a successor member of the Committee and shall notify the Trustees, in writing, of the appointment of any such successor.

(f) Qualifications for Members of the Committee.

Any successor member of the Committee must satisfy the following requirements: Such successor must be at least twenty-one (21) years of age.

No member of the Committee, other than the first Chairman, shall be permitted to serve as such after reaching seventy-five (75) years of age and shall be automatically treated as removed from such membership upon the earlier of (i) December 31 of the year in which such member attains such age; or (ii) the designation and appointment of such member's successor as provided herein. Such retiring member and the remaining members of the Committee shall designate and appoint such retiring member's successor in accordance with the provisions of this Article.

    (g)   Compensation of Committee.

The members of the Committee shall be entitled to reasonable compensation for their services rendered as such and for reimbursement of their out-of-pocket expenses reasonably incurred in connection with such services. Such compensation and reimbursement shall be paid out of the trust property or income.

ARTICLE XII

RECORDS AND ACCOUNTING

The Trustees shall keep accurate accounts of its Trusteeship and, after Settlor's death, shall have them audited annually by a firm of certified public accountants or chartered accountants of good repute to be selected by the Trustees and the expenses of such audit shall be paid either out of the capital or income of this trust as the Trustees may decide to be appropriate. It is intended that such accounting and audit shall comply with the requirements of Barbados Law. All records and accounts shall be open to inspection by the Committee.

ARTICLE XIII

COMPENSATION OF TRUSTEES; AUTHORIZATION TO ACT IN OTHER CAPACITIES; POWER TO OBTAIN RELEASES AND INDEMNITIES

    (a)   Compensation of Trustees.

A Trustee of this trust shall be entitled to be reasonably remunerated, and reimbursed and indemnified for expenditures as follows:

    (1)   On the basis of any agreement entered into by correspondence or otherwise between such person or corporation and the Settlor on or before the appointment of such person or corporation as Trustees and in default of any such express agreement then;

(2)   On the basis of the terms and conditions as to the acceptance of Trusteeship and remuneration chargeable therefor published by such person or corporation and current at the date of the appointment of such person or corporation as Trustees and in default of any such published terms and conditions then;

(3)   On the basis of a reasonable recompense to trust business transacted, time expended, and acts and things done by such person or corporation including time expended and acts and things done on behalf of such person or corporation by any partner of any such person or by any corporation subsidiary to or associated with any such corporation and also;

4)   To be reimbursed for any expenditure properly incurred in the transaction of trust business, in the execution or administration of the said trust or in the exercise of the said powers and discretions;

(5)   To deduct and retain from any money from time to time under the control of the Trustees and included in or forming part of the trust property or income or subject to any trust created under the powers and discretions in this trust agreement contained a sum equal to the amount of any such remuneration and expenditure as aforesaid then due and owing; and

(6)   To be indemnified out of the trust property or income or out of any money investments or property for the time being subject to any trust created under the powers and discretions contained in this trust agreement in respect of any expenditure properly incurred as mentioned in subparagraph (a) (iv) of this Article.

(b)   Corporate Trustees.

A corporation being a successor or substituted Trustees hereof may transact in its own office on behalf of the trust any business which by its constitution it is authorized to undertake upon the same terms as would for the time being be made with an ordinary customer and may retain on current or deposit account or advance at interest all moneys necessary or convenient to be retained or advanced in connection with the trust premises.

(c)   Indemnification of Trustees and the Advisory Committee.

Except as otherwise required by law, no Trustee nor any member of the Advisory Committee shall be responsible or liable for the acts or omissions of any other of the Trustees or the members of the Committee or of any predecessor or of a custodian, agent, depository or counsel selected with reasonable care. Except as otherwise required by law, no Trustees nor any member of the Committee shall be liable for any acts or omissions in connection with the subject matter hereof except in the case of such Trustees' or such Committee member's fraud negligence or intentional or willful disregard of the provisions hereof. Except as limited in this paragraph (c), the Trustees and the members of the Committee shall be indemnified out of the trust property or income for all reasonable costs, damages, legal fees, expenses and liabilities, which in good faith, and without fault in its or their part, the Trustees or the Committee members may incur or sustain in connection with its or their performance under this agreement.

14

ARTICLE XIV

THIRD-PARTIES

Any person may rely upon a copy, certified by a notary public or an officer of a court, of the executed original (or executed counterpart) of this trust agreement held by the Trustees, and of any of the notations on it and writings attached to it, as fully as he might rely on the original documents themselves. Any such person may rely fully upon any statements of fact certified by anyone who appears from such documents or from such certified copy to be a trustee under this trust agreement. No one dealing with the Trustees need inquire concerning the validity of anything the Trustees purport to do. No one dealing with the Trustees needs to see the application of anything paid or transferred to or upon the order of the Trustees or the trust.

ARTICLE XV

SETTLOR EXCLUSION

Notwithstanding anything to the contrary hereinbefore contained no discretion or power by this trust conferred on the Trustees shall be exercised and no provision of this trust shall operate so as to cause any part of the income or principal of the trust fund to become payable to or applicable for the benefit of the Settlor or any spouse of the Settlor or any person who shall contribute to the trust fund or the spouse of any such person.

ARTICLE XVI

NOTICE TO TRUSTEES

Communications, correspondence, directions, notices, consents, designations, appointments, statements, releases, or other documents to be delivered to the Trustees may be delivered to _____ at the address set forth in SCHEDULE B hereto or such other address as the Trustees or any successor thereto shall designate in writing to the Committee.

ARTICLE XVII

APPLICATION OF INTERNATIONAL TRUSTS ACT

Pursuant to section 4 (a) of the International Trusts Act-1995 of the laws of Barbados as amended (the "International Trusts Act"), the trust being a duly qualified international trust as defined therein, which complies with all the requirements of section 2(1)(c) of the International Trusts Act, it is hereby expressly declared that the International Trusts Act applies to this trust.

IN WITNESS WHEREOF, the Settlor and the Trustees have executed this Agreement as of the date first-above written.

SETTLOR:

_____

TRUSTEE:

_____

TRUSTEE:

_____

Bermuda Purpose Trust Template

THE   TRUST

DEED OF TRUST

BETWEEN

And

TRUST COMPANY LIMITED

2

TABLE OF CONTENTS

HEADINGS

THIS DEED OF TRUST is made the   day of   two thousand _____

BETWEEN:

        (hereinafter called "the Settlor") of the first part, and

        _____ TRUST COMPANY LIMITED, a company incorporated under the laws of Bermuda and having its registered office at Hamilton, Bermuda (hereinafter called "the Original Trustees") of the other part

WHEREAS:

(a)   The Settlor intends hereby to create a purpose trust within the meaning of the Trusts (Special Provisions) Act 1989 in the manner hereinafter appearing and with this intention has paid on or before the date hereof the sum of ten thousand United States Dollars (US $10,000.00) (hereinafter called "the Initial Property") to the Trustees (as hereinafter defined) to be held by the Trustees upon the trusts and with and subject to the powers and provisions hereinafter contained; and

(b)   Further property may hereafter from time to time be paid or transferred to or otherwise vested in the Trustees (as hereinafter defined) to be held upon the trusts of this Trust.

NOW THIS DEED WITNNESSES as follows: -

1.   DEFINITIONS AND INTERPRETATION

    (1)   In this Deed where the context so admits or requires:-

        (a)   "charity" means any body (corporate or unincorporate) established exclusively for the purposes recognised as charitable by the Proper Law of this Trust;

        (b)   "company" means any body incorporated or established in any part of the world which has legal existence independent of that of its members;

        (c)   "Emergency Trustees" means the person appointed as an Emergency Trustee in accordance with the provisions of Clauses 17 and 18 hereof;

(d)   "person" means any individual or any body or persons corporate of unincorporate and without prejudice to the generality of the foregoing includes charities;

(e)   "Proper Law of this Trust" means the law of the jurisdiction governing this Trust as stipulated in Clause 15(1) hereof or as otherwise declared under the provisions of Clause 15(3) hereof and the rights of all persons hereunder and the constructions and effect of each and every provision hereof shall be subject to the applicable Proper Law;

(f)   "the Protector" shall be the person or persons appointed as Protector of this Trust pursuant to Clauses 13 & 14 of this Trust and shall initially be

of Hamilton, Bermuda or such other person or persons who is or are appointed as a Protector or as joint Protectors in accordance with the provisions of this Trust;

(g)   "the Termination Date" means (i) the day on which expires the period of one hundred (100) years from and after the date of this Trust (which period shall be perpetuity period applicable to this Trust for the purposes of the Perpetuities and Accumulations Act 1989 of Bermuda) (ii) such earlier date after a period of a minimum of five (5) years from the date hereof as the Protector in his or its absolute discretion by deed delivered to the Trustees declares to be the Termination Date;

(h)   "the Trustees" means the Original Trustees or other Trustee or Trustees for the time being of this Trust;

(i)   "the Trust Fund" means:-

    (a)   the Initial Property;

    (b)   all money, investments or other property hereinafter paid or transferred by any person or persons to or so as to be under the control of and (in either case) accepted by the Trustees as additions to the Trust Fund;

    (c)   all accumulations (if any) of income which shall be held as an accretion to the capital of the Trust Fund;

    (d)   the money, investments and property from time to time representing the said money investments property additions and accumulations; and

(j)   "this Trust" means the trust created by these presents.

(2)   In the interpretation and construction of this Trust (i) words in the singular shall include the plural and words in the plural shall include the singular (ii) words importing the masculine gender shall include the feminine and (iii) the clause headings are inserted for ease of reference only shall be ignored.

2.   TRUSTS FOR INVESTMENT

(1)   The Trustees shall hold all investments comprised in the Trust Fund UPON TRUST at such discretion either to retain the same in the existing state thereof for such period as they shall think fit or at any time or times to sell the same or any part thereof but subject to Clauses 4,5 and 6 hereof.

(2)   The Trustees shall hold the net proceeds of any sale of investments comprised in the Trust Fund and all other monies held or received by them as capital monies UPON TRUST to invest the same at their discretion in or upon any of the investments authorised by this Trust with power to vary or transpose such investments for or in to any others of a like nature.

3.   DECLARATION OF TRUST

The Trustees shall hold the Trust Fund and the income thereof upon the trusts and with and subject to the powers and provisions contained in this Trust,

4.   PURPOSES OF THE TRUST

(1)   The principal purpose of this Trust is to promote the following objects for a minimum of five (5) years:

(a)   to promote _____ and to financially support research into _____; and

(b)   to promote humanitarian interests in general throughout the world, and in particular to assist students who are in financial need to obtain an education (at elementary, secondary and post-secondary levels) and to further their education based on their meritorious efforts.

(2)   In furtherance of such purposes, the promotion of the following additional specific purposes (which shall also be purposes independent from the principal purposes listed above) of this Trust are:-

  (a)   to incorporate and subscribe for the entire beneficial interest in the share capital of a corporation to be incorporated under the laws of _____ with investment holding objects and with the objects of _____(hereinafter called "the Company");

  (b)   to hold and retain (whether through a nominee or otherwise) the entire beneficial interest in the shares of the Company;

  (c)   to promote and support the activities of the Company in the fulfillment of its objects and in furtherance of the purposes hereof shall engage the Company from time to time by (without limitation to the generality of the foregoing) the exercise of rights as shareholder thereof and providing such financial support and assistance as considered advisable by the Trustees in their absolute discretion.

5.   TRUSTS TO PAY OR APPLY AND TO ACCUMULATE

(1)   The Trustees shall until Termination Date pay or apply the capital and income of the Trust Fund in furtherance of the purposes aforesaid in such proportions and at such times and from time to time and generally in such manner as the Trustees in their absolute discretion think fit provided that the Trustees shall make distributions on at least an annual basis out of the Trust Fund in furtherance of the purposes hereof in the minimum amount of United States Dollars _____(US$_____) subject always to the limit of the Trust Fund from time to time.

(2)   The Trustees shall until Termination Date hold any income of the Trust Fund not so paid or applied pursuant to Clause 5(1) of this Trust upon trust to accumulate and hold the same as an accretion to the capital of the Trust Fund by investing the same and the resulting income thereof in any investments hereby authorised with power to vary the same for others similarly authorised.

6.	ULTIMATE TRUSTS

(1)	If the whole or any part of the capital or income of the Trust Fund shall be otherwise undisposed of on the Termination Date the Trustees shall subject to the powers of this Trust or by law vested in the Trustees and each and every exercise thereof hold the same upon trust to pay or transfer the same charity, charities, individuals or other persons as the Protector before the Termination Date in his or its absolute discretion shall determine and direct the Trustees by written instrument, PROVIDED THAT such distribution shall be made absolutely and in no circumstances in contravention of the rule against perpetuities and FURTHER PROVIDED that no appointment of any part of the Trust Fund shall be paid to the Protector or for his personal benefit and FURTHER PROVIDED that if the Protector fails to direct the Trustees before the Termination Date or at all the Trust Fund shall be held for such charity or charities as the Trustee shall determine.

(2)	The Trustees shall not be held liable for any breach of duty or loss or damage to any third party caused by virtue caused virtue of or as a result of any distribution made pursuant to the direction of the Protector.

(3)	The Trustees shall not have the responsibility or any duty to investigate or ascertain whether any distribution directed to be made by the Protector under this Clause 6 is properly in furtherance of the purposes hereof.

7.	ADMINISTRATIVE POWERS

The Trustees shall in addition and without prejudice to all other powers at law have the powers and immunities set out in the First Schedule hereto and additionally the powers and provisions of the Schedule to section 17 of The Trusts (Special Provisions) Act 1989 (except those contained in Clauses 1, 3, 4(2), 4(7) and 4(9) thereof) shall be incorporated herein by reference to form the Second Schedule hereto and renumbered to follow sequentially without the incorporation of the above mentioned excepted clauses, provided that all references to a beneficiary or beneficiaries in such Schedule shall be deemed to include the purposes of this Trust.

8.	ADMINISTRATION OF TRUSTEE MEETINGS AND RECORDS

(1)	The Trustees shall make such rules as they shall deem appropriate to regulate:-

      (a)   meetings of the Trustees (including all matters relating to time, place, manner, procedure and agenda);

      (b)   the delegation of any part and all powers of the Trustees to a committee or committees or to an officer or officers (in the case of a sole corporate Trustee) of the Trustees which are established to act on behalf of the Trustees to manage the administration of the Trust or for such other specific or particular purpose in furtherance of the purpose s of the Trust;

      (c)   the administration of the Trust generally.

(2)   The Trustees shall keep at its offices in Bermuda the following:-

      (a)   A copy of this Deed of Trust and any amending or supplemental instruments.

      (b)   Such documents as are sufficient to show the true financial position of the assets held in the Trust Fund for each financial year together with details of distributions of capital and income made by the Trustees during the financial year.

(3)   The Trustees shall enter the details of this Trust as required by the Trusts (Special Provisions) Act 1989 on a register kept for that purpose by the Trustees.

9.   MAJORITY DECISIONS OF THE TRUSTEES

(1)   In the event that there shall be more than two Trustees hereof in office from time to time every decision, resolution or exercise of a power or discretion required to be or capable of being made by the Trustees shall be validly made if so made by a majority in number of the Trustees and any instrument executed in pursuance of any such decision, resolution or exercise shall have binding legal effect (as if executed by all the Trustees) if it shall be executed by a majority in number of the Trustees but not so as to render any of the Trustees hereof liable for any act or thing done or omitted without his consent by reason of the provisions of this paragraph or for any act in which he joins for conformity only.

(2)   A resolution in writing signed by a majority of the Trustees shall be as valid and effective as if it had been passed at a meeting of the Trustees duly convened and held and any such resolution may consist of one or more documents in similar form each signed by one or more of the Trustees.

10. TRUSTEES' AND PROTECTOR'S REMUNERATION

(1) Any Trustee or Protector hereof being a bank or corporation or other person engaged in any profession or business shall be entitled to charge and be paid all usual professional or other charges for services done by him or his firm or it in relation to the trusts hereof including a fee for acting as such Trustee or Protector and such fee in the case of a corporate Trustee or corporate Protector to be in accordance with its usual scale of fees as shall from time to time be in effect or in the absence of any usual scale of fees or if it shall be agreed otherwise then the fees shall be as may be agreed in the case of the Trustees with the Protector.

(2) The Trustees shall have the power to pay any Trustee or Protector hereof entitled to remuneration in accordance with sub-clause (1) above by the appropriation of or procuring the distribution of funds out of the Trust Fund as an expense of the proper administration of this Trust (and which shall include the arranging for payment by a Company or other legal entity held by the Trustees as part of the Trust Fund).

(3) Any new or additional Trustee appointed under the provisions hereof or by a court or competent jurisdiction shall have such powers, rights and benefits as to remuneration or otherwise at or prior to his or its appointment as may be agreed in writing (in the case of a Trustee appointed as hereinbefore provided) between such new or additional Trustee and the person or persons making such appointment or (in the case of a Trustee appointed by a court) as the order appointing such Trustee may direct or in the absence of such agreement in the case of a corporate Trustee in accordance with its usual scale of fees as shall from time to time be in effect.

11. TRUSTEE LIABILITY

(1) In the professed execution of the trusts and powers hereof no Trustee hereof and no director officer or employee of any corporate Trustee hereof shall be liable for any loss to the Trust Fund arising by reason of any improper investment made in good faith or for the negligence of any agent employed by him or by any other Trustee hereof although the employment of such agent was not strictly necessary or expedient or by reason of any mistake or omission made in good faith by any Trustee hereof or by any director officer or employee of any corporate Trustee hereof or by reason of any other matter or thing except for willful default fraud or

willful negligence on the part of the Trustee or director, officer or employee of a corporate Trustee who is sought to be made liable.

(2)　The Trustees hereof the directors, officers, and employers of any corporate Trustee hereof and each of them, their respective heirs, personal representatives, assigns and successors shall be wholly indemnified out of the Trust Fund in respect of any liability or loss which they may suffer by virtue of or arising out of any mistake or omission they may have made in good faith in the course of carrying out their duties as Trustees hereof or as directors, officers or employees of any corporate Trustee hereof except for loss or liability arising due to their own willful default fraud or willful negligence.

12.　APPOINTMENT REMOVAL RETIREMENT AND RESIGNATION OF TRUSTEES

(1)　Any person may be appointed a Trustee of this Trust whether resident or incorporated (as the case may be) within or outside the jurisdiction of the Proper Law of this Trust PROVIDED THAT so long ad the Proper Law shall be the law of Bermuda any sole Trustee hereof or at least one of the Trustees shall be a designated person within the meaning given to that expression by The Trusts (Special Provisions) Act 1989.

(2)　The power of appointing a new or additional Trustee or new additional Trustees of this Trust shall be vested in the Protector and such power shall be exercisable by instrument in writing.

(3)　The Protector shall have the power to remove any Trustee of this Trust upon delivery of written notice to such Trustee provided that upon such removal so long as the Proper Law shall be the Law of Bermuda there shall be at least one Trustee remaining who shall be a designated person as aforesaid.

(4)　The person or persons exercising the powers granted in sub-clauses (2) and (3) above shall promptly give written notice thereof to the other then serving Trustee or Trustees (if any).

(5)　Acts and deeds done or executed for the proper vesting of the Trust Fund in new or additional Trustees shall be done and executed by the continuing or retiring Trustee or Trustees at the expense of the income or capital of the Trust Fund PROVIDED ALWAYS that in the event of the resignation, retirement or removal of any Trustee hereunder such outgoing Trustees and every director officer and employee of any outgoing corporate Trustee shall be entitled to receive from the new Trustee or Trustees and from the continuing Trustee and Trustees (if any) an indemnity against any and all liabilities in respect of any costs, claims, expenses, or debts or probate, succession, estate or any other duties, impositions or taxes of whatever nature which are then or may thereafter become payable out of the capital or income of the Trust Fund and shall not be bound to do or to execute any such acts or deeds as aforesaid except upon his or its receipt of such indemnity.

(6)   If a Trustee ceases to be a Trustee hereof such Trustee and in the case of a corporate Trustee every director, officer and employee thereof shall be released from all claims, demands, actions, proceedings and accounts of any such kind on the part of any person (whether in existence or not) actually or prospectively interested under this Trust for or in respect of the Trust Fund or the income of the Trust Fund or the trusts of this Trust or any act or thing done or omitted in execution or purported execution of such trusts other than and excepting only actions which

(a)   arise from any willful default, willful negligence fraud or fraudulent breach of trust in which such Trustee or in the case of a corporate Trustee any of its directors officers or employees was a party or privy or

(b)   are brought to recover from such Trustee trust property or the proceeds of trust property in the possession of such Trustee or previously received by such Trustee or in the case of a corporate Trustee any of its directors, officers and employees and converted to his or its use.

(7)   A Trustee desiring to withdraw and be discharged from the trusts hereof may resign as Trustee by giving notice of resignation in writing to the continuing Trustees (if any) and the person or persons then having the power to appoint new Trustees and after the expiration of thirty days from the date of so giving notice (or such shorter period as may be agreed in writing between the Trustee giving notice and the person or persons then having the power to appoint new Trustees) the Trustee who has so given notice shall cease to be a Trustee to all intents and purposes except as to acts and deeds necessary for the proper vesting of the Trust Fund in the continuing or new Trustee or Trustees or otherwise as the case may require PROVIDED THAT so long as the Proper Law shall be the Law of Bermuda there shall then be at least one Trustee remaining who is a designated person as aforesaid and if there shall not then be such a person remaining the

12

Trustee so resigning will not cease to be a Trustee until there shall be such a person acting as a Trustee hereof.

13. PROTECTORS

(1) (a) Each Protector hereof shall have the power to nominate a successor by instrument in writing revocable or irrevocable (which may be effective on death without submission to probate) or by nomination in the relevant Protector's Last Will and Testament and delivered to any other person then serving as a Protector hereof, the Trustees and to the successor named therein and if the Protector so nominating shall for any reason cease to act as a Protector hereof then the person who is the subject of such nomination that has not been revoked shall forthwith become and be Protector hereof.

(b) If more than one Protector is in office at any one time they shall act jointly and any references to the Protector shall be read to include reference to the joint Protectors as the case may be.

(c) If only one Protector is in office at any one time, he or she or it may act singly in exercising any powers granted to the Protector hereunder.

(d) _____ and _____ shall have the power to remove any Protector of this Trust upon delivery of written notice to such Protector and to the Trustees of this Trust and the said written notice shall be jointly signed by _____and by _____ and in the event of one of them being unable to act due to death or illness, the other shall be able to exercise such power without the other's consent.

(e) In the event that there is no Protector in office and no such successor Protector shall have been nominated by any Protector previously in office the Trustees shall have the power exercisable in their absolute discretion by deed to appoint any person or persons who is or are not a Trustee or Trustees hereof to be the Protector.

(f) Any Protector hereof may resign by giving notice thereof in writing to any other person then serving as Protector, the Trustees and any successor who is the subject of any nomination under sub-Clause (1)(a) immediately above that has not been revoked and after the expiration of thirty (30) days from the date of the Trustees receiving such notice (or such shorter period as may be agreed in writing between the person giving notice and the Trustees) the person who has so given such notice shall thereafter cease to be a Protector hereof.

(g)   Any person serving as a Protector hereof shall immediately cease to be a Protector if such person dies (or being a company is dissolved) or is the subject of an insolvency, bankruptcy or like proceedings whether voluntary or involuntary resigns becomes of unsound mind or otherwise becomes unable to fulfill office of the Protector hereunder.

(2)   If there shall at any time be no Protector then this Trust shall during such time as there shall be no Protector (but no further or otherwise) be read and construed as if all references to the Protector were omitted from this Trust Deed.

(3)   In addition to the powers specifically conferred on the Protector by this Trust the Protector shall have the power to request information and accounts from the Trustees (which information and accounts shall forthwith be supplied to the Protector).

(4)   (a)   The Protector shall not owe any fiduciary duty towards and shall not be accountable to any person or persons from time to time interested hereunder or to the Trustees for any act or omission or commission of the Protector in relation to the powers given to the Protector by this Trust to the intent that any person acting as a Protector hereof (in the absence of fraud, dishonesty willful default or willful negligence on the part of such person) shall be free from any liability whatsoever in relation to such powers.

        (b)   The Protector shall be wholly indemnified and held harmless out of the Trust Fund or as otherwise provided from any losses, damages or judgement debt arising out of any action or suit in a court of law based upon or in connection with the Protector's powers or duties under this Trust in the absence of its fraud, dishonesty willful default or willful negligence.

14

14. ADDITIONAL DUTIES OF PROTECTOR

(1)   The person or persons from time to time serving as the Protector shall also be the Enforcer ("the Enforcer") being the person or persons charged with the duty of enforcing the trusts of this Trust as required by Section 13(1)(e) of the Trusts (Special Provisions) Act 1989 and during such times as there is more than one such person or persons so serving they shall act jointly when performing their duties as Enforcer.

(2)   Any of the persons serving from time to time as the Protector may delegate by revocable or irrevocable instrument in writing to any other person who is not a Trustee hereof the duties, responsibilities and discretions of Enforcer for such period and on such terms and conditions as the person so delegating thinks fit.

15. PROPER LAW AND POWER TO CHANGE SITUS OF PROPER LAW

(1)   Subject to the following provisions of this clause this Trust is established under the laws of Bermuda and the construction and effect of this Trust shall be subject to the jurisdiction of and construed in accordance with the laws of Bermuda.

(2)   Subject to the following provisions of this Clause the Courts of Bermuda shall be the forum for the administration of this Trust.

(3)   The Trustees shall upon the written instruction of the Protector at any time and from time to time declare by deed that the trusts, powers and the construction and effect of this Trust shall from the date of such declaration take effect in accordance with the law of any other jurisdiction in any part of the world and as from the date of such declaration the law of the jurisdiction named therein shall be the Proper Law governing the Trust and the Courts in that jurisdiction shall be the forum for the administration of this Trust (subject to the provisions of this sub-clause and sub-clause (5) hereof) and until any further declaration is made PROVIDED THAT notwithstanding anything herein contained and notwithstanding any written direction of the Protector the Trustees for the time being shall not have the power to make any declaration which might directly of indirectly result in this Trust becoming according to the law thereupon becoming applicable hereto illegal, void or voidable or which might in any way change the purposes or objects of this Trust otherwise than in accordance with the terms hereof AND PROVIDED FURTHER that so often as any such declaration as

aforesaid shall be made the Trustees shall be at liberty to make such consequential alterations or additions in or to the trusts, powers and provisions of this Trust as the Trustees may consider necessary or desirable to ensure so far as may be possible that the trusts, powers and provisions of this Trust shall (mutatis mutandis) be as valid and effective as they were under the law of Bermuda immediately prior to such declaration.

(4)   The Trustees shall have the power with the written consent of the Protector (subject to the application (if any) of the rule against perpetuities) to carry on the general administration of these trusts in any jurisdiction in the world whether or not such jurisdiction is for the time being the Proper Law of this Trust or the courts of such jurisdiction are for the time being the forum for the administration of these trusts and whether or not the Trustees or any of them are for the time being resident or domiciled in or otherwise connected with such jurisdiction.

(5)   The Trustees may at any time with the written consent of the Protector declare by deed that from the date of such declaration the forum for the administration of this Trust shall be the courts of any jurisdiction in the world whether or not such courts are of the jurisdiction which is for the time being the Proper Law of this Trust.

16.   IRREVOCABILITY

This Trust shall be irrevocable PROVIDED ALWAYS THAT notwithstanding anything hereinbefore contained or implied the Protector may at such time as he, it or they shall in their absolute discretion think fit (with the consent of the Trustees) by deed executed before the Termination Date vary, amend, alter or change the purposes or the administrative provisions herein contained and substituting such new or modified purposes or administrative provisions whatsoever concerning the Trust Fund and the income thereof as he, it or they shall think fit.

17.   APPOINTMENT OF EMERGENCY TRUSTEES

(1)   At any time prior to the Termination Date the Protector may by deed delivered to the Trustees appoint a person or persons to be the Emergency Trustees of this Trust PROVIDED THAT no person may be so appointed to be an Emergency Trustee who is resident in a territory in which an Emergency Event (as defined below) has occurred within the previous year of such appointment and

PROVIDED ALWAYS THAT the jurisdiction chosen by the Protector shall contain the necessary legislative provisions to administer this trust.

(2) In the event that an Emergency Trustee has not been appointed by the Protector, then _____Trust Company Limited of _____ shall be appointed as Emergency Trustee of this Trust in accordance with Clause 18 hereof.

(3) An Emergency Trustee shall become a Trustee under this Trust immediately upon the ceasing of a Trustee continuing as a Trustee in accordance with Clause 18 hereof.

(4) An Emergency Trustee (not having become one of the Trustees) may at any time resign by giving written notice to the Protector (if any) and the Trustees and may at any time be removed from office by written notice given by the Protector and received by the Emergency Trustee who is to be removed from office.

18. EMERGENCY EVENTS

(1) Any Trustee hereof shall automatically cease to be a Trustee in the happening of any of the following events ("Emergency Event") within the territory where such Trustee is incorporated (in the case of a corporate Trustee) or resident in the case of an individual that is to say:-

    (a) the invasion of such territory by military forces;

    (b) the enactment of any law or the taking of any action by or on the part of any governmental authority agency or officer of or within the said territory the aim or purpose or effect of which is (or would be if such Trustee had sole control of the assets comprising the Trust Fund);

        (i) to acquire expropriate or confiscate any of the assets comprising the Trust Fund or any part thereof;

        (ii) to jeopardise or interfere with or hamper the free exercise by such Trustee of its fiduciary obligations powers and discretions;

        (iii) the restriction suspension abrogation withdrawal cancellation or rescission of any exemption relief or contract in relation to the trusts of this Trust in respect of the Trust Fund or any part thereof whether in respect of exchange or currency control or any other matter;

        (iv)   to levy any tax or duty on the capital or income of the Trust Fund (in excess of 20 per centum thereof);

    (c)   the nationalism or attempted nationalisation of the Trustee or other substantial intervention in its affairs by a government official or a government body or agency;

    (d)   the occurrence in that territory of civil war or of violent civil disturbances which shall cause or appear likely to cause a serious and prolonged interference with the ability of the Trustee to function as such;

    (e)   the acquisition by the government or any other public authority of that territory of a controlling interest in the Trustee;

    (f)   to determine or substantially restrict the power of the Trustee to transfer assets comprising income or capital of the Trust Fund out of that territory for the purpose of investment or distribution.

(2)   Upon such Trustees ceasing to be a Trustee pursuant to this Clause such Trustee shall be divested of title to the Trust Fund which shall automatically vest in Emergency Trustees had been the Original Trustee hereof and the forum for the administration and the Proper Law of this Trust shall notwithstanding any other provisions of this Trust forthwith be deemed to be the place of residence or incorporation (if a corporation) of such Emergency Trustees or such other jurisdiction or territory which designated under the Deed appointing Emergency Trustees.

(3)   Notwithstanding paragraphs (a) and (b) of this Clause 18 a certificate in writing issued by the Protector no later than the 14 days following the happening of an Emergency Event to the effect that paragraphs (a) and (b) of this Clause 18 shall not be deemed to have applied notwithstanding the happening of any such Emergency Event and shall be conclusive for the purpose of reinstating as a Trustee hereof the Trustee automatically removed under the provisions of paragraph (1) of this Clause.

(4)   The Protector shall be obliged to make his endeavours to deliver any certificate issued under sub-clause (c) above to the Emergency Trustee and to the reinstated Trustee as soon as practicable.

19.　　NAME

　　　　The name of this Trust shall be "THE　　　　　　　TRUST" or such other name as
　　　　the Trustees shall from time to time decide.

IN WITNESS WHEROF the parties hereto have hereunto set their hands and seals or caused their
Common Seals to be affixed (as the case may be) the day and year first above written.

FIRST SCHEDULE

IN furtherance of the purposes of this Trust but no further or otherwise the Trustees shall have the
following additional powers:-

(i)　　To borrow money subject to such consents as may be required by law
and further subject to the prior written consent of the Protector on such
terms as to interest, repayment or otherwise as the Trustees may think fit
without security or (subject as aforesaid) upon the security of the whole
or any part or parts of the Trust Fund and to use such money so borrowed
for any purpose for which capital of the Trust Fund may be used.

(ii)　　To employ any person, firm or company not being a Trustee to manage
or assist in managing the Trust Fund upon such reasonable terms as the
Trustees think fit and to pay a secretary and other such officials or staff
not being a Trustee as the Trustees may in their discretion from time to
time determine and to enter into agreements and to fix such reasonable
salaries as the Trustees may deem proper and to enter into any service
agreements which they shall consider to be necessary including power to
determine any such employment upon such terms as the Trustees may
decide and to make all reasonable and necessary provisions for the
payment of pensions and superannuation to or on behalf of employees
and their widows or widowers and dependants

(iii)　　To apply capital or income in insuring any buildings or other property to
their full value.

(iv)　　To make contributions as they may think fit or otherwise to assist (and
whether out of capital or income) towards the purposes of this Trust.

(v)　　To invest any moneys for the time being comprised in the Trust Fund
and also in the hands of the Trustees and for the time being unapplied in

the names or under the control of the Trustees in or upon any investments authorised by this deed with power to vary or transpose investments for or into others of any nature so authorised.

(vi)   To engage in any trade or venture in the nature of trade whether solely or jointly with any other person and whether of not by way of partnership under the jurisdiction of the Proper Law of this Trust or elsewhere and make such arrangements in connection therewith as they think fit and may delegate any exercise of this power to any one or more of their number or to a company or partnership formed for this purpose PROVIDED THAT the persons carrying on any trade or venture in the nature of trade authorised by this power shall have power to determine what are the distributable profits thereof and so much of the distributable profits as accrue to the Trustees (and no more) shall be income of the Trust Fund for the purposes of this Trust and any power vested in the Trustees under this Trust shall (where applicable) extend to any arrangements in connection with any such company or partnership as aforesaid and in particular but without prejudice to the generality of the foregoing the Trustees' powers of borrowing and charging shall extend to any borrowing arrangements made in connection with such company or partnership as aforesaid and whether made severally or jointly with others or with unequal liability.

(vii)   To accept as a good discharge in respect of any funds granted or donated to any charity the receipt of the treasurer or secretary or other authorised officer for the time being of such charity.

(viii)   To do all such lawful acts or things as shall further the attainment of the purposes of this Trust and so far as may be necessary to do such acts or things in collaboration with any person.

(ix)   From time to time and at such time intervals as they shall in their sole discretion think fit cause the financial documents and accounts kept by them to be examined or audited by such person or persons as they shall designate and to pay the costs of such examination or audit out of the capital or income of the Trust Fund.

20

SECOND SCHEDULE

Further administrative powers incorporated by reference
to the Trusts (Special Provisions) Act 1989.

SIGNED, SEALED and DELIVERED   )
by   in the presence of   )
)
)
)
)
)

Witness

THE COMMON SEAL of _____   )
Trust Company Limited was hereunto   )
affixed in the presence of:)
)
)
)
)